Belief, Bodies, and Being

Belief, Bodies, and Being

FEMINIST REFLECTIONS ON EMBODIMENT

EDITED BY

DEBORAH ORR, LINDA LOPEZ MCALISTER,
EILEEN KAHL, AND KATHLEEN EARLE

ROWMAN & LITTLEFIELD PUBLISHERS, INC
Lanham • Boulder • New York • Toronto • Oxford

＃ 61757944   1-23-07

ROWMAN & LITTLEFIELD PUBLISHERS, INC.

Published in the United States of America
by Rowman & Littlefield Publishers, Inc.
A wholly owned subsidiary of The Rowman & Littlefield Publishing Group, Inc.
4501 Forbes Boulevard, Suite 200, Lanham, Maryland 20706
www.rowmanlittlefield.com

PO Box 317
Oxford
OX2 9RU, UK

British Library Cataloguing in Publication Information Available

Library of Congress Cataloging-in-Publication Data

Orr, Deborah, 1946-
  Belief, bodies, and being : feminist reflections on embodiment / edited by
  Deborah Orr ... [et al.].
    p. cm.
  Includes bibliographical references and index.
  ISBN-13: 978-0-7425-1414-0 (cloth : alk. paper)
  ISBN-13: 978-0-7425-1415-7 (pbk. : alk. paper)
  ISBN-10: 0-7425-1414-5 (cloth : alk. paper)
  ISBN-10: 0-7425-1415-3 (pbk. : alk. paper)
  1. Feminist theory. 2. Body, Human.   I. Title
HQ1190 .B465 2006
306.4—dc22   2005027601

Printed in the United States of America

The paper used in this publication meets the minimum requirements of American
National Standard for Information Sciences—Permanence of Paper for Printed Library
Materials, ANSI/NISO Z39.48-1992.

Contents

Preface

This book could not have existed thirty years ago. For one thing, there were hardly any women philosophers in the United States in those days and even fewer women were able to find academic positions in philosophy in European countries. In 1974, while I was on a sabbatical at the University of Würzburg, Dr. Wiebke Schrader and I organized a meeting of German women philosophers. First we had to cull the catalogs of German universities and the membership list of the *Deutsche Gesellschaft für Philosophie* to find women's names for our shockingly short invitation list. Our keynote speaker was a man! That was because we didn't know any German women philosophers of stature, so we invited Dr, Eberhardt Ave-Lallemant of the University of Munich to speak about his teacher Dr. Hedwig Conrad-Martius (1888—1966), the first German woman to earn her doctorate in philosophy and the first to teach at a German university. To our great joy, about fifteen women philosophers gathered in Würzburg on that Saturday in April, 1974, to share their work, their interests, their professional concerns and to get to know one another. Among them were Prof. Dr. Elfriede Tielsch of the Technical University of Berlin and Brigitte Weishaupt, then a graduate student in Frankfurt, now a professor at the Eidgenössischen Technische Hochschule Zürich (ETH).

As a result of that meeting, under the leadership of Drs. Tielsch, Weisshaupt, and Schrader, the German Association of Women Philosophers (*Deutsche Assoziation von Philosophinnen*) was established and its first Symposium was held in Würzburg in 1980. As time went on, more symposia were held and philosophers from other countries began to participate, so the organization changed its name to the International Association of Women Philosophers (IAPh). It has organized eleven international symposia in seven different countries since 1980. The papers contained in this volume were originally presented by IAPh members at the Eighth IAPh Symposium held in conjunction with the World Congress of Philosophy in Boston, MA in 1998.

The proceedings of almost all of the previous IAPh symposia have been published in the countries in which the symposia were held shortly after the symposium took place. The publishing industry in the United States operates rather differently than publishers in European countries, however, and it became clear early on that it would be prohibitively expensive if not downright impossible to publish the complete proceedings of the conference during which nearly 200 papers were presented by women philosophers from eighteen different countries. It was decided that, as an alternative mode of publication, we would invite the presenters to submit their papers for possible publication in four thematic volumes. Since I had just completed eight years as editor of *Hypatia:A Journal of Feminist Philosophy,* I had an excellent group of experienced assistant editors at hand who were willing to work on the project: Eileen Kahl, Kathleen Earle, and Christa Elrod Rainwater. We reviewed papers for and developed four volumes on the themes, the body, identity, ethics, and history of women philosophers. Rowman & Littlefield offered to contract with us to publish the first two of these collections. When I retired from my position at the University of South Florida I expected to have time to undertake the final tasks leading to publication. Unfortunately, I encountered a series of health and family problems which prevented me from carrying out this plan and, reluctantly, I felt I had to withdraw from the project. I had to come to terms with the fact that, in all likelihood, these volumes would never be published.

Then, in 2002, Dr. Deborah Orr of York University in Toronto agreed to take over the project. Just imagine—a woman philosopher in shining armor! Thanks to her efforts, now at least some of the fine work from that wonderful week in Boston will finally appear in print. Wherever necessary the papers have been revised and updated so this collection remains timely and relevant. What is particularly special about these volumes is that they contain the perspectives of women philosophers from a far wider variety of countries and cultures than is usually found in such collections. I look forward eagerly to the long-delayed publication of this volume, and the publication of the subsequent volumes in this series.

Linda López McAlister
Albuquerque, NM, 2004

Acknowledgments

This volume has been many years in the making and since I was not involved, except as a contributor, in the earlier work, I am unable to fully acknowledge all those who worked on it simply because I do not know who they are. First and foremost among those I do know, I would like to thank Linda López McAlister for her fine work both in organizing the IAPh Conference in Boston, where these papers were given, and for all of her efforts in bringing the earlier draft of the book together. She has been an ongoing source of help to me during my work on this volume, and, I'd also like to say, a genuine inspiration to me as a feminist Wittgenstein scholar.

We would especially like to thank *Hypatia: A Journal of Feminist Philosophy* for their sponsorship of the conference.

The original draft of *Beliefs, Bodies, and Being* was put together by Linda López McAlister, as chief editor, Eileen Kahl, and Kathleen Earle. When I took over editing the volume I asked all contributors to review their papers in order to bring them up to date. Thus many changes were made and I take full responsibility for errors created during that process. I would like to thank Eileen Kahl in particular for volunteering to come back into the project and index the book.

Bettina Schmitz has been my liaison with IAPh throughout the course of the preparation of the book and has been of invaluable assistance.

A special thank-you must be extended to our editor at Rowman and Littlefield, Eve DeVaro Fowler, for her infinite patience and the many courtesies she extended during this process. She has our gratitude for agreeing to honor the original contract for this volume in spite of the long time lapse, and for arranging an advance to cover the reprint permission fee for one of the papers.

Veronica Vasterling's paper, "Butler's Sophisticated Constructivism: A Critical Assessment' is reprinted with permission of *Hypatia. A Journal of Feminist Philosophy*. We are grateful to *Hypatia* for granting this permission for a nominal fee.

We also thank *Signs· Journal of Women in Culture and Society* for greatly reducing their reprint permission fee for "Posthumanist Performativity: Toward an Understanding of How Matter Comes to Matter" by Karen Barad.

Last, but far from least, a debt of gratitude is owed all the contributors to this volume both for their fine work and for their patience with the process of completing the book.

Chapter 1

Thinking through the Body:
An Introduction to
Beliefs, Bodies, and Being

Deborah Orr

With the work of Parmenides (c. 515–399 B.C.E.) Western philosophy, and the culture which it both reflects and informs, began to articulate a metaphysic, a logic, and an epistemology which would systematically disadvantage women for the next twenty-five hundred years. Parmenides posited a dualistic metaphysics and a complementary epistemology organized around two and only two logically coherent possibilities, the way of "is" and the way of "is not" (A or ~A). This is the first recorded theorization of what philosopher Karen Warren (1988) shows is the "logic of domination" that structures Western culture to this day. In the poem in which he presents his theory Parmenides first schematized the logic of domination of patriarchal culture by dividing "reality" and our talk about it into mutually exclusive and oppositional pairs (what "is/ what "is not"). These are arranged in a value hierarchy (what "is" is one, eternal, indivisible, imperishable, unchanging, and grounds Truth/ what "is not" is multiple, temporal, changing, mixed, ultimately non-existent, and grounds error and "mortal belief"). This hierarchy implicitly assumes "a structure of argumentation which explains, justifies, and maintains the subordination of an 'inferior' group ['is not'] by a 'superior' group ['is'] *on the grounds* of the (alleged) superiority and inferiority of the respective groups" (see Warren, 1988, 32, Warren's italics). With this binaristic formulation and the rejection of the way of "is not" as unintelligible, Parmenides is able "to lay claim to the knowledge of a truth not attained by the ordinary run of mortals" (Kirk et al, 1991, 243). In his day, as is still very much the case in our own, it was the privileged, elite male who could access the higher truth. He achieved this access through the use of his mind ("is", A) only, to the exclusion of his senses ("is not", ~A), thereby deserting the realm of the body and of "ordinary mortals."

With the articulation of his metaphysical scheme Parmenides claimed to have discovered the nature of the "reality" that lay behind mere "appearance". "Mortal belief", expressed in the speech of the hoi polloi, could make no such claim for it merely reflected the unreliable, ever shifting world of appearances. While only fragments of Parmenides' master work have survived, leaving the context of fragment 17 unclear, with "[o]n the right boys, on the left girls . . ." (Kirk et al, 260), he is clearly marking out sex as one of his binaristic pairs. Since it was girls and women, along with slaves, servants, and foreigners, who were denied access to the education and the leisure on which the newly discovered life of the mind depended, Parmenides' metaphysical divide reflected, and at the same time justified and entrenched, the existing social order: As he might also have put it, "on the right those who work with their minds (intellectuals), on the left those who work with their bodies." In the contemporary terminology of Simone de Beauvoir, woman is thus constructed as "Other," the oppositional category to the elite male Norm, defined in terms of deficiency and lack.

Beauvoir's notion of the Other has performed two important functions for contemporary feminists. First, it captures the logical structure of "woman" that has circulated in various formations since before the time of Parmenides. Appropriately, Beauvoir quotes Lévinas' androcentric and privileged description of Otherness from his *Temps et l'Autre*,

> Is there not a case in which otherness, alterity [*altérité*], unquestionably marks the nature of a being, as its essence, an instance of otherness not consisting purely and simply in the opposition of two species of the same genus? I think that the feminine represents the contrary in its absolute sense, this contrariness being in no wise affected by any relation between it and its correlative and thus remaining absolutely other. Sex is not a certain specific difference . . . no more is the sexual difference a mere contradiction.   Nor does this difference lie in the duality of two complementary terms, for two complementary terms imply a pre-existing whole. . . . Otherness reaches its full flowering in the feminine, a term of the same rank as consciousness but of opposite meaning. (quoted in Beauvoir, 1970, xvi).

To say, as Lévinas does, that the feminine is "contrary" is to express that absolute, essentialized difference which is captured in the A/~A formulation. The feminine (~A) can never be assimilated to the masculine Norm (A) without loosing its character as feminine. At the same time, to retain femininity is to retain inferiority and subordination. Thus the problematic issuing from this for contemporary, and particularity postliberal and postmodernist, feminists has been to provide a theorization of the feminine that would recognize and valorize the full humanity of women while subverting Parmenides' logic of domination.

But so powerful has this structuring of the contrary nature of the feminine been that it could be made to survive the radical metaphysical shifts that Western culture has undergone since the days of Parmenides, Plato, and subsequent philosophical upholders of the patriarchal tradition. Femininity has not always been ontologically rooted in the female body. As Thomas Laqueur has amply demonstrated (1990), until roughly the onset of the Enlightenment period and the concomitant ascendancy of the materialism favored by the New Science, male and female bodies were seen as epiphenomenal byproducts of the ontologically and epistemologically primary category of "gender"[1] or social role. The "one sex model" that dominated the premodern cultural orientation is succinctly captured by Galen, "Turn outward the woman's, turn inward, so to speak, and fold double the man's [genital organs], and you will find the same in both in every respect" (quoted in Laqueur, 1990, 25). This privileging of social role or gender over body was not merely enabled by dominant premodern cultural ideologies: In intellectual contexts such as the functional metaphysic of Aristotle in which form (body) followed function (social role), and the theology of Augustine in which not only was each being placed to fulfill the role assigned to it by God, but materiality in all of its manifestations, including the body, was subordinated to spirit, the privileging of social role over epiphenomenal body was the only position that made sense.

With the European Enlightenment came a general suspicion of theologically grounded explanations, the overthrow of social institutions that supported and derived power from them, and the growth of material science. But the areligious, even antireligious, tenor of the new, secular order deprived patriarchal power of its justification as God's will. Thus a serious power vacuum arose in gender politics with the loss of such props as Augustine's declaration that "the divine instructor teaches [that] those who are concerned for others give commands, the husband to his wife, the parents to their children, the masters to their servants, while those who are objects of concern obey; for example, the women their husbands, the children their parents, the servants their masters" (1974, 105). But, if nature abhors a vacuum, so does the social order, and theorists such as Jean Jacques Rousseau moved with alacrity to fill it.

The new materialism found expression in Rousseau's biologism, an articulation of the new "two sex model" in which the body is primary and gender and social role epiphenomenal. For those enlightened citizens who had rejected god and embraced science there was an obvious truth to such statements as, "The sameness and the difference [in biological sex] cannot but have an effect on mentality" (Rousseau, 1956, 131). And from this it was but a short step for Rousseau to reinstate the old order: "It is the part of the one to be active and strong, and of the other to be passive and weak. Accept this principle and it follows in the *second* place that woman is intended to please man [but] [m]asterfulness is his special attribute. He pleases by the very fact that he is strong. This is not the law of love, I admit. But it is the law of nature, which is more ancient than love" (131, italics in original).

Rousseau's biologism was quickly challenged by Mary Wollstonecraft, who grounded her critique in the corrupting influence of the property-based class system that also structured gender relations. The dependence on men that makes women "cunning, mean, and selfish" (Wollstonecraft, 1986, 155) also corrupts men, she argued. Hinting at a constructionist theory of gender, Wollstonecraft maintained that women's independence of male control, combined with the development of their rational capacity, will render them "more observant daughters, more affectionate sisters, more faithful wives, more reasonable mothers—in a word, better citizens" (164). That is, under the proper circumstances, ones that fostered the development of her rational capacity, women could be a lot more like men. In 1969, less than eighty years later, John Stuart Mill articulated a recognizably modernist form of gender construction theory. Because of the benefits they derive from the subservience of women, Mill argued, men "enslave the minds" of women (Mill, 1986, 232) by bringing them up from infancy to believe that "their ideal of character is the very opposite to that of men; not self-will, and government by self-control, but submission, and yielding to the control of others. All the moralities tell them that it is the duty of women, and all the current sentimentalities that it is their nature, to live for others; to make complete abnegation of themselves, and to have no life but in their affections" (232). In consequence, "[w]hat is now called the nature of women is an eminently artificial thing—the result of forced repression in some directions, unnatural stimulation in others (238).

Thus we can see in this brief history the maintenance, despite radically different ontological and epistemological orders, of gendered power relations grounded in a binaristic logic. Whether theorized as given in the nature of things or inscribed in the language we speak, the feminine as Other seems doomed to either subordination in the status quo, or erasure through assimilation to the contrary Norm. The problem only deepened with the development of postmodernist and poststructuralist positions which foregrounded the role of language/discourse in the construction of feminine being. Notoriously, while many of these attempts have, through their valorization of language, theoretically subverted the rigid binaristic structures handed down from the time of Parmenides, they have done so at the expense of alienation from, even the erasure of, the body. And so we can see that, with her notion of woman as Other, Simone de Beauvior has performed a second important function for feminists by alerting us to *a*, if not *the*, central problem with which femininists have grappled from the onset of mid-twentieth century second-wave feminism, which her work signals, through contemporary postmodernist and poststructuralist critique and theory. For women that problem, or complex of problems, is to find a way to articulate a reality of their own and then to translate their experience and vision into social praxis. But what is the solution? Can this project be affected either through, or by evading, the language that has been constructed at its deepest logical level to denigrate and control her while erasing her voice and experience? Or can feminists construct a symbolic more appropriate to their experience: One that will allow for the flourishing of women's lives? Can we provide a more adequate theorization of the female body or, more correctly, the different bodies of women? Do we even have access to our own bodies? How might we understand the relationship between corporeality and the hitherto gendered categories of space and time? And, for constructionist theories of the subject, what are the possibilities of ethical and political action? This is the central complex of issues taken up by the essays in this volume.

The feminist philosophers in this volume write with an acknowledged debt to postmodernism and poststructuralism, but at the same time take a critical distance from it. Their work is informed by the critiques of the purported objectivity and universalizability of the ahistorical truths produced by transcendent reason that have been developed by earlier philosophers. At the same time they share a willingness to deconstruct and refine the advances made by some of the leading postmodernist feminists (see also Nicholson, 1990). While the essays in this volume critically engage with work of such eminent thinkers as Luce Irigaray, Julia Kristeva, Judith Butler, and others, this engagement undertakes supplimentation, revision, and elaboration of their theories rather than either naive acceptance or rejection. What this signals is not an attempt at "theory building" in the sense of pre-Kuhnian theories of science, but rather the recognition of the need for an ongoing reflexivity in feminist theory and praxis.

In "Getting Real: How Matter Comes to Matter" Karen Barad contends that "language has been granted too much power" (11). Her project in this paper is to bring matter into a revised theory of performativity, thus expanding the usefulness of Judith Butler's work for both science studies and for feminist and queer theory through redressing the matter/language imbalance that she identifies in Butler's work. Barad seeks to affect this by providing an account of the materiality of both inanimate matter and human bodies together with an expanded account of regulatory practices that will supplement the discursive dimension with an account of their materiality. She holds that what emerges from this is an "ontology of agential reality" which goes beyond Butler by theorizing not only citationality but also intra-activity, and that allows for an emergent account of agency. Thus Barad provides a posthumanist notion of performativity in which language is not more trustworthy than matter. In her paper Barad contests a range of key binarisms of the dominant philosophical discourse including active/passive, subject/object, human/nonhuman, and epistemology/ontology.

In company with Karen Barad, Margrit Shildrick also problematizes matter and the body. In her "Monstrous Reflections on the Mirror of the Self-Same" she queries modernity's Cartesian erasure of corporeality and its discourse of the single and bounded subject. She engages the work of Irigaray, especially her exploration of the significance of touch, both to contest that modernist construction, and also to foreground issues arising from morphological differences which are not reducible to issues of sex/uality and which, she argues, have been ignored by feminist essentialists, constructionists, and phenomenologists. Specifically, Shildrick introduces the case of conjoined twins as an example of the "monstrous other," occupant of Anzaldua's borderlands and "insult to the norms of human corporeality," a figure which is both self and other and so represents our psychical experience of the "always already incorporation of otherness." In discrediting the Cartesian subject and turning to the other within, the monstrous and strange which is both self and alien, Shildrick reveals both our vulnerability and the possibility of engaging in an "ethics of risk."

In her paper Käthe Trettin proposes an ontological theory, the Ontology of Tropes, to address two issues in feminist theory, the Individuality Problem, that is, how to provide an account of individual features, e.g., particular womennesses, with general properties or generic concepts, and the Generality Problem which concerns the reference of generic "woman" and plural "women." Trettin's strategy is to provide a particularist and realist theory by improving on Natalie Stoljar's Resemblance Nominalism through the use of tropes as constituents of resemblance classes. This yields what she calls an Ontology of Individual Qualities that can explicate gender differences and similarities.

As her title suggests, in "Re-situating the Feminine in Contemporary French Philosophy" Louise Burchill surveys standard conceptualizations of the feminine and proposes an alternative. Grounded in the work of Deleuze and Guattari, Burchill argues that grasping the philosophical function in French texts of "the feminine" as a "conceptual persona" calls for an understanding of what it "personifies," that is, complexes of space and time. She holds that "the philosophical operation of "the feminine" can be qualified as that of a *schema* in the sense Kant gives to this term in the *Critique of Pure Reason* as a (pure) spatio-temporal determination that corresponds to a concept" (84). Exploring the ramifications of this, she argues that French philosophers deemed it possible to "extract from the attributes associated with 'women' as a psychosocial type a determination of time or temporality radically at odds with the conception of time shared by both common sense and metaphysics . . . it was judged capable of questioning the notion of time as a linear and homogeneous succession of present moments . . ." (85). Burchill then, however, suggests that the new conception of time (or proto-temporalization) that the French philosophers want to promote under the name of "difference" (or "differance") is nevertheless put into question by this very functioning of the feminine as a schema, insofar as this highlights a spatial modality that proves to be irreducible to the proto-temporalization in question. In this light, she examines the destiny reserved to Plato's notion of the *chora* in the French philosophical configuration, concentrating on the work of Kristeva, Derrida, and Irigaray, for this clearly shows the way in which the French authors—in order to claim the Platonic notion as a precursor of their own conception of a "pre-ontological site in which differentiation in general is produced"—are forced to disqualify Plato's conception of a nondifferentiated "originary spatiality" and to introduce a vector or movement of temporalization within this primordial spatial medium. In this sense, then, the very recourse to the feminine as a schema of a different ordering of time and space was to confront the contemporary French philosophers with the question of whether the proto-temporalizing process they thereby sought to transpose in intuitive terms was not itself dependent upon a more primordial "spatium."

In "To Take a Chance with Meaning under the Veil of Words: Transpositions, Mothers and Learning in Julia Kristeva's Theory of Language" Bettina Schmitz is concerned with how we can use the word "mother" from a feminist and critical perspective. This investigation, she stresses, is important for both women and men. She utilized Kristeva's linguistic theory to probe this concept, although she maintains that we must transgress Kristeva. In carrying out her project Schmitz argues that, with her focus on materiality/corporeality, we can go beyond and, at the same time correct, much poststructuralist theory. In her words, "we have to take into consideration that the first ordering of the subject is not based on itself but on another and that this other in most societies and for most people is the mother" (128). Thus an exploration of the child's early relationship with its mother's body will be of paramount theoretical importance.

Jana Braziel explores the material and the spatial as constructions of *le feminine* (the feminine) and argues that her study shows that not only time but also generation, motion, and temporality are set up for revaluation by the feminine's affiliation with the spatial and the material. Her paper, "Being and Time, Non-Being and Space. . . Introductory Notes Toward an Ontological Study of 'Woman' and *Chora*" is part of a larger work in which she draws especially upon the work of Luce Irigary, Judith Butler, Elizabeth Grosz, and Jacqueline Zita to address feminist and queer deconstructions of space and time as gendered philosophical categories. While her concern is with, in some sense, the ostensible "origins of 'western thought,'" she clarifies in a note that "I do not seek a pre-patriarchal, or pre-discursive, space or time; I do not seek a spatio-temporal 'before' as another ontological ground; I merely seek to reveal these beginnings as one of many *choric becomings*; one of many *sophic spaces*; and in this sense only, do I seek to *unravel time*, a time constructed as interior, immutable, transcendent and as the prime movements of an unmoved mover, to use Aristotleian terms" (fn. 1).

The ethical is a thematic running through many of the papers of this volume: Tonja van den Ende foregrounds it in "In Search of the Body in the Cave: Luce Irigaray's Ethics of Embodiment." She observes that, with the exception of Irigaray's *Speculum of the Other Woman,* unease with the possibility of essentialism and the devaluation of specific bodies (female, black, etc.) resulted in a neglect by feminists of this crucial topic until the appearance of groundbreaking works by Butler, Grosz, and Gatens in the nineties. Since, as Irigaray's work and also more recent feminist theory has claimed to have shown, there is no such thing as either "the human subject" or "the human body," we must now begin to interrogate the relation between bodies and identities. This is the task she sets herself. She undertakes to, first, show that Irigaray's work, with its focus on sexual difference, does not theoretically exclude treatment of other forms of difference. She then moves to supplement the body of feminist deconstructive theories of difference by foregrounding the lived experience of difference that is central to identity formation. Finally, she addresses the implications of her theory for ethics. In company with Irigaray, Tonja van den Ende argues for an embodied ethics that begins from the lived experience of relationship. She is now able to supplement Irigaray's position with recognition of difference for a relational ethics.

Harkening back to Simone de Beauvoir's formulation in *The Second Sex* that "One is not born but rather becomes a woman," Annemie Halsema undertakes to reconsider the role of the body in the accounts of gender identity developed by Judith Butler and Luce Irigaray. In "Reconsidering the Notion of the Body in Anti-Essentialism With the Help of Luce Irigaray and Judith Butler" she argues that, while Butler's notion of materialization overcomes the dualism of matter and constructionism, her reflections on the body are less than fully satisfying. She maintains that Irigaray's phenomenological approach to embodied identity offers a more promising direction for her project. The thesis of her work is that feminist anti-essentialism requires a new notion of the body which theorizes it as neither fully constructed nor as entirely outside of discourse and construction. Bringing the work of Irigaray and Butler into conversation enables Halsema to provide such an account.

Veronica Vasterling assesses a closely related set of problems to those considered by Annemie Halsema. Vasterling starts with the debate carried out between Butler, Benhabib, Cornell, and Fraser in *Feminist Contentions* (1995) around issues of subjectivity, agency, political action (how can we understand resistance on Butler's account?), and normativity (e.g., how can we make value judgments, especially about regimes of subjugation?). In "Butler's Sophisticated Constructionism: A Critical Assessment" Vasterling argues that Butler has successfully refuted the charge of linguistic monism which underpins much of the criticism leveled at her work, but at the price of advocating an epistemological position which is both too restrictive, and which generates negative consequences for feminist and queer theories of the body. However, she finds in Butler's Dutch interview (Costera Meijer and Prins, 1998) the possibility of an interpretation along the lines of a Kantian position, in Butler's words, "as it has been taken up by Derrida" (279), that opens up the promise of a potentially more fruitful phenomenological approach to the key issues of the intelligibility and accessibility of the body. Vasterling holds that the resolution of these issues along such Derridean lines may allow the "unintelligible body" to serve a critical and creative function. Developing this line of argument she concludes that Butler's "Derridean conception of language" does allow for a politically engaged account of agency.

Although we tend to think of constructivist theory, and so the issue of gender, as of fairly contemporary origin, Saskia Wendel argues in "A Critique of Feminist Radical Constructionism" that it is of much older provenance. Wendel demonstrates that constructivist theory can be traced back to the nominalist-realist controversy. A key issue in the nominalist-realist debate was the status of universals: are they merely constructs, or do they have an independent existence? Through a comparison with the work of William of Ockham (c. 1285–1349), who denied the existence of universals outside the mind, she maintains that the work of Judith Butler can be placed in the nominalist camp. Further, she argues that, with her negation of subjectivity and valorization of discourse, Butler moves closer to the extreme idealism of George Berkeley, who is often considered Ockham's theoretical successor. It is, Wendel argues, when Butler claims that the bearer of acts is discourse itself, which constitutes the subject, rather than 'spirit' or a 'recognizing subject' as Berkeley theorized, that her positions "mutates into extreme idealism" (186). Consequently Wendel argues for the necessity of a moderate realism in order to achieve a practicable approach to current issues surrounding sex and gender.

As several other contributors to this volume have done, Lanei Rodemeyer addresses the importance of theorizing space and time in her "Applying Time to Feminist Philosophy of the Body." Noting the dominant traditions' affiliation of time with masculinity and space with femininity, an articulation, once again, of the mind/active/masculine as opposed to the body/passive/feminine binaristic schema, Rodemeyer seeks to reveal the passive and intersubjective aspects of time and to bring temporality into feminist discussions of corporeality. A major strategy of her paper is to cite Susan Bordo's notion of the "slender body," specifically eating disorders as a manifestation of the battle between "mind" and "body," in order to discuss the interrelations of temporality and corporeality. Subsequent to this discussion, which reveals both the active and passive nature of temporal consciousness and of the body, she concludes by arguing that temporality and corporeality can only ever be analytically separated for in actuality they are always "intertwined."

Finally, in her paper "Diotima, Wittgenstein, and a Language for Liberation," Deborah Orr reads Diotima's speech in Plato's *Symposium* through the lens of Wittgenstein's work on conceptual grammar. Orr's position is that Diotima's words cannot appropriately be construed on either the referential model of meaning appropriate to Platonism, or through poststructuralist theory. Wittgenstein's work on pretheoretical language provides a "middle way" of reading Diotima that avoids the distortions of either of those approaches through recognizing embodiment and human "natural history" on the one hand, and, on the other, the role of the acquisition of language-games for the construction of the self. Orr argues that Diotima of Mantinea was possibly the first woman philosopher to contest the nascent patriarchal order of the ancient world; however, her work has been systematically misread by generations of philosophers in ways that render it a support for, rather than a radical critique of, that order. Orr examinations several major areas of affinity in the work of Diotima and Wittgenstein: (1) methodology, (2) the rejection of binaries and hierarchy, (3) human ontology and linguistic practice, (4) personal identity and epistemology, and (5) the therapeutic and ethico-religious purpose of their philosophy. The aim of her paper is to show that, once she is understood on her own terms, feminists will find a valuable message in Diotima's words, one which can advance feminist theory and praxis. This message is one of human maturation and the growth of love from the narrow obsession with beautiful bodies and physical procreation, toward an ever-widening concern with the creation of the circumstances and conditions in which human beings can flourish.

Early first-wave feminists have provided us with fertile resources of theory, models for praxis, and creative production. The almost immediate critiques of their work developed by women of color, lesbian and queer theorists, Latinas, those suffering socio-economic disadvantage, and many others have only served to strengthen and enrich the feminist movement. Their work and that of their early second wave critics continues to inform and inspire that of each new generation. The papers in this volume continue that tradition of productive critique of those who came before, critique that aims to strengthen the understanding and the voice of women through addressing the issues, both theoretical and practical, with which we are faced.

Note

1 Although Laqueur (1990) uses the term "gender" throughout his work, much of what characterizes gender as identity in modernity, especially its growing individualism and internalization, was not a part of the experience of premodern Western people.

Bibliography

Augustine *The City of God.* Book XIX. Pp. 89–113 in *Philosophy in the Middle Ages· The Christian, Islamic, and Jewish Traditions*, edited by Arthur Hyman and James J. Walsh. Indianapolis: Hackett Publishing Company, 1974

Benhabib, Seyla, Judith Butler, Drucilla Cornell, Nancy Fraser. *Feminist Contentions A Philosophical Exchange.* New York and London: Routledge, 1995

De Beauvoir, Simone. *The Second Sex.* New York: Bantam Books, 1970

Costera Meijer, Irene and Baukje Prins. "How Bodies Come to Matter: An Interview with Judith Butler." *Signs* 23, no. 2 (Winter 1998): 275–286.

Kirk, G. S., J. E. Raven, M. Schofield, editors. *The Presocratic Philosophers· A Critical History with a Selection of Texts.* Cambridge: Cambridge University Press, 1991.

Laqueur, Thomas *Making Sex: Body and Gender from the Greeks to Freud.* Cambridge, Massachusetts, and London, England: Harvard University Press. 1990

Mill, John Stuart *The Subjection of Women.* Pp. 217–317 in *Mary Wollstonecraft, A Vindication of the Rights of Woman, John Stuart Mill, The Subjection of Women*, introduced by Mary Warnock. London and Melbourne: Everyman's Library, 1985.

Nicholson, Linda J., editor *Feminism/Postmodernism.* Routledge: New York and London, 1990

Rousseau, Jean Jacques *Emile.* In *The Emile of Jean Jacques Rousseau Selections*, translated and edited by William Boyd. New York: Teachers College Press, 1956.

Warren, Karen J "Critical Thinking and Feminism." *Informal Logic* 10, no. 1 (1988): 31–44

Wollstonecraft, Mary. *The Subjection of Women* Pp. 1–215 in *Mary Wollstonecraft, A Vindication of the Rights of Woman, John Stuart Mill, The Subjection of Women*, introduced by Mary Warnock. London and Melbourne: Everyman's Library, 1985.

Chapter 2

Posthumanist Performativity: Toward an Understanding of How Matter Comes to Matter

Karen Barad

> Where did we ever get the strange idea that nature—as opposed to culture—is ahistorical and timeless? We are far too impressed by our own cleverness and self-consciousness . . . We need to stop telling ourselves the same old anthropocentric bedtime stories.
>
> —Steve Shaviro, 1997

Language has been granted too much power. The linguistic turn, the semiotic turn, the interpretative turn, the cultural turn: it seems that at every turn lately every "thing"—even materiality—is turned into a matter of language or some other form of cultural representation. The ubiquitous puns on "matter" do not, alas, mark a rethinking of the key concepts (materiality and signification) and the relationship between them. Rather, it seems to be symptomatic of the extent to which matters of "fact" (so to speak) have been replaced with matters of signification (no scare quotes here). Language matters. Discourse matters. Culture matters. There is an important sense in which the only thing that does not seem to matter anymore is matter.

What compels the belief that we have a direct access to cultural representations and their content that we lack toward the things represented? How did language come to be more trustworthy than matter? Why are language and culture granted their own agency and historicity while matter is figured as passive and immutable, or at best inherits a potential for change derivatively from language and culture? How does one even go about inquiring after the material conditions that have led us to such a brute reversal of naturalist beliefs when materiality itself is always already figured within a linguistic domain as its condition of possibility?

It is hard to deny that the power of language has been substantial. One might argue too substantial, or perhaps more to the point, too substantializing. Neither an exaggerated faith in the power of language nor the expressed concern that language is being granted too much power is a novel apprehension specifically attached to the early twenty-first century. For example, during the nineteenth century Nietzsche warned against the mistaken tendency to take grammar too seriously: allowing linguistic structure to shape or determine our understanding of the world, believing that the subject and predicate structure of language reflects a prior ontological reality of substance and attribute. The belief that grammatical categories reflect the underlying structure of the world is a continuing seductive habit of mind worth questioning. Indeed, the representationalist belief in the power of words to mirror preexisting phenomena is the metaphysical substrate that supports social constructivist, as well as traditional realist, beliefs. Significantly, social constructivism has been the object of intense scrutiny within both feminist and science studies circles where considerable and informed dissatisfaction has been voiced.[1]

A *performative* understanding of discursive practices challenges the representationalist belief in the power of words to represent preexisting things. Performativity, properly construed, is not an invitation to turn everything (including material bodies) into words; on the contrary, performativity is precisely a contestation of the excessive power granted to language to determine what is real. Hence, in ironic contrast to the misconception that would equate performativity with a form of linguistic monism that takes language to be the stuff of reality, performativity is actually a contestation of the unexamined habits of mind that grant language and other forms of representation more power in determining our ontologies than they deserve.[2]

The move toward performative alternatives to representationalism shifts the focus from questions of correspondence between descriptions and reality (e.g., do they mirror nature or culture?) to matters of practices/doings/actions. I would argue that these approaches also bring to the forefront important questions of ontology, materiality, and agency, while social constructivist approaches get caught up in the geometrical optics of reflection where, much like the infinite play of images between two facing mirrors, the epistemological gets bounced back and forth, but nothing more is seen. Moving away from the representationalist trap of geometrical optics, I shift the focus to physical optics, to questions of diffraction rather than reflection. Diffractively reading the insights of feminist and queer theory and science studies approaches through one another entails thinking the "social" and the "scientific" together in an illuminating way. What often appears as separate entities (and separate sets of concerns) with sharp edges does not actually entail a relation of absolute exteriority at all. Like the diffraction patterns illuminating the indefinite nature of boundaries—displaying shadows in "light" regions and bright spots in "dark" regions—the relation of the social and the scientific is a relation of "exteriority within." This is not a static relationality but a doing—the enactment of boundaries—that always entails constitutive exclusions and therefore requisite questions of accountability.[3] My aim is to contribute to efforts to sharpen the theoretical tool of performativity for science studies and feminist and queer theory endeavors alike, and to promote their mutual consideration. In this article, I offer an elaboration of performativity—a materialist, naturalist, and posthumanist elaboration—that allows matter its due as an active participant in the world's becoming, in its ongoing "intra-activity."[4] It is vitally important that we understand how matter matters.

From Representationalism to Performativity

> People represent. That is part of what it is to
> be a person. . . . Not *homo faber*, I say, but
> *homo depictor*.
> —Ian Hacking, 1983, 144, 132

Liberal social theories and theories of scientific knowledge alike owe much to the idea that the world is composed of individuals—presumed to exist before the law, or the discovery of the law—awaiting/inviting representation. The idea that beings exist as individuals with inherent attributes, anterior to their representation, is a metaphysical presupposition that underlies the belief in political, linguistic, and epistemological forms of representationalism. Or, to put the point the other way around, representationalism is the belief in the ontological distinction between representations and that which they purport to represent; in particular, that which is represented is held to be independent of all practices of representing. That is, there are assumed to be two distinct and independent kinds of entities—representations and entities to be represented. The system of representation is sometimes explicitly theorized in terms of a tripartite arrangement. For example, in addition to knowledge (i.e., representations), on the one hand, and the known (i.e., that which is purportedly represented), on the other, the existence of a knower (i.e., someone who does the representing) is sometimes made explicit. When this happens it becomes clear that representations serve a mediating function between independently existing entities. This taken-for-granted ontological gap generates questions of the accuracy of representations. For example, does scientific knowledge accurately represent an independently existing reality? Does language accurately represent its referent? Does a given political representative, legal counsel, or piece of legislation accurately represent the interests of the people allegedly represented?

Representationalism has received significant challenge from feminists, poststructuralists, postcolonial critics, and queer theorists. The names of Michel Foucault and Judith Butler are frequently associated with such questioning. Butler sums up the problematics of political representationalism as follows:

> Foucault points out that juridical systems of power *produce* the subjects they subsequently come to represent. Juridical notions of power appear to regulate political life in purely negative terms. . . . But the subjects regulated by such structures are, by virtue of being subjected to them, formed, defined, and reproduced in accordance with the requirements of those structures. If this analysis is right, then the juridical formation of language and politics that represents women as "the subject" of feminism is itself a discursive formation and effect of a given version of representationalist politics. And the feminist subject turns out to be discursively constituted by the very political system that is supposed to facilitate its emancipation (1990, 2).

In an attempt to remedy this difficulty, critical social theorists struggle to formulate understandings of the possibilities for political intervention that go beyond the framework of representationalism.

The fact that representationalism has come under suspicion in the domain of science studies is less well-known but of no less significance. Critical examination of representationalism did not emerge until the study of science shifted its focus from the nature and production of scientific knowledge to the study of the detailed dynamics of the actual practice of science. This significant shift is one way to coarsely characterize the difference in emphasis between separate multiple disciplinary studies of science (e.g., history of science, philosophy of science, sociology of science) and science studies. This is not to say that all science studies approaches are critical of representationalism; many such studies accept representationalism unquestioningly. For example, there are countless studies on the nature of scientific representations (including how scientists produce them, interpret them, and otherwise make use of them) that take for granted the underlying philosophical viewpoint that gives way to this focus—namely, representationalism. On the other hand, there has been a concerted effort by some science studies researchers to move beyond representationalism.

Ian Hacking's *Representing and Intervening* (1983) brought the question of the limitations of representationalist thinking about the nature of science to the forefront. The most sustained and thoroughgoing critique of representationalism in philosophy of science and science studies is to be found in the work of philosopher of science Joseph Rouse. Rouse has taken the lead in interrogating the constraints that representationalist thinking places on theorizing the nature of scientific practices.[5] For example, while the hackneyed debate between scientific realism and social constructivism moved frictionlessly from philosophy of science to science studies, Rouse (1996) has pointed out that these adversarial positions have more in common than their proponents acknowledge. Indeed, they share representationalist assumptions that foster such endless debates: both scientific realists and social constructivists believe that scientific knowledge (in its multiple representational forms such as theoretical concepts, graphs, particle tracks, photographic images) mediates our access to the material world; where they differ is on the question of referent, whether scientific knowledge represents things in the world as they really are (i.e., "Nature") or "objects" that are the product of social activities (i.e., "Culture"), but both groups subscribe to representationalism.

Representationalism is so deeply entrenched within Western culture that it has taken on a commonsense appeal. It seems inescapable, if not downright natural. But representationalism (like "nature itself," not merely our representations of it!) has a history. Hacking traces the philosophical problem of representations to the Democritean dream of atoms and the void. According to Hacking's anthropological philosophy, representations were unproblematic prior to Democritus: "the word 'real' first meant just unqualified likeness" (142). With Democritus's atomic theory emerges the possibility of a gap between representations and represented—"appearance" makes its first appearance. Is the table a solid mass made of wood or an aggregate of discrete entities moving in the void? Atomism poses the question of which representation is real. The problem of realism in philosophy is a product of the atomistic worldview.

Rouse identifies representationalism as a Cartesian by-product—a particularly inconspicuous consequence of the Cartesian division between "internal" and "external" that breaks along the line of the knowing subject. Rouse brings to light the asymmetrical faith in word over world that underlines the nature of Cartesian doubt:

> I want to encourage doubt about [the] presumption that representations (that is, their meaning or content) are more accessible to us than the things they supposedly represent. If there is no magic language through which we can unerringly reach out directly to its referents, why should we think there is nevertheless a language that magically enables us to reach out directly to its sense or representational content? The presumption that we can know what we mean, or what our verbal performances say, more readily than we can know the objects those sayings are about is a Cartesian legacy, a linguistic variation on Descartes' insistence that we have a direct and privileged access to the contents of our thoughts that we lack towards the "external" world. (1996, 209)

In other words, the asymmetrical faith in our access to representations over things is a contingent fact of history and not a logical necessity; that is, it is simply a Cartesian habit of mind. It takes a healthy skepticism toward Cartesian doubt to be able to begin to see an alternative.[6]

Indeed, it is possible to develop coherent philosophical positions that deny that there are representations on the one hand and ontologically separate entities awaiting representation on the other. A performative understanding, which shifts the focus from linguistic representations to discursive practices, is one such alternative. In particular, the search for alternatives to social constructivism has prompted performative approaches in feminist and queer studies, as well as in science studies. Judith Butler's name is most often associated with the term *performativity* in feminist and queer theory circles. And while Andrew Pickering has been one of the very few science studies scholars to take ownership of this term, there is surely a sense in which science studies theorists such as Donna Haraway, Bruno Latour, and Joseph Rouse also propound performative understandings of the nature of scientific practices.[7] Indeed, *performativity* has become a ubiquitous term in literary studies, theater studies, and the nascent interdisciplinary area of performance studies, prompting the question as to whether all performances are performative.[8] In this article, I propose a specifically posthumanist notion of performativity—one that incorporates important material and discursive, social and scientific, human and nonhuman, and natural and cultural factors. A posthumanist account calls into question the givenness of the differential categories of "human" and "nonhuman," examining the practices through which these differential boundaries are stabilized and destabilized.[9] Donna Haraway's scholarly opus—from primates to cyborgs to companion species—epitomizes this point.

If performativity is linked not only to the formation of the subject but also to the production of the matter of bodies, as Butler's account of "materialization" and Haraway's notion of "materialized refiguration" suggest, then it is all the more important that we understand the nature of this production.[10] Foucault's analytic of power links discursive practices to the materiality of the body. However, his account is constrained by several important factors that severely limit the potential of his analysis and Butler's performative elaboration, thereby forestalling an understanding of precisely *how* discursive practices produce material bodies.

If Foucault, in queering Marx, positions the body as the locus of productive forces, the site where the large-scale organization of power links up with local practices, then it would seem that any robust theory of the materialization of bodies would necessarily take account of *how the body's materiality*—for example, its anatomy and physiology—*and other material forces actively matter to the processes of materialization*. Indeed, as Foucault makes crystal clear in the last chapter of *The History of Sexuality* (vol. 1), he is not out to deny the relevance of the physical body but, on the contrary, to

> show how the deployments of power are directly connected to the body—to bodies, functions, physiological processes, sensations, and pleasures; far from the body having to be effaced, what is needed is to make it visible through an analysis in which the biological and the historical are not consecutive to one another . . . but are bound together in an increasingly complex fashion in accordance with the development of the modern technologies of power that take life as their objective. Hence, I do not envision a "history of mentalities" that would take account of bodies only through the manner in which they have been perceived and given meaning and value; but a "history of bodies" and the manner in which what is most material and most vital in them has been invested. (1980a, 15–52)

On the other hand, Foucault does not tell us in what way the biological and the historical are "bound together" such that one is not consecutive to the other. What is it about the materiality of bodies that makes it susceptible to the enactment of biological and historical forces simultaneously? To what degree does the matter of bodies have its own historicity? Are social forces the only ones susceptible to change? Are not biological forces in some sense always already historical ones? Could it be that there is some important sense in which historical forces are always already biological? What would it mean to even ask such a question given the strong social constructivist undercurrent in certain interdisciplinary circles in the early twenty-first century? For all Foucault's emphasis on the political anatomy of disciplinary power, he too fails to offer an account of the body's historicity in which its very materiality plays an *active* role in the workings of power. This implicit reinscription of matter's passivity is a mark of extant elements of representationalism that haunt his largely postrepresentationalist account.[11] This deficiency is importantly related to his failure to theorize the relationship between "discursive" and "nondiscursive" practices. As materialist feminist theorist Rosemary Hennessey insists in offering her critique of Foucault, "a rigorous materialist theory of the body cannot stop with the assertion that the body is always discursively constructed. It also needs to explain how the discursive construction of the body is related to nondiscursive practices in ways that vary widely from one social formation to another" (1993, 46).

Crucial to understanding the workings of power is an understanding of the nature of power in the fullness of its materiality. To restrict power's productivity to the limited domain of the "social," for example, or to figure matter as merely an end product rather than an active factor in further materializations is to cheat matter out of the fullness of its capacity. How might we understand not only how human bodily contours are constituted through psychic processes but how even the very atoms that make up the biological body come to matter and, more generally, how matter makes itself felt? It is difficult to imagine how psychic and sociohistorical forces alone could account for the production of matter. Surely it is the case—even when the focus is restricted to the materiality of "human" bodies—that there are "natural," not merely "social," forces that matter. Indeed, there is a host of material-discursive forces—including ones that get labeled "social," "cultural," "psychic," "economic," "natural," "physical," "biological," "geopolitical," and "geological"—that may be important to particular (entangled) processes of materialization. If we follow disciplinary habits of tracing disciplinary-defined causes through to the corresponding disciplinary-defined effects, we will miss all the crucial intra-actions among these forces that fly in the face of any specific set of disciplinary concerns.[12]

What is needed is a robust account of the materialization of *all* bodies — "human" and "nonhuman"—and the material-discursive practices by which their differential constitutions are marked. This will require an understanding of the nature of the relationship between discursive practices and material phenomena, an accounting of "nonhuman" as well as "human" forms of agency, and an understanding of the precise causal nature of productive practices that takes account of the fullness of matter's implication in its ongoing historicity. My contribution toward the development of such an understanding is based on a philosophical account that I have been calling "agential realism." Agential realism is an account of technoscientific and other practices that takes feminist, antiracist, poststructuralist, queer, Marxist, science studies, and scientific insights seriously, building specifically on important insights from Niels Bohr, Judith Butler, Michel Foucault, Donna Haraway, Vicki Kirby, Joseph Rouse, and others.[13] It is clearly not possible to fully explicate these ideas here. My more limited goal in this article is to use the notion of performativity as a diffraction grating for reading important insights from feminist and queer studies and science studies through one another while simultaneously proposing a materialist and posthumanist reworking of the notion of performativity. This entails a reworking of the familiar notions of discursive practices, materialization, agency, and causality, among others.

I begin by issuing a direct challenge to the metaphysical underpinnings of representationalism, proposing an agential realist ontology as an alternative. In the following section I offer a posthumanist performative reformulation of the notion of discursive practices and materiality and theorize a specific causal relationship between them. In the final section I discuss the agential realist conceptions of causality and agency that are vital to understanding the productive nature of material-discursive practices, including technoscientific ones.

Toward a Performative Metaphysics

> As long as we stick to things and words we can believe that we are speaking of what we see, that we see what we are speaking of, and that the two are linked.
> —Giles Deleuze, 1988, 65

> "Words and things" is the entirely serious title of a problem.
> —Michel Foucault, 1972, 49

Representationalism separates the world into the ontologically disjoint domains of words and things, leaving itself with the dilemma of their linkage such that knowledge is possible. If words are untethered from the material world, how do representations gain a foothold? If we no longer believe that the world is teeming with inherent resemblances whose signatures are inscribed on the face of the world, things already emblazoned with signs, words lying in wait like so many pebbles of sand on a beach there to be discovered, but rather that the knowing subject is enmeshed in a thick web of representations such that the mind cannot see its way to objects that are now forever out of reach and all that is visible is the sticky problem of humanity's own captivity within language, then it begins to become apparent that representationalism is a prisoner of the problematic metaphysics it postulates. Like the frustrated would-be runner in Zeno's paradox, representationalism never seems to be able to get any closer to solving the problem it poses because it is caught in the impossibility of stepping outward from its metaphysical starting place. Perhaps it would be better to begin with a different starting point, a different metaphysics.[14]

Thingification—the turning of relations into "things," "entities," "relata"— infects much of the way we understand the world and our relationship to it.[15] Why do we think that the existence of relations requires relata? Does the persistent distrust of nature, materiality, and the body that pervades much of contemporary theorizing and a sizable amount of the history of Western thought feed off of this cultural proclivity? In this section, I present a relational ontology that rejects the metaphysics of relata, of "words" and "things." On an agential realist account, it is once again possible to acknowledge nature, the body, and materiality in the fullness of their becoming without resorting to the optics of transparency or opacity, the geometries of absolute exteriority or interiority, and the theoretization of the human as either pure cause or pure effect while at the same time remaining resolutely accountable for the role "we" play in the intertwined practices of knowing and becoming.

The postulation of individually determinate entities with inherent properties is the hallmark of atomistic metaphysics. Atomism hails from Democritus.[16] According to Democritus the properties of all things derive from the properties of the smallest unit—atoms (the "uncuttable" or "inseparable"). Liberal social theories and scientific theories alike owe much to the idea that the world is composed of individuals with separately attributable properties. An entangled web of scientific, social, ethical, and political practices, and our understanding of them, hinges on the various/differential instantiations of this presupposition. Much hangs in the balance in contesting its seeming inevitability.

Physicist Niels Bohr won the Nobel Prize for his quantum model of the atom, which marks the beginning of his seminal contributions to the development of the quantum theory.[17] Bohr's philosophy-physics (the two were inseparable for him) poses a radical challenge not only to Newtonian physics but also to Cartesian epistemology and its representationalist triadic structure of words, knowers, and things. Crucially, in a stunning reversal of his intellectual forefather's schema, Bohr rejects the atomistic metaphysics that takes "things" as ontologically basic entities. For Bohr, things do not have inherently determinate boundaries or properties, and words do not have inherently determinate meanings. Bohr also calls into question the related Cartesian belief in the inherent distinction between subject and object, and knower and known.

It might be said that the epistemological framework that Bohr develops rejects both the transparency of language and the transparency of measurement; however, even more fundamentally, it rejects the presupposition that language and measurement perform mediating functions. Language does not represent states of affairs, and measurements do not represent measurement-independent states of being. Bohr develops his epistemological framework without giving in to the despair of nihilism or the sticky web of relativism. With brilliance and finesse, Bohr finds a way to hold on to the possibility of objective knowledge while the grand structures of Newtonian physics and representationalism begin to crumble.

Bohr's break with Newton, Descartes, and Democritus is not based in "mere idle philosophical reflection" but on new empirical findings in the domain of atomic physics that came to light during the first quarter of the twentieth century. Bohr's struggle to provide a theoretical understanding of these findings resulted in his radical proposal that an entirely new epistemological framework is required. Unfortunately, Bohr does not explore crucial ontological dimensions of his insights but rather focuses on their epistemological import. I have mined his writings for his implicit ontological views and have elaborated on them in the development of an agential realist ontology. In this section, I present a quick overview of important aspects of Bohr's account and move on to an explication of an agential realist ontology. This relational ontology is the basis for my posthumanist performative account of the production of material bodies. This account refuses the representationalist fixation on "words" and "things" and the problematic of their relationality, advocating instead *a causal relationship between specific exclusionary practices embodied as specific material configurations of the world* (i.e., discursive practices/(con)figurations rather than "words") *and specific material phenomena* (i.e., relations rather than "things"). This causal relationship between the apparatuses of bodily production and the phenomena produced is one of "agential intra-action." The details follow.

According to Bohr, *theoretical concepts* (e.g., "position" and "momentum") are not ideational in character but rather *are specific physical arrangements.*[18] For example, the notion of "position" cannot be presumed to be a well-defined abstract concept, nor can it be presumed to be an inherent attribute of independently existing objects. Rather, "position" only has meaning when a rigid apparatus with fixed parts is used (e.g., a ruler is nailed to a fixed table in the laboratory, thereby establishing a fixed frame of reference for specifying "position"). And furthermore, any measurement of "position" using this apparatus cannot be attributed to some abstract independently existing "object" but rather is a property of the *phenomenon*—the inseparability of "observed object" and "agencies of observation." Similarly, "momentum" is only meaningful as a material arrangement involving movable parts. Hence, the simultaneous indeterminacy of "position" and "momentum" (what is commonly referred to as the Heisenberg uncertainty principle) is a straightforward matter of the material exclusion of "position" and "momentum" arrangements (one requiring fixed parts and the complementary arrangement requiring movable parts).[19]

Therefore, according to Bohr, the primary epistemological unit is not independent objects with inherent boundaries and properties but rather *phenomena*. On my agential realist elaboration, phenomena do not merely mark the epistemological inseparability of "observer" and "observed"; rather, *phenomena are the ontological inseparability of agentially intra-acting "components."* That is, phenomena are ontologically primitive relations— relations without preexisting relata.[20] The notion of *intra-action* (in contrast to the usual "interaction," which presumes the prior existence of independent entities/relata) represents a profound conceptual shift. It is through specific agential intra-actions that the boundaries and properties of the "components" of phenomena become determinate and that particular embodied concepts become meaningful. A specific intra-action (involving a specific material configuration of the "apparatus of observation") enacts an *agential cut* (in contrast to the Cartesian cut—an inherent distinction—between subject and object) effecting a separation between "subject" and "object." That is, the agential cut enacts a *local* resolution *within* the phenomenon of the inherent ontological indeterminacy. In other words, relata do not preexist relations; rather, relata-within-phenomena emerge through specific intra-actions. Crucially then, intra-actions enact *agential separability*—the local condition of *exteriority-within-phenomena*. The notion of agential separability is of fundamental importance, for in the absence of a classical ontological condition of exteriority between observer and observed it provides the condition for the possibility of objectivity. Moreover, the agential cut enacts a local causal structure among "components" of a phenomenon in the marking of the "measuring agencies" ("effect") by the "measured object" ("cause"). Hence, *the notion of intra-actions constitutes a reworking of the traditional notion of causality.*[21]

In my further elaboration of this agential realist ontology, I argue that phenomena are not the mere result of laboratory exercises engineered by human subjects. Nor can the apparatuses that produce phenomena be understood as observational devices or mere laboratory instruments. Although space constraints do not allow an in-depth discussion of the agential realist understanding of the nature of apparatuses, since apparatuses play such a crucial, indeed constitutive, role in the production of phenomena, I present an overview of the agential realist theoretization of apparatuses before moving on to the question of the nature of phenomena. The proposed elaboration enables an exploration of the implications of the agential realist ontology beyond those specific to understanding the nature of scientific practices. In fact, agential realism offers an understanding of the nature of material-discursive practices, such as those very practices through which different distinctions get drawn, including those between the "social" and the "scientific."[22]

Apparatuses are not inscription devices, scientific instruments set in place before the action happens, or machines that mediate the dialectic of resistance and accommodation. They are neither neutral probes of the natural world nor structures that deterministically impose some particular outcome. In my further elaboration of Bohr's insights, apparatuses are not mere static arrangements *in* the world, but rather *apparatuses are dynamic (re)configurings of the world, specific agential practices/intra-actions/performances through which specific exclusionary boundaries are enacted*. Apparatuses have no inherent "outside" boundary. This indeterminacy of the "outside" boundary represents the impossibility of closure—the ongoing intra-activity in the iterative reconfiguring of the apparatus of bodily production. Apparatuses are open-ended practices.

Importantly, apparatuses are themselves phenomena. For example, as scientists are well aware, apparatuses are not preformed interchangeable objects that sit atop a shelf waiting to serve a particular purpose. Apparatuses are constituted through particular practices that are perpetually open to rearrangements, rearticulations, and other reworkings. This is part of the creativity and difficulty of doing science: getting the instrumentation to work in a particular way for a particular purpose (which is always open to the possibility of being changed during the experiment as different insights are gained). Furthermore, any particular apparatus is always in the process of intra-acting with other apparatuses, and the enfolding of locally stabilized phenomena (which may be traded across laboratories, cultures, or geopolitical spaces only to find themselves differently materializing) into subsequent iterations of particular practices constitutes important shifts in the particular apparatus in question and therefore in the nature of the intra-actions that result in the production of new phenomena, and so on. Boundaries do not sit still.

With this background we can now return to the question of the nature of phenomena. Phenomena are produced through agential intra-actions of multiple apparatuses of bodily production. Agential intra-actions are specific causal material enactments that may or may not involve "humans." Indeed, it is through such practices that the differential boundaries between "humans" and "nonhumans," "culture" and "nature," the "social" and the "scientific" are constituted. Phenomena are constitutive of reality. Reality is not composed of things-in-themselves or things-behind-phenomena but "things"-in-phenomena.[23] The world *is* intra-activity in its differential mattering. It is through specific intra-actions that a differential sense of being is enacted in the ongoing ebb and flow of agency. That is, it is through specific intra-actions that phenomena come to matter—in both senses of the word. The world is a dynamic process of intra-activity in the ongoing reconfiguring of locally determinate causal structures with determinate boundaries, properties, meanings, and patterns of marks on bodies. This ongoing flow of agency through which "part" of the world makes itself differentially intelligible to another "part" of the world and through which local causal structures, boundaries, and properties are stabilized and destabilized does not take place in space and time but in the making of spacetime itself. The world is an ongoing open process of mattering through which "mattering" itself acquires meaning and form in the realization of different agential possibilities. Temporality and spatiality emerge in this processual historicity. Relations of exteriority, connectivity, and exclusion are reconfigured. The changing topologies of the world entail an ongoing reworking of the very nature of dynamics.

In summary, the universe is agential intra-activity in its becoming. The primary ontological units are not "things" but phenomena—dynamic topological reconfigurings/entanglements/relationalities/(re)articulations. And the primary semantic units are not "words" but material-discursive practices through which boundaries are constituted. This dynamism *is* agency. Agency is not an attribute but the ongoing reconfigurings of the world. On the basis of this performative metaphysics, in the next section I propose a posthumanist refiguration of the nature of materiality and discursivity and the relationship between them, and a posthumanist account of performativity.

A Posthumanist Account of Material-Discursive Practices

Discursive practices are often confused with linguistic expression, and meaning is often thought to be a property of words. Hence, discursive practices and meanings are said to be peculiarly human phenomena. But if this were true, how would it be possible to take account of the boundary-making practices by which the differential constitution of "humans" and nonhumans" are enacted? It would be one thing if the notion of constitution were to be understood in purely epistemic terms, but it is entirely unsatisfactory when questions of ontology are on the table. If "humans" refers to phenomena, not independent entities with inherent properties but rather beings in their differential becoming, particular material (re)configurings of the world with shifting boundaries and properties that stabilize and destabilize along with specific material changes in what it means to be human, then the notion of discursivity cannot be founded on an inherent distinction between humans and nonhumans. In this section, I propose a posthumanist account of discursive practices. I also outline a concordant reworking of the notion of materiality and hint at an agential realist approach to understanding the relationship between discursive practices and material phenomena.

Meaning is not a property of individual words or groups of words. Meaning is neither intralinguistically conferred nor extralinguistically referenced. Semantic contentfulness is not achieved through the thoughts or performances of individual agents but rather through particular discursive practices. With the inspiration of Bohr's insights, it would also be tempting to add the following agential realist points: meaning is not ideational but rather specific material (re)configurings of the world, and semantic indeterminacy, like ontological indeterminacy, is only locally resolvable through specific intra-actions. But before proceeding, it is probably worth taking a moment to dispel some misconceptions about the nature of discursive practices.

Discourse is not a synonym for language.[24] Discourse does not refer to linguistic or signifying systems, grammars, speech acts, or conversations. To think of discourse as mere spoken or written words forming descriptive statements is to enact the mistake of representationalist thinking. Discourse is not what is said; it is that which constrains and enables what can be said. Discursive practices define what counts as meaningful statements. Statements are not the mere utterances of the originating consciousness of a unified subject; rather, statements and subjects emerge from a field of possibilities. This field of possibilities is not static or singular but rather is a dynamic and contingent multiplicity.

According to Foucault, discursive practices are the local sociohistorical material conditions that enable and constrain disciplinary knowledge practices such as speaking, writing, thinking, calculating, measuring, filtering, and concentrating. Discursive practices produce, rather than merely describe, the "subjects" and "objects" of knowledge practices. On Foucault's account these "conditions" are immanent and historical rather than transcendental or phenomenological. That is, they are not conditions in the sense of transcendental, ahistorical, cross-cultural, abstract laws defining the possibilities of experience (Kant), but rather they are actual historically situated social conditions.

Foucault's account of discursive practices has some provocative resonances (and some fruitful dissonances) with Bohr's account of apparatuses and the role they play in the material production of bodies and meanings. For Bohr, apparatuses are particular physical arrangements that give meaning to certain concepts to the exclusion of others; they are the local physical conditions that enable and constrain knowledge practices such as conceptualizing and measuring; they are productive of (and part of) the phenomena produced; they enact a local cut that produces "objects" of particular knowledge practices within the particular phenomena produced. On the basis of his profound insight that "concepts" (which are actual physical arrangements) and "things" do not have determinate boundaries, properties, or meanings apart from their mutual intra-actions, Bohr offers a new epistemological framework that calls into question the dualisms of object/subject, knower/known, nature/culture, and word/world.

Bohr's insight that concepts are not ideational but rather are actual physical arrangements is clearly an insistence on the materiality of meaning making that goes beyond what is usually meant by the frequently heard contemporary refrain that writing and talking are material practices. Nor is Bohr merely claiming that discourse is "supported" or "sustained" by material practices, as Foucault seems to suggest (though the nature of this "support" is not specified), or that nondiscursive (background) practices determine discursive practices, as some existential-pragmatic philosophers purport.[25] Rather, Bohr's point entails a much more intimate relationship between concepts and materiality. In order to better understand the nature of this relationship, it is important to shift the focus from linguistic concepts to discursive practices.

On an agential realist elaboration of Bohr's theoretical framework, apparatuses are not static arrangements in the world that embody particular concepts to the exclusion of others; rather, apparatuses are specific material practices through which local semantic and ontological determinacy are intra-actively enacted. That is, apparatuses are the exclusionary practices of mattering through which intelligibility and materiality are constituted. Apparatuses are material (re)configurings/discursive practices that produce material phenomena in their discursively differentiated becoming. A phenomenon is a dynamic relationality that is locally determinate in its matter and meaning as mutually determined (within a particular phenomenon) through specific causal intra-actions. Outside of particular agential intra-actions, "words" and "things" are indeterminate. Hence, the notions of materiality and discursivity must be reworked in a way that acknowledges their mutual entailment. In particular, on an agential realist account, both materiality and discursive practices are rethought in terms of intra-activity.

On an agential realist account, *discursive practices are specific material (re)configurings of the world through which local determinations of boundaries, properties, and meanings are differentially enacted. That is, discursive practices are ongoing agential intra-actions of the world through which local determinacy is enacted within the phenomena produced. Discursive practices are causal intra-actions*—they enact local causal structures through which one "component" (the "effect") of the phenomenon is marked by another "component" (the "cause") in their differential articulation. Meaning is not a property of individual words or groups of words but an ongoing performance of the world in its differential intelligibility. In its causal intra-activity, "part" of the world becomes determinately bounded and propertied in its emergent intelligibility to another "part" of the world. Discursive practices are boundary-making practices that have no finality in the ongoing dynamics of agential intra-activity.

Discursive practices are not speech acts, linguistic representations, or even linguistic performances, bearing some unspecified relationship to material practices. Discursive practices are not anthropomorphic placeholders for the projected agency of individual subjects, culture, or language. Indeed, they are not human-based practices. On the contrary, agential realism's posthumanist account of discursive practices does not fix the boundary between "human" and "nonhuman" before the analysis ever gets off the ground but rather enables (indeed demands) a genealogical analysis of the discursive emergence of the "human." "Human bodies" and "human subjects" do not preexist as such; nor are they mere end products. "Humans" are neither pure cause nor pure effect but part of the world in its open-ended becoming.

Matter, like meaning, is not an individually articulated or static entity. Matter is not little bits of nature, or a blank slate, surface, or site passively awaiting signification; nor is it an uncontested ground for scientific, feminist, or Marxist theories. Matter is not a support, location, referent, or source of sustainability for discourse. Matter is not immutable or passive. It does not require the mark of an external force like culture or history to complete it. Matter is always already an ongoing historicity.[26]

On an agential realist account, matter does not refer to a fixed substance; rather, *matter is substance in its intra-active becoming—not a thing, but a doing, a congealing of agency. Matter is a stabilizing and destabilizing process of iterative intra-activity.* Phenomena—the smallest material units (relational "atoms")—come to matter through this process of ongoing intra-activity. That is, *matter refers to the materiality/materialization of phenomena*, not to an inherent fixed property of abstract independently existing objects of Newtonian physics (the modernist realization of the Democritean dream of atoms and the void).

Matter is not simply "a kind of citationality" (Butler, 1993, 15), the surface effect of human bodies, or the end product of linguistic or discursive acts. Material constraints and exclusions and the material dimensions of regulatory practices are important factors in the process of materialization. The dynamics of intra-activity entails matter as an *active* "agent" in its ongoing materialization.

Boundary-making practices, that is, discursive practices, are fully implicated in the dynamics of intra-activity through which phenomena come to matter. In other words, materiality is discursive (i.e., material phenomena are inseparable from the apparatuses of bodily production: matter emerges out of and includes as part of its being the ongoing reconfiguring of boundaries), just as discursive practices are always already material (i.e., they are ongoing material (re)configurings of the world). Discursive practices and material phenomena do not stand in a relationship of externality to one another; rather, the material and the discursive are mutually implicated in the dynamics of intra-activity. But nor are they reducible to one another. The relationship between the material and the discursive is one of mutual entailment. Neither is articulated/articulable in the absence of the other; matter and meaning are mutually articulated. Neither discursive practices nor material phenomena are ontologically or epistemologically prior. Neither can be explained in terms of the other. Neither has privileged status in determining the other.

Apparatuses of bodily production and the phenomena they produce are material-discursive in nature. *Material-discursive practices are specific iterative enactments—agential intra-actions—through which matter is differentially engaged and articulated (in the emergence of boundaries and meanings), reconfiguring the material-discursive field of possibilities in the iterative dynamics of intra-activity that is agency.* Intra-actions are causally constraining nondeterministic enactments through which matter-in-the-process-of-becoming is sedimented out and enfolded in further materializations.[27]

Material conditions matter, not because they "support" particular discourses that are the actual generative factors in the formation of bodies but rather because *matter comes to matter* through the iterative intraactivity of the world in its becoming. The point is not merely that there are important material factors in addition to discursive ones; rather, the issue is the conjoined material-discursive nature of constraints, conditions, and practices. The fact that material and discursive constraints and exclusions are intertwined points to the limited validity of analyses that attempt to determine individual effects of material or discursive factors.[28] Furthermore, the conceptualization of materiality offered by agential realism makes it possible to take account of material constraints and conditions once again without reinscribing traditional empiricist assumptions concerning the transparent or immediate given-ness of the world and without falling into the analytical stalemate that simply calls for a recognition of our mediated access to the world and then rests its case. The ubiquitous pronouncements proclaiming that experience or the material world is "mediated" have offered precious little guidance about how to proceed. The notion of mediation has for too long stood in the way of a more thoroughgoing accounting of the empirical world. The reconceptualization of materiality offered here makes it possible to take the empirical world seriously once again, but this time with the understanding that the objective referent is phenomena, not the seeming "immediately given-ness" of the world.

All bodies, not merely "human" bodies, come to matter through the world's iterative intra-activity—its performativity. This is true not only of the surface or contours of the body but also of the body in the fullness of its physicality, including the very "atoms" of its being. Bodies are not objects with inherent boundaries and properties; they are material-discursive phenomena. "Human" bodies are not inherently different from "nonhuman" ones. What constitutes the "human" (and the "nonhuman") is not a fixed or pregiven notion, but nor is it a free-floating ideality. What is at issue is not some ill-defined process by which human-based linguistic practices (materially supported in some unspecified way) manage to produce substantive bodies/bodily substances but rather a material dynamics of intra-activity: material apparatuses produce material phenomena through specific causal intra-actions, where "material" is always already material-discursive—*that is what it means to matter*. Theories that focus exclusively on the materialization of "human" bodies miss the crucial point that the very practices by which the differential boundaries of the "human" and the "nonhuman" are drawn are always already implicated in particular materializations. The differential constitution of the "human" ("nonhuman") is always accompanied by particular exclusions and always open to contestation. This is a result of the nondeterministic causal nature of agential intra-actions, a crucial point that I take up in the next section.

The Nature of Production and the Production of Nature:
Agency and Causality

What is the nature of causality on this account? What possibilities exist for agency, for intervening in the world's becoming? Where do the issues of responsibility and accountability enter in?

Agential intra-actions are causal enactments. Recall that an agential cut effects a local separability of different "component parts" of the phenomenon, one of which ("the cause") expresses itself in effecting and marking the other ("the effect"). In a scientific context this process is known as a "measurement." (Indeed, the notion of "measurement" is nothing more or less than a causal intra-action.)[29] Whether it is thought of as a "measurement," or as part of the universe making itself intelligible to another part in its ongoing differentiating intelligibility and materialization, is a matter of preference.[30] Either way, what is important about causal intra-actions is the fact that marks are left on bodies. Objectivity means being accountable to marks on bodies.

This causal structure differs in important respects from the common choices of absolute exteriority and absolute interiority and of determinism and free will. In the case of the geometry of absolute exteriority, the claim that cultural practices produce material bodies starts with the metaphysical presumption of the ontological distinction of the former set from the latter. The inscription model of constructivism is of this kind: culture is figured as an external force acting on passive nature. There is an ambiguity in this model as to whether nature exists in any prediscursive form prior to its marking by culture. If there is such an antecedent entity then its very existence marks the inherent limit of constructivism. In this case, the rhetoric should be softened to more accurately reflect the fact that the force of culture "shapes" or "inscribes" nature but does not materially *produce* it. On the other hand, if there is no preexistent nature, then it behooves those who advocate such a theory to explain how it is that culture can materially produce that from which it is allegedly ontologically distinct, namely nature. What is the mechanism of this production? The other usual alternative is also not attractive: the geometry of absolute interiority amounts to a reduction of the effect to its cause, or in this case nature to culture, or matter to language, which amounts to one form or another of idealism.

Agential separability presents an alternative to these unsatisfactory options.[31] It postulates a sense of "exteriority within," one that rejects the previous geometries and opens up a much larger space that is more appropriately thought of as a changing topology.[32] More specifically, *agential separability* is a matter of *exteriority within* (*material-discursive*) *phenomena*. Hence, no priority is given to either materiality or discursivity.[33] There is no geometrical relation of absolute exteriority between a "causal apparatus" and a "body effected," nor an idealistic collapse of the two, but rather an ongoing topological dynamics that enfolds the spacetime manifold upon itself, a result of the fact that the apparatuses of bodily production (which are themselves phenomena) are (also) part of the phenomena they produce. Matter plays an active, indeed agential, role in its iterative materialization, but this is not the only reason that the space of agency is much larger than that postulated in many other critical social theories.[34] Intra-actions always entail particular exclusions, and exclusions foreclose any possibility of determinism, providing the condition of an open future.[35] Therefore, intra-actions are constraining but not determining. That is, intra-activity is neither a matter of strict determinism nor unconstrained freedom. The future is radically open at every turn. This open sense of futurity does not depend on the clash or collision of cultural demands; rather, it is inherent in the nature of intra-activity—even when apparatuses are primarily reinforcing, agency is not foreclosed. Hence, the notion of intra-actions reformulates the traditional notion of causality and opens up a space, indeed a relatively large space, for material-discursive forms of agency.

A posthumanist formulation of performativity makes evident the importance of taking account of "human," "nonhuman," and "cyborgian" forms of agency (indeed all such material-discursive forms). This is both possible and necessary because agency is a matter of changes in the apparatuses of bodily production, and such changes take place through various intra-actions, some of which remake the boundaries that delineate the differential constitution of the "human." Holding the category "human" fixed excludes an entire range of possibilities in advance, eliding important dimensions of the workings of power.

On an agential realist account, agency is cut loose from its traditional humanist orbit. Agency is not aligned with human intentionality or subjectivity. Nor does it merely entail resignification or other specific kinds of moves within a social geometry of antihumanism. Agency is a matter of intra-acting; it is an enactment, not something that someone or something has. Agency cannot be designated as an attribute of "subjects" or "objects" (as they do not preexist as such). Agency is not an attribute whatsoever—it is "doing"/"being" in its intra-activity. Agency is the enactment of iterative changes to particular practices through the dynamics of intra-activity. Agency is about the possibilities and accountability entailed in reconfiguring material-discursive apparatuses of bodily production, including the boundary articulations and exclusions that are marked by those practices in the enactment of a causal structure. Particular possibilities for acting exist at every moment, and these changing possibilities entail a responsibility to intervene in the world's becoming, to contest and rework what matters and what is excluded from mattering.

Conclusions

Feminist studies, queer studies, science studies, cultural studies, and critical social theory scholars are among those who struggle with the difficulty of coming to terms with the weightiness of the world. On the one hand, there is an expressed desire to recognize and reclaim matter and its kindred reviled Others exiled from the familiar and comforting domains of culture, mind, and history, not simply to altruistically advocate on behalf of the subaltern but in the hopes of finding a way to account for our own finitude. Can we identify the limits and constraints, if not the grounds, of discourse-knowledge in its productivity? But despite its substance, in the end, according to many contemporary attempts at its salvation, it is not matter that reels in the unruliness of infinite possibilities; rather, it is the very existence of finitude that gets defined as matter. Caught once again looking at mirrors, it is either the face of transcendence or our own image. It is as if there are no alternative ways to conceptualize matter: the only options seem to be the naïveté of empiricism or the same old narcissistic bedtime stories.

I have proposed a posthumanist materialist account of performativity that challenges the positioning of materiality as either a given or a mere effect of human agency. On an agential realist account, materiality is an active factor in processes of materialization. Nature is neither a passive surface awaiting the mark of culture nor the end product of cultural performances. The belief that nature is mute and immutable and that all prospects for significance and change reside in culture is a reinscription of the nature/culture dualism that feminists have actively contested. Nor, similarly, can a human/nonhuman distinction be hardwired into any theory that claims to take account of matter in the fullness of its historicity. Feminist science studies scholars in particular have emphasized that foundational inscriptions of the nature/culture dualism foreclose the understanding of how "nature" and "culture" are formed, an understanding that is crucial to both feminist and scientific analyses. They have also emphasized that the notion of "formation" in no way denies the material reality of either "nature" or "culture." Hence, any performative account worth its salt would be ill advised to incorporate such anthropocentric values in its foundations.

A crucial part of the performative account that I have proposed is a rethinking of the notions of discursive practices and material phenomena and the relationship between them. On an agential realist account, discursive practices are not human-based activities but rather specific material (re)configurings of the world through which local determinations of boundaries, properties, and meanings are differentially enacted. And matter is not a fixed essence; rather, matter is substance in its intra-active becoming—not a thing but a doing, a congealing of agency. And performativity is not understood as iterative citationality (Butler) but rather iterative intra-activity.

On an agential realist account of technoscientific practices, the "knower" does not stand in a relation of absolute externality to the natural world being investigated—there is no such exterior observational point.[36] It is therefore not absolute exteriority that is the condition of possibility for objectivity but rather agential separability—exteriority within phenomena.[37] "We" are not outside observers of the world. Nor are we simply located at particular places *in* the world; rather, we are part *of* the world in its ongoing intra-activity. This is a point Niels Bohr tried to get at in his insistence that our epistemology must take account of the fact that we are a part of that nature we seek to understand. Unfortunately, however, he cuts short important posthumanist implications of this insight in his ultimately humanist understanding of the "we." Vicki Kirby eloquently articulates this important posthumanist point: "I'm trying to complicate the locatability of human identity as a here and now, an enclosed and finished product, a causal force upon Nature. Or even . . . as something within Nature. I don't want the human to be in Nature, as if Nature is a container. Identity is inherently unstable, differentiated, dispersed, and yet strangely coherent. If I say 'this is Nature itself,' an expression that usually denotes a prescriptive essentialism and that's why we avoid it, I've actually animated this 'itself' and even suggested that 'thinking' isn't the other of nature. Nature performs itself differently."[38]

The particular configuration that an apparatus takes is not an arbitrary construction of "our" choosing; nor is it the result of causally deterministic power structures. "Humans" do not simply assemble different apparatuses for satisfying particular knowledge projects but are themselves specific local parts of the world's ongoing reconfiguring. To the degree that laboratory manipulations, observational interventions, concepts, or other human practices have a role to play it is as part of the material configuration of the world in its intra-active becoming. "Humans" are part of the world bodyspace in its dynamic structuration.

There is an important sense in which practices of knowing cannot be fully claimed as human practices, not simply because we use nonhuman elements in our practices but because knowing is a matter of part of the world making itself intelligible to another part. Practices of knowing and being are not isolatable, but rather they are mutually implicated. We do not obtain knowledge by standing outside of the world; we know because "we" are *of* the world. We are part of the world in its differential becoming. The separation of epistemology from ontology is a reverberation of a metaphysics that assumes an inherent difference between human and nonhuman, subject and object, mind and body, matter and discourse. *Onto-epistem-ology*—the study of practices of knowing in being—is probably a better way to think about the kind of understandings that are needed to come to terms with how specific intra-actions matter.

Notes

1. Dissatisfaction surfaces in the literature in the 1980s. See, e.g., Donna Haraway's "Gender for a Marxist Dictionary The Sexual Politics of a Word" (originally published 1987) and "Situated Knowledges: The Science Question in Feminism and the Privilege of Partial Perspective" (originally published 1988); both reprinted in Haraway 1991. See also Butler (1989)

2. This is not to dismiss the valid concern that certain specific performative accounts grant too much power to language. Rather, the point is that this is not an inherent feature of performativity but an ironic malady.

3. Haraway proposes the notion of diffraction as a metaphor for rethinking the geometry and optics of relationality: "[F]eminist theorist Trinh Minh-ha . . . was looking for a way to figure 'difference' as a 'critical difference within,' and not as special taxonomic marks grounding difference as apartheid . . Diffraction does not produce 'the same' displaced, as reflection and refraction do. Diffraction is a mapping of interference, not of replication, reflection, or reproduction A diffraction pattern does not map where differences appear, but rather maps where the effects of differences appear" (1992, 300). Haraway (1997) promotes the notion of diffraction to a fourth semiotic category. Inspired by her suggestions for usefully deploying this rich and fascinating physical phenomenon to think about differences that matter, I further elaborate the notion of diffraction as a mutated critical tool of analysis (though not as a fourth semiotic category) in my forthcoming book (Barad forthcoming).

4. See Rouse (2002) on rethinking naturalism The neologism *intra-activity* is defined below.

5. Rouse begins his interrogation of representationalism in *Knowledge and Power* (1987). He examines how a representationalist understanding of knowledge gets in the way of understanding the nature of the relationship between power and knowledge. He continues his critique of representationalism and the development of an alternative understanding of the nature of scientific practices in *Engaging Science* (1996). Rouse proposes that we understand science practice as ongoing patterns of situated activity, an idea that is then further elaborated in *How Scientific Practices Matter* (2002).

6. The allure of representationalism may make it difficult to imagine alternatives. I discuss performative alternatives below, but these are not the only ones. A concrete historical example may be helpful at this juncture. Foucault points out that in sixteenth-century Europe, language was not thought of as a medium; rather, it was simply "one of the figurations of the world" (1970, 56), an idea that reverberates in a mutated form in the posthumanist performative account that I offer.

7. Andrew Pickering (1995) explicitly eschews the representationalist idiom in favor of a performative idiom. It is important to note, however, that Pickering's notion of performativity would not be recognizable as such to poststructuralists, despite their shared embrace of performativity as a remedy to representationalism, and despite their shared rejection of humanism. Pickering's appropriation of the term does not include any acknowledgment of its politically important—arguably inherently queer—genealogy (see Sedgwick 1993) or why it has been and continues to be important to contemporary critical theorists, especially feminist and queer studies scholars/activists Indeed, he evacuates its important political historicity along with many of its crucial insights. In particular, Pickering ignores important discursive dimensions, including questions of meaning, intelligibility, significance, identity formation, and power, which are central to poststructuralist invocations of "performativity " And he takes for granted the humanist notion of agency as a property of individual entities (such as humans, but also weather systems, scallops, and stereos), which poststructuralists problematize. On the other hand, poststructuralist approaches fail to take account of "nonhuman agency," which is a central focus of Pickering's account. See Barad (forthcoming) for a more detailed discussion.

8. The notion of performativity has a distinguished career in philosophy that most of these multiple and various engagements acknowledge. Performativity's lineage is generally traced to the British philosopher J L Austin's interest in speech acts, particularly the relationship between saying and doing. Jacques Derrida is usually cited next as offering important poststructuralist amendments Butler elaborates Derrida's

notion of performativity through Foucault's understanding of the productive effects of regulatory power in theorizing the notion of identity performatively Butler introduces her notion of gender performativity in *Gender Trouble*, where she proposes that we understand gender not as a thing or a set of free-floating attributes, not as an essence— but rather as a "doing": "gender is itself a kind of becoming or activity . . gender ought not to be conceived as a noun or a substantial thing or a static cultural marker, but rather as an incessant and repeated action of some sort" (1990, 112). In *Bodies That Matter* (1993) Butler argues for a linkage between gender performativity and the materialization of sexed bodies. Eve Kosofsky Sedgwick (1993) argues that performativity's genealogy is inherently queer.

9. This notion of posthumanism differs from Pickering's idiosyncratic assignment of a "posthumanist space [as] a space in which the human actors are still there but now inextricably entangled with the nonhuman, no longer at the center of the action calling the shots" (26). However, the decentering of the human is but one element of posthumanism. (Note that Pickering's notion of "entanglement" is explicitly epistemological, not ontological. What is at issue for him in dubbing his account "posthumanist" is the fact that it is attentive to the mutual accommodation, or responsiveness, of human and nonhuman agents.)

10. It could be argued that "materialized refiguration" is an enterprised up (Haraway's term) version of "materialization," while the notion of "materialization" hints at a richer account of the former. Indeed, it is possible to read my posthumanist performative account along these lines, as a diffractive elaboration of Butler's and Haraway's crucial insights.

11 . See also Butler (1989).

12. The conjunctive term *material-discursive* and other agential realist terms like *intra-action* are defined below.

13. This essay outlines issues I developed in earlier publications including Barad 1996, 1998a, 1998b, 2001b, and in my forthcoming book (Barad forthcoming).

14. It is no secret that *metaphysics* has been a term of opprobrium through most of the twentieth century. This positivist legacy lives on even in the heart of its detractors. Poststructuralists are simply the newest signatories of its death warrant. Yet, however strong one's dislike of metaphysics, it will not abide by any death sentence, and so it is ignored at one's peril. Indeed, new "experimental metaphysics" research is taking place in physics laboratories in the United States and abroad, calling into question the common belief that there is an inherent boundary between the "physical" and the "metaphysical" (see Barad forthcoming). This fact should not be too surprising to those of us who remember that the term metaphysics does not have some highbrow origins in the history of philosophy but, rather, originally referred to the writings of Aristotle that came after his writings on physics, in the arrangement made by Andronicus of Rhodes about three centuries after Aristotle's death.

15. *Relata* are would-be antecedent components of relations. According to metaphysical atomism, individual relata always preexist any relations that may hold between them.

16. Atomism is said to have originated with Leucippus and was further elaborated by Democritus, devotee of democracy, who also explored its anthropological and ethical implications. Democritus's atomic theory is often identified as the most mature pre-Socratic philosophy, directly influencing Plato and Epicurus, who transmitted it into the early modern period Atomic theory is also said to form the cornerstone of modern science.

17. Niels Bohr (1885–1962), a contemporary of Einstein, was one of the founders of quantum physics and also the most widely accepted interpretation of the quantum theory, which goes by the name of the Copenhagen interpretation (after the home of Bohr's

internationally acclaimed physics institute that bears his name). On my reading of Bohr's philosophy-physics, Bohr can be understood as proposing a protoperformative account of scientific practices.

18. Bohr argues on the basis of this single crucial insight, together with the empirical finding of an inherent discontinuity in measurement "intra-actions," that one must reject the presumed inherent separability of observer and observed, knower and known. See Barad 1996, forthcoming.

19. The so-called uncertainty principle in quantum physics is not a matter of "uncertainty" at all but rather of indeterminacy. See Barad 1995, 1996, forthcoming.

20. That is, relations are not secondarily derived from independently existing "relata," but rather the mutual ontological dependence of "relata"—the relation—is the ontological primitive As discussed below, relata only exist within phenomena as a result of specific intra-actions (i.e., there are no independent relata, only relata-within-relations)

21. A concrete example may be helpful. When light passes through a two-slit diffraction grating and forms a diffraction pattern it is said to exhibit wavelike behavior But there is also evidence that light exhibits particlelike characteristics, called *photons*. If one wanted to test this hypothesis, the diffraction apparatus could be modified in such a way as to allow a determination of which slit a given photon passes through (since particles only go through a single slit at a time). The result of running this experiment is that the diffraction pattern is destroyed! Classically, these two results together seem contradictory—frustrating efforts to specify the true ontological nature of light. Bohr resolves this wave-particle duality paradox as follows: the objective referent is not some abstract, independently existing entity but rather the phenomenon of light intra-acting with the apparatus. The first apparatus gives determinate meaning to the notion of "wave," while the second provides determinate meaning to the notion of "particle." The notions of "wave" and "particle" do not refer to inherent characteristics of an object that precedes its intra-action. *There are no such independently existing objects with inherent characteristics.* The two different apparatuses effect different cuts, that is, draw different distinctions delineating the "measured object" from the "measuring instrument." In other words, they differ in their local material resolutions of the inherent ontological indeterminacy. There is no conflict because the two different results mark different intra-actions. See Barad (1996, forthcoming) for more details.

22. This elaboration is not based on an analogical extrapolation. Rather, I argue that such anthropocentric restrictions to laboratory investigations are not justified and indeed defy the logic of Bohr's own insights. See Barad forthcoming.

23. Because phenomena constitute the ontological primitives, it makes no sense to talk about independently existing things as somehow behind or as the causes of phenomena. In essence, there are no noumena, only phenomena. Agential realist phenomena are neither Kant's phenomena nor the phenomenologist's phenomena

24. I am concerned here with the Foucauldian notion of discourse (discursive practices), not formalist and empirical approaches stemming from Anglo-American linguistics, sociolinguistics, and sociology.

25. Foucault makes a distinction between "discursive" and "nondiscursive" practices, where the latter category is reduced to social institutional practices: "The term 'institution' is generally applied to every kind of more-or-less constrained behaviour, everything that functions in a society as a system of constraint and that isn't utterance, in short, *all the field of the non-discursive social, is an institution*" (1980b, 197–198; my italics). This specific social science demarcation is not particularly illuminating in the case of agential realism's posthumanist account, which is not limited to the realm of the social In fact, it makes no sense to speak of the "nondiscursive" unless one is willing to jettison the notion of causality in its intra-active conception

26 In her critique of constructivism within feminist theory Judith Butler puts forward an account of materialization that seeks to acknowledge these important points. Reworking the notion of matter as a process of materialization brings to the fore the importance of recognizing matter in its historicity and directly challenges representationalism's construal of matter as a passive blank site awaiting the active inscription of culture and the representationalist positioning of the relationship between materiality and discourse as one of absolute exteriority. Unfortunately, however, Butler's theory ultimately reinscribes matter as a passive product of discursive practices rather than as an active agent participating in the very process of materialization. This deficiency is symptomatic of an incomplete assessment of important causal factors and an incomplete reworking of "causality" in understanding the nature of discursive practices (and material phenomena) in their productivity. Furthermore, Butler's theory of materiality is limited to an account of the materialization of human bodies or, more accurately, to the construction of the contours of the human body. Agential realism's relational ontology enables a further reworking of the notion of materialization that acknowledges the existence of important linkages between discursive practices and material phenomena without the anthropocentric limitations of Butler's theory.

27. The nature of causal intra-actions is discussed further in the next section.

28. See Barad (1998b, 2001a, 2001b, forthcoming) for examples.

29 I am grateful to Joe Rouse for putting this point so elegantly (private conversation). Rouse (2002) suggests that measurement need not be a term about laboratory operations, that before answering whether or not something is a measurement a prior question must be considered, namely, What constitutes a measurement of what?

30 Intelligibility is not a human-based affair. It is a matter of differential articulations and differential responsiveness/engagement. Vicki Kirby (1997) makes a similar point.

31. Butler also rejects both of these options, proposing an alternative that she calls the "constitutive outside." The "constitutive outside" is an exteriority *within language*—it is the "that which" to which language is impelled to respond in the repeated attempt to capture the persistent loss or absence of that which cannot be captured. It is this persistent demand for, and inevitable failure of, language to resolve that demand that opens up a space for resignification—a form of agency—within the terms of that reiteration. But the fact that language itself is an enclosure that contains the constitutive outside amounts to an unfortunate reinscription of matter as subservient to the play of language and displays a commitment to an unacceptable anthropocentrism, reducing the possibilities for agency to resignification.

32 Geometry is concerned with shapes and sizes (this is true even of the non-Euclidean varieties, such as geometries built on curved surfaces like spheres rather than on flat planes), whereas topology investigates questions of connectivity and boundaries. Although spatiality is often thought of geometrically, particularly in terms of the characteristics of enclosures (like size and shape), this is only one way of thinking about space. Topological features of manifolds can be extremely important. For example, two points that seem far apart geometrically may, given a particular connectivity of the spatial manifold, actually be proximate to one another (as, e.g., in the case of cosmological objects called "wormholes").

33. In contrast to Butler's "constitutive outside," for example.

34. For example, the space of agency is much larger than that postulated by Butler's or Louis Althusser's theories. There is more to agency than the possibilities of linguistic resignification, and the circumvention of deterministic outcome does not require a clash of apparatuses/discursive demands (i.e., overdetermination).

35. This is true at the atomic level as well Indeed, as Bohr emphasizes, the mutual exclusivity of "position" and "momentum" is what makes the notion of causality in

quantum physics profoundly different from the determinist sense of causality of classical Newtonian physics.

36. Others have made this point as well, e.g., Haraway (1991); Kirby (1997); Rouse (2002); and Bohr.

37. The notion of agential separability, which is predicated on the agential realist notion of intra-actions, has far-reaching consequences. Indeed, it can be shown to play a critical role in the resolution of the "measurement problem" and other long-standing problems in quantum theory. See Barad forthcoming.

38. Vicki Kirby (private communication, 2002). Kirby's sustained interrogation of the tenacious nature/culture binary is unparalleled. See Kirby (1997) for a remarkable "materialist" (my description) reading of Derridean theory.

Bibliography

Barad, Karen. "A Feminist Approach to Teaching Quantum Physics." Pp. 43–75 in *Teaching the Majority. Breaking the Gender Barrier in Science, Mathematics, and Engineering*, edited by Sue V. Rosser. Athene Series. New York: Teacher's College Press, 1995.

———. "Meeting the Universe Halfway: Realism and Social Constructivism without Contradiction " Pp. 161–194 in *Feminism, Science, and the Philosophy of Science*, edited by Lynn Hankinson and Jack Nelson. Dordrecht, Holland: Kluwer Press, 1996.

———. "Agential Realism: Feminist Interventions in Understanding Scientific Practices." Pp. 1–11 in *The Science Studies Reader*, edited by Mario Biagioli. New York: Routledge, 1998a.

———. "Getting Real: Technoscientific Practices and the Materialization of Reality." *differences A Journal of Feminist Cultural Studies* 10, no. 2 (1998b): 87—126.

———. "Performing Culture/Performing Nature: Using the Piezoelectric Crystal of Ultrasound Technologies as a Transducer between Science Studies and Queer Theories " Pp 98–114, in *Digital Anatomy*, edited by Christina Lammar,Vienna: Turia & Kant, 2001a.

———. "Re(con)figuring Space, Time, and Matter " Pp. 75—109, in *Feminist Locations. Global and Local, Theory and Practice*, edited by Marianne DeKoven. New Brunswick, N.J.: Rutgers University Press, 2001b.

———. *Meeting the Universe Halfway*. Durham: Duke University Press. Forthcoming.

Butler, Judith. "Foucault and the Paradox of Bodily Inscriptions." *Journal of Philosophy* 86, no. 11 (1989): 601–607.

———. *Gender Trouble· Feminism and the Subversion of Identity* New York: Routledge, 1990

———. *Bodies That Matter· On the Discursive Limits of "Sex"* New York: Routledge, 1993.

Deleuze, Giles. *Foucault*. Translated by Seán Hand. Minneapolis: University of Minnesota Press, 1988.

Foucault, Michel. *The Order of Things· An Archaeology of the Human Sciences*. New York: Vintage Books, 1970.

———. *The Archaeology of Knowledge and the Discourse on Language*. Translated by A. M. Sheridan Smith. New York: Pantheon Books, 1972.

———. *The History of Sexuality*. Vol. 1. *An Introduction*. Translated by Robert Hurley. New York: Vintage Books, 1980a.

————. *Power/Knowledge. Selected Interviews and Other Writings, 1972–1977.* Edited by Colin Gordon. New York: Pantheon Books, 1980b.

Hacking, Ian. *Representing and Intervening Introductory Topics in the Philosophy of Natural Science* Cambridge: Cambridge University Press, 1983.

Haraway, Donna. *Simians, Cyborgs, and Women The Reinvention of Nature.* New York: Routledge, 1991.

————. "The Promises of Monsters· A Regenerative Politics for Inappropriate/d Others." Pp. 295–337 in *Cultural Studies*, edited by Lawrence Grossberg, Cory Nelson, and Paula Treichler. New York: Routledge, 1992

————. Modest_Witness@Second_Millenium.FemaleMan_Meets_OncoMouse: *Feminism and Technoscience* New York: Routledge, 1997.

Hennessey, Rosemary. *Materialist Feminism and the Politics of Discourse.* New York: Routledge, 1993.

Kirby, Vicki. *Telling Flesh· The Substance of the Corporeal.* New York: Routledge, 1997.

Pickering, Andrew. *The Mangle of Practice Time, Agency, and Science.* Chicago: University of Chicago Press, 1995.

Rouse, Joseph. *Knowledge and Power: Toward a Political Philosophy of Science.* Ithaca, N.Y.: Cornell University Press, 1987.

————. *Engaging Science: How to Understand Its Practices Philosophically.* Ithaca, N.Y.: Cornell University Press, 1996

————. *How Scientific Practices Matter Reclaiming Philosophical Naturalism.* Chicago: University of Chicago Press, 2002

Sedgwick, Eve Kosofsky. "Queer Performativity: Henry James's *The Art of the Novel.*" *GLQ* 1(1):1–16, 1993.

Shaviro, Steve. *Doom Patrols A Theoretical Fiction about Postmodernism.* New York: Serpent's Tail, 1997. Available on-line at http://www.dhalgren.com/Doom/.

Chapter 3

Monstrous Reflections on the Mirror of the Self-Same

Margrit Shildrick

What are the figures of difference that haunt philosophy, and what would it mean to reflect on, rework, and valorize them? Within the context of a more general elevation of the body as a focus of scholarship, many feminist theorists have identified the erasure of the corporeal from the founding moment of western modernity—I refer to the take-up of the Cartesian split between mind and body—as a paradigmatic element in the oppression of women, and indeed others.[1] And as the sustained deconstruction of the seminal texts of philosophy has shown, from the classical era to the present century, the masculinist retreat from the body and from embodiment has denied to women access to subjectivity itself. In recent years, then, many feminist philosophers have reexamined gender indifference and developed new insights, which mobilize a reinstatement of the feminine. And yet for all the emphasis now given to embodied sexual difference as the grounds for a specific reassessment of the conventional paradigms of ontology, epistemology, and ethics, the body that is recovered in its difference, remains, nevertheless, highly normative. It is as though the body in question may be read solely through its sexuality or its relationship to reproduction in order to establish an adequate alternative to masculinist standards of disembodied subjectivity. Whether the feminist approach has appealed to a more or less nuanced form of essentialism, to notions of the body as a social construct, or to a phenomenology of the body that emphasizes corporeal being-in-the-world, all seem to me to have failed to engage with the issues arising from morphological differences that are not reducible to questions of sex/uality.

In contrast, what I want to do in this paper, is to address the consequences—ontological, epistemological, and ethical—of viewing all bodies not as either reducible to the same or as the absolute other, but as non-assimilable, and yet finally as undecidable. By engaging with a specifically feminist take up of the insights of poststructuralism and postmodernism, particularly in relation to the work of Luce Irigaray, I shall suggest that the reincorporation into our terms of reference of what might be called monstrous bodies—by which is meant those bodies that in their gross failure to approximate to corporeal norms are radically excluded—demands a fundamental reevaluation of the self-same, and of the relationship between self and other. Where normative embodiment has hitherto seemed to guarantee individual autonomous selfhood, monstrosity in all its forms—hybrid creatures, conjoined twins, human clones, cyborg embodiment, and others—disrupts the notions of separation and distinction that underlie such claims. So long as the monstrous remains the absolute other in its corporeal difference it poses few problems—in other words it is so distanced in its difference that it can clearly be put into an oppositional category of not-me; but once it begins to resemble us, or reflect back aspects of ourselves that are repressed, then its indeterminate status— neither wholly self nor wholly other—becomes deeply disturbing. In other words, what is at stake, is not simply the status of those bodies which might be termed monstrous, but the being in the body of us all. To valorize the monster, then, is to challenge the parameters of the subject as defined within logocentric discourse.[2]

When I first started researching the notion of the monstrous body, initially through archival texts, it was to ask just what it was that the monster signifies– *monstrare* itself means "to show forth"—that gives rise to a transhistorical and simultaneous fascination and fear. In other words, why is it that like the feminine, monsters are both the unspoken of western discourse, and at the same time always haunting its margins, seductive and threatening at the same time. In turning to both contemporary biomedical sources and to historical archives, I want to wrench those texts away from their conventional readings, away from the specific disciplinary receptions that are taken to mark the limits of their intelligibility. By asking what metaphors and rhetorical devices such texts carry, what form of imaginary is mobilized, the intention, as Derrida punningly puts it, is to "interrogate the hierarchives." The question of the "reality" or otherwise of such monstrous creatures has not been at issue, and my approach is unashamedly postmodernist in that I understand *all* bodies to be discursively constructed rather than given. It is not simply that corporeality is a dynamic process that belies the static universalization of the body image, but that all bodies are in some sense phantasmatic. Nonetheless, to mark my primary concern as being with the *meaning* of the corporeal, and to concur with Liz Grosz that "(bodies) are materialities that are uncontainable in physicalist terms alone" (1994, xi), should not be taken to exclude the substantial and tangible. Indeed, it is not just that the somewhat abstract theorizations of postmodernism contest the dominant body image of modernity, but that, in addition to the monstrous bodies of the past, the radically new possibilities of embodiment that are emerging in the era of postmodernity, through such techniques as cloning, transsexual surgery, genetic engineering, and xenotransplantation, suggest that the body is not only being superseded, but was unstable all along.

What then is the ontological and epistemological status of the body in the modern period? Despite the conventional lack of theoretical interest in the corporeal except as the mechanical housing of the subject, the privileged transcendence of the self is reliant on a predictable and determinate corporeality that can be so taken for granted that it may in effect be forgotten. Above all the body must be self-contained, complete in and of itself, and clearly distinct from other bodies, and moreover, there can be no doubt as to which minds and bodies go together (Shildrick, 1999). Bounded by the closure of normative embodiment that guarantees self-identity, the subject itself is marked out by individuality and autonomy. I will merely note here that in the western logos such a subject is intrinsically masculine. As he surveys his world he sees only that which reflects of his own self-presence, the confirmation of his own wholeness and completion. For Luce Irigaray, that metaphor of the mirror is central to her understanding of how the history of philosophy is structured by a series of exclusions. Throughout her deconstructive critique she asserts that the quality of reduplication that sustains the logos is predicated on and perpetuates a move in which the feminine is merely the reflective surface, the other of the same whose only function is the reproduction—in all its senses—of masculine subjectivity: "Mother-matter-nature must go on forever nourishing speculation. But this resource is also rejected as the waste product of reflection, cast outside as what resists it" (1985b, 77). It is an image that at best speaks to the passivity of women, at worst to their erasure. And yet an opening onto the feminine remains, for as Baudrillard warns, and as Irigaray is very well aware in her own strategy of mimicry, "(t)here is always sorcery at work in the mirror. . . . Reproduction is diabolical in its essence; it makes something fundamental vacillate" (1988, 182). Though the two dimensional plain of the mirror may seem to faithfully reiterate the original,[3] it has in its unrepresented excess always the potential for subversion.

It is the image of the mirror as a hard reflective surface that is taken up by Lacan (1977) as that which metaphorically and literally inaugurates the accession to being in the world as a subject, a singular self in a singular body. Where the early infant is unable to recognize the distinctions between self and other, and experiences only fragmentary and uncoordinated motor impulses, the mirror stage founds the ego as "both a map of the body's surface and a reflection of the image of the other's body" (Grosz, 1994, 38). Nonetheless, both the corporeal unities that it posits, and identity itself are fictional: misrecognition is at the heart of subjectivity. Although Lacan explicitly saw his account of the formation of the subject as counterposed to the disembodied *Cogito*, the body-images that are (mis)recognized in his model enact their own exclusions, again most particularly of the feminine. But it is not simply that the feminine is represented only as a lack—the nothing to be seen with nothing of itself to reflect—it is also the site of an unruly excess that must be repressed if the project of emergent subjectivity is to succeed. The conventional model of subjectivity—be it Cartesian or Lacanian—has no room for corporeal being that is either uncontrollable or less than perfect. It is an image that disavows existential vulnerability. The supposedly intrinsic leakiness of women's bodies is, then, a threat to well Being, a breach in the boundaries of selfhood that blurs the distinctions between self and other, and between one corpus and another. In her potent analysis of the denial in the masculine imaginary of matter and of the mother as the originary place of embodiment, Luce Irigaray asserts that the horror of fluidity is characteristic of the male: "All threaten to deform, propagate, evaporate, consume him, to flow out of him and into another who cannot be easily be held on to" (1985a, "Volume-Fluidity", 237). Danger lies in any loss of the hard, smooth reflective surfaces that reduplicate but never vary the subject. And just as uncontainable feminine excess must be erased from the clean and proper masculinist subject, so too must the disturbingly fluid corporeality of the monstrous.

The conflation of women with monsters should come as no surprise and has a long history in western discourse. The term monstrosity was used by Aristotle to mean not just those bodies which were malformed by disease, accident, or birth, but more widely to describe all beings that are a deviation from the common course of Nature: "Anyone who does not take after his parents is really in a way a monstrosity, since in these cases Nature has . . . strayed from the generic type" (*G.A* 4.3.767b, 1953, 401). They had failed in other words, the law of resemblances. And insofar as Aristotle marked excess and deficiency more generally as conditions of moral failing, the traditional characterization of monstrosity in terms of excess, deficiency, or displacement suggests, not only bodily imperfection, but an improper being.[4] The Aristotelian insistence that such beings lie within the realm of natural science, that they are curiosities of nature rather than opposed to it, does not preclude, however, a subsequent history in which monstrosities are widely understood as prodigies, as the marvelous signifiers of god's will, the ominous markers of good or ill to come. Even within that discourse of the supernatural, then, monsters are taken to reflect back at least some contingent truths of the human condition. Nonetheless, although the question of the humanity of human-born monsters—and particularly possession of a soul—was widely debated throughout the medieval and early modern period, they were indisputably the other whose anomalous bodies served to fix the normalcy of the standard model. For all that the failure to provide a copy of the original was the proximate cause of the ascription of monstrosity, such creatures functioned ideally as the other of the same, as boundary markers that secured rather than threatened the integrity of the normatively embodied subject.

It is by now widely accepted that the western logos is structured according to an infinite series of binaries which ground all knowledge in the play of sameness and difference. And it is only by making such distinctions, by having a clear sense of self and other, that we are enabled to mark out the parameters of self-identity. At first sight then, the monstrous represents an indisputable case of otherness, which though it may engender the fear of the unknown, serves in its separation and distinction the very positive function of securing the boundaries of the self. We know what we are by what we are not. And yet the monstrous is not simply alien, but arouses always the contradictory responses of denial *and* recognition, disgust *and* empathy, exclusion *and* identification. From the natural science of Aristotle through to present day medical discourse, which seeks to categorize and explain the pathology of abnormal corporeality, there is another more disruptive intuition that the monstrous cannot be confined in the place of the other. Moreover, as postmodernist theory makes clear, the predictable, knowable body with which we think ourselves familiar is an achievement secured only by the processes of normalization that must seek to abject, name, and exclude the monstrous other. What makes that other monstrous, then, is not so much its morphological difference and *un*familiarity, as the disruptive threat of its return. It is in its failure to occupy the place of the absolute other, in its incomplete abjection, that the monster marks the impossibility of the modernist self. Monsters haunt us, not because they represent an external threat—and indeed some are always benign—but because they stir recognition within, a sense of our openness and vulnerability that western discourse insists on covering over. And in that very ambiguity of sliding between self and other, monsters signify not the difference that defines the self-same, but rather the *différance* in its Derridean sense that undoes all distinction and speaks to indifferentiation.

Monsters, then, are what Freud would call the uncanny which he defines as "that class of the frightening which leads back to what is known of old and long familiar" (quoted in Kristeva, 1990, 183). Like the feminine, the monstrous may remain the other, unreflected as itself, but it is nonetheless evident as the *unheimlich*, as the anxiety-provoking double. And it is not simply that monsters are always there in our conscious appraisal of the external world, but that they are the other within. The image that looks back at us from the mirror may be our own disturbing and half-recognized selves. It is as though in looking for a reflection of our own secure subjecthood in what we are not, we see instead the leaks and flows, the vulnerabilities in our own embodied being. The other others—the feminine, the monstrous, the unclean—both resist exclusion and contest the closure of self-identity. Julia Kristeva's analysis of the abject— "something rejected from which one does not part. . . . Imaginary uncanniness and real threat, it beckons to us and ends up engulfing us" (1982, 4) could equally be a description of the monstrous. In her more recent book *Strangers to Ourselves*, Kristeva develops her early concept of the abject to give a psychical account of the oft times negative and fearful human relationship to the irreconcilable other. The potentially catastrophic encounter with that which appears foreign to us—the stuff of violent aversions of every kind—is not so much an engagement with an alien outside as an expression of the disavowal of the "improper" facet of our own unconscious. Just as Derrida sees *différance* as the trace within, so Kristeva understands the phenomenon of strangeness to be the interior presence of what she calls the "other scene," that, as she puts it: "integrates within the assumed unity of human beings an *otherness* that is both biological *and* symbolic and becomes an integral part of the *same*. . . ." (1990, 181). What is at issue then is that our ambivalent response to the external manifestation of the strange, of the monster, is an effect of the gap between our understanding of ourselves as whole and separate, and the psychical experience of the always already incorporation of otherness. Moreover, that other within is simultaneously both integrated with and irreducible to the self.

It is with that sense of ambivalence in mind, an ambivalence that figures a deep-seated anxiety about the corporeal as such, that we should understand modernist attempts to fix the epistemology and ontology of the monstrous. If the price of a unified self-image, illusory though it may be, is repression, then the subject must be in a relationship of mastery over all that is alien to the clean and proper self. An overview of the empirical parameters of the debate around monstrosity reveals that it was taken up, during the early modern period, by a highly positivist discourse. The desire for the certainty of closure was not of course new—legal and clerical scholars had long debated the civil and spiritual status of monsters—but the advent of Enlightenment science seemed to promise a discourse, which would explain and normalize the marvelous and prodigious. In the move away from metaphysical speculation, the body itself became the privileged object of an intense visual regime dedicated to uncovering new truths, and naturally occuring monstrosities were studied empirically as aberrations that would throw light on the normal (Daston, 1991). For Francis Bacon, for example, the categorization of "errors, vagaries, prodigies" and "deviating instances" (*Novum Organum*, 1620), served both to define and give power over what should be central to the normative body. Although in one sense the domain of science appears to treat the anomalous body with a new degree of neutrality, the very fact that any epistemological category, such as that which constitutes the proper form of humanity, works on the basis of exclusion, should alert us to its ethical underpinnings. The desire for mastery over the excessive other, so explicit in Baconian taxonomies, is no less a motivating force in the present day response to corporeal difference, as I shall shortly discuss with regard to conjoined twins. Moreover, as I have indicated, the monstrous signifies much more than simple difference, and its challenge is not so much epistemological as ontological.

Despite the best endeavors, then, of the domesticating scientific impulses, that which is monstrous evades the limits of classificatory systems and remains on the side of the unthought, which is neither properly reflective nor reflected in itself, neither entirely absent nor present. As I have argued elsewhere (Shildrick, 1996), the monstrous occupies what Gloria Anzaldua calls the borderlands, the location of "those who cross over, pass over, go through the confines of the 'normal'" (1987, 3). Its alterity is not that of the absolute other, but of the far more disturbing figure of the inbetween that is both self and other. Describing the unthought of western culture, Foucault refers to the Other as "not only a brother, but a twin, born, not of man, nor in man, but beside him and at the same time, in an identical newness, in an unavoidable duality" (1970, 326). This is the selfsame in its constituent parts, seeing in the mirror not the authorized reflection that constructs and defines the parameters of self-presence, but an unnerving double that is yet irreducible to the bounded subject. It is not simply that the self is split, but that duality is the condition of becoming. As such, the monstrous is always with us, our own necessary ontological excess. Can we, then, begin to theorize material monsters and the concept of the monstrous in the same register?

Taking up the cue from Foucault, I want now to consider the specific case of conjoined twins as a kind of limit case in our understanding of the self/other relationship, in which uncertainty is exemplified in a particularly acute form. Not surprisingly, corporeal excess in any form—extraordinary height, extra digits or limbs, for example, is unsettling; and the incidence of concorporation in which both bodies are visibly human is highly disruptive to western notions of individual agency and personal identity. The use of the word monstrous to describe such twins has extensive historical precedence,[5] but my point here, far from wishing to reiterate the negative charge of that term, is to contest the binary that opposes the monstrous to the normal. Rather than conjoined twins being absolutely other to ourselves - and as I have said no monster is wholly alien—they seem to manifest an arrested moment of the split between self and other, the very mirroring process that underlies all identity (Lacan, 1977). In terms of the post-Enlightenment understanding of selfhood, the question then is whether one or both should be considered autonomous persons. If we accept the conventional Lockean definition of a person as one who possesses a sense of self as the continuing subject of its own experiences, then to demarcate conjoined twins as two persons begs the question. It is not clear that such twins do always distinguish one self from another, nor that there are separate experiences or independent agency. Moreover, the complex interrelationship between body and self, which is most often ignored in the philosophical tradition, is highly pertinent in the cases of those concorporate bodies whose morphology defies a commonsense division.

It is in the light of these considerations that I turn to the case of the Irish conjoined twins, Katie and Eilish Holton, whose early childhood and subsequent separation features in two television documentaries.[6] Given their particular morphology, the term "conjunction" is perhaps less than adequate, and concorporation indeed seems a more accurate description. The twins' embodiment is, then, a monstrous insult to the norms of human corporeality; it is an other mode of being that undermines the binary of sameness/difference in which the self-same finds affirmation. Moreover, despite a taken-for-granted assumption that separation is in the best interests of the children, the claim that they are either physically or existentially disabled would be at least contestable. Nonetheless, the normative desire that each twin should be functionally autonomous, and that their supposedly individual selves should be liberated from an abnormal morphology, is powerful enough to risk innovative surgical intervention on a massive scale. As they are not one, then they must become two. It is only the passing reflection that "although we value individuality, they might not value it. They might prefer togetherness" (*Katie and Eilish: Siamese Twins*, 1993) that disturbs such certainty. Yet even that recognition prompts no thought of more fluid forms of subjectivity, but expresses only an acknowledgment that the twins' negotiation of their environment depends on co-operative intentionality. It is as though two autonomous subjects, trapped as it were in a fleshy bondage, have contracted to act as one. For all the twins' current contentment and evident pleasure in their mutual touch, surgery goes ahead. Separation is followed by the death of Katie, while for Eilish final success depends on the resealing of her body and the recontainment of her self.

What this often very moving narrative speaks to is the power of ontological anxiety in the face, not simply of corporeal excessiveness (Shildrick, 1999), but of the putative threat of monstrous engulfment. It is the loss of the interval between self and other, the ambiguity at the heart of concorporation, that frustrates the mapping of both the singular subject and of the pair. The recurrent refrain that Katie and Eilish are nevertheless two individuals is, then, a refusal of undecidability, an attempt both metaphorical and ultimately literal to *see* them as both existentially and corporeally distinct.[7] But even as we institute a specular model of being, is it not contested by Freud's remark that "the ego is first and foremost a bodily ego" (1923, 26), that is, the psychic location of the introjected sensation of touching and being touched? Although the phenomenological specificity of the twins' concorporate being is scarcely acknowledged, it is through the psychic endurance of mutual touch that Katie remains incorporated as an absent presence in the life of Eilish. The positivity of the indivisible tactility of their co-existence as self/other survives to contest the continuing stress on concorporation as obstructive. When asked what she remembers of her twin, Eilish directly echoes Irigaray's words—"I carry you with me everywhere. . . . You are there, like my skin" (1985b, 216)—in her own response: "She used to bring me round everywhere." And though the poignancy of that moment is swiftly interrupted by an older sibling who declares: "Eilish couldn't go wherever she wanted," that normative voice is clearly disrupted. For Eilish, in this and other instances, the corporeal memory of her twin stands against— guards against perhaps we should say—the closure of the self.

That is not of course to say that such twins, and others whose morphology defies normative categories of embodiment, should be denied personhood; rather it is the defining parameters of the self, still more of the subject, in western discourse that are inadequate to embodied difference. The assumption, in the case of conjoined twins for example, that there are two individuals obstructed by a single monstrous body, covers over the significance of both the psychic investments in body image, and "the phenomenological sense of being-in-the-world, in which corporeal extension is indivisible from subjecthood and identity" (Shildrick, 1999). In short, there is no clear distinction to be made between corporeal exteriority and psychical interiority. Moreover, if, as Merleau-Ponty (1964) asserts, identity is realized only as the lived body is immersed in the lived bodies of others, then concorporation is scarcely hostile to that model. In contrast, the dominant discourse of the singular and bounded subject, together with the privileging of corporeal self-determination, where exclusive property rights in one's own body stage the meeting with the other, enact a closure that suspends more open and ambiguous modes of existence. Though in the majority of cases, the drive is to see conjoined twins as two persons,[8] it might be more appropriate to say instead that the symbolic distinction between self and other that is taken to found identity in difference is deferred by the persistence of identification. For conjoined twins, the other-self is indivisible, not just as a facet of early infanthood, but as the very texture of experiential being. And where in general the Lacanian mirror stage marks "the assumption of the armour of an alienating identity" (1977, 4) that inaugurates an illusory corporeal integrity and singularity,[9] for conjoined twins the undecidable other-self is figured in a very different kind of reflection that calls for a reconfiguration of ontological and ethical paradigms.

Is there, then, a quite different way of understanding the significance of concorporate bodies and of overcoming the interval of the Lacanian mirror? Luce Irigaray seems to me to offer a way forward in her exploration of touch, which she claims both as characteristic of the feminine and as the substratum of all the senses. It is, in Cathy Vasseleu's words, "a scene which defies reduction to the discriminations of vision" (1998, 17). Despite her strong critique of Merleau-Ponty's apparent privileging of sight in *The Visible and the Invisible*, Irigaray concurs with him in marking the tactile as that which precedes, or perhaps more accurately defers, the separation of the subject from its objects (Irigaray, 1992, 108; Merleau-Ponty, 1962, 1968). In contradistinction to the disjunction intrinsic to the specular image, touch is always chiasmatic. It is not only, as Merleau-Ponty puts it, that "(t)actile experience . . . adheres to the surface of our body; we cannot unfold it before us and it never quite becomes an object" (1962, 316), but in addition that the hand that touches is also touched. That double sensation is especially evident in the contact between animate surfaces. The subject accordingly is in a mutually constitutive relationship with its objects, intertwined one with the other through touch. And yet, for Merleau-Ponty, a form of hierarchy remains in that reversibility. The irreducible flip that he proposes between the active and the passive is premised on the image of one hand *reaching out* to touch the other, not on two surfaces that are always already touching.

In contrast, Irigaray's specific displacement of Merleau-Ponty's active hand by her own image of two hands touching as though in prayer (Irigaray, 1993) provides an account more adequate to the issue of concorporation. For Irigaray, directly, it is the question of a specifically feminine desire that is addressed through the image of bodily contact, not necessarily as an anatomical event, but in the imaginary. Nonetheless, her evocation of feminine morphology as always already concorporate—"the birth that is never accomplished, the body never created once and for all, the form never definitively completed" (1985b, 217)—is highly pertinent to the problematic of (self)identity. For the body she proposes, the interval of the mirror is displaced, just as it might be for conjoined twins in an alternative cultural discourse. Instead of the flat, reflective surface that Irigaray sees as a weapon that wards off touching and holds back fluidity (1993, 65), what is mobilized is the plasticity of three dimensional contact. The masculinist economy of subject and object finds no place in a corporeality mediated by touch, by mucous, and by the mingling of blood. It is not that Irigaray recommends indifferentiation, for in that lies potential paralysis; rather it is a move to difference otherwise, where subject-object relations might be rewritten as the contiguity between subjects. What matters is that the inflexible and distancing reflection of modernist discourse should be reconfigured as a fluid and open mediation. As Irigaray puts it: "If being means permanent advent between us, our bodies become living mirrors. Sense mirrors where the outline of the other is profiled through touch. No longer the site of a frozen, fixed appropriation and expropriation" (1992, 77).

In the light of the potential of late twentieth century biotechnology to radically vary the body, the need to reconfigure relational economies may be of especial urgency. I am not claiming that morphological difference has become more acceptable, but on the contrary that the processes of normalization that are correlative to the stable bounded subject are potentially even more powerful and call for greater resistance. And yet there are alternative ways forward. One significant achievement of postmodernism and its feminist uptake has been to deconstruct the rigidity of both the mind/body split, and the post-Enlightenment model of an autonomous, fully self-present, and invulnerable subject, in favor of undecidable and fluid forms of embodiment that frustrate the mirroring of the selfsame. There is no certain reduplication. What the monstrous in all its forms reflects is that the singular disembodied subject is in any case an unachievable construct of modernity, and that instead our necessarily embodied identities are never secured, and our bodies never one. To resist closure, to be open to the trace of the other within, the other that is both self and irreducibly alien in its excess, to resist the normalization of the strange, is to accept vulnerability. It is the very possibility of our becoming, for ourselves and with others, and it calls finally for the willingness to engage in an ethics of risk.

Notes

1. To some extent this means that my comments might be applicable to differences that are not addressed directly, but at the same time it is necessary to be wary of conflating those differences and overriding their own specificities.

2. Some of the material following has been developed further in *Embodying the Monster Encounters with the Vulnerable Self* (Shildrick, 2002).

3 As Derrida has made clear, reiteration is not in any case a faithful copy. See, for example, *Limited Inc* (Derrida, 1988), and Judith Butler's *Bodies that Matter* (1993) for a detailed exposition.

4. The application of Aristotelian ethics to material conditions did not however preclude the possibility of redemption. Augustine for example believed that God would restore monsters in perfect form at the Resurrection (*City of God*, 1966).

5. See Thijssen (1987) for the Aristotelian account for example.

6. For a fuller account of this case see Shildrick (1999).

7 Indeed, in another well-documented case of conjoined twins, the postoperative strategy was to position a mirror next to the bed of each recovering twin, ostensibly to minimize distress at the loss of the other-self, but also to reflect back a "whole" and separate self (*ITN* report, 21 July 1998).

8. In cases where it is not self-evident that there are two consciousnesses, the matter is less clear. For a more detailed account of "parasitic" twinning and of the so-called Bengali boy who had a single body, but two heads joined at the crown rather than the neck, see Shildrick (1999).

9. Merleau-Ponty (1964) takes a less deterministic view of the mirror stage, in which the inauguration of difference is always offset by a continuing mutuality of being-in-the-world with others

Bibliography

Anzaldúa, Gloria. *Borderlands/La Frontera· The Mestiza*. San Francisco: Spinsters, 1987.

Aristotle. *De Generatione Animalium*. Translated by A. L. Peck. London: Heinemann, 1953.

Augustine *The City of God*. Edited and translated by Philip Levine. Cambridge: Loeb Classical Library, 1966.

Bacon, Francis. *Novum Organum* In *The ,Works of Francis Bacon*, edited by Basil Montagu. London, 1825–1834

Baudrillard, Jean. *Selected Writings*, Edited by Mark Poster. Stanford, Calif.: Stanford University Press, 1988

Butler, Judith. *Bodies That Matter· On the Discursive Limits of 'Sex '* London: Routledge, 1993.

Daston, Lorraine. "Marvellous Facts and Miraculous Evidence in Early Modern Europe". *Critical Inquiry* 18 (1991): 93–124.

Derrida, Jacques. *Limited Inc* Edited by G. Graff. Evanston, Ill. Northwestern University Press, 1988.

Foucault, Michel. *The Order of Things*. Translated by M. Sheridan. London: Tavistock, 1970.

Freud, Sigmund. "The Uncanny" (1919). In *The Standard Edition of the Complete Psychological Works of Sigmund Freud*, edited by James Strachey . Vol. 17 London: Hogarth Press, 1953–1966.

———. "The Ego and the Id" (1923). In *The Standard Edition of the Complete Psychological Works of Sigmund Freud*, edited by James Strachey. Vol. 19. London: Hogarth Press, 1953–1966.

Grosz, Elizabeth. *Volatile Bodies Toward a Corporeal Feminism*. Bloomington: Indiana University Press, 1994.

Irigaray, Luce. "Volume-Fluidity." In *Speculum of the Other Woman*, translated by G. C. Gill. New York: Cornell University Press, 1985a.

———. *This Sex Which Is Not One*. New York: Cornell University Press, 1985b.

———. *Elemental Passions*, translated by J. Collie and J. Still. London: Athlone Press, 1992.

———. *Sex and Genealogies*, translated G. C. Gill. New York: Columbia University Press, 1993.

Kristeva, Julia. *Powers of Horror An Essay on Abjection*. New York: Columbia University Press, 1982.

———. *Strangers to Ourselves*. London: Harvester Wheatsheaf, 1990.

Lacan, Jacques. "The mirror stage as formative of the function of the I". In *Ecrits. A Selection*, translated by Alan Sheridan. New York: W.W. Norton, 1977.

Merleau-Ponty, Maurice. *The Phenomenology of Perception*. London: Routledge and Kegan Paul, 1962.

———. *The Primacy of Perception* Evanston: Northwestern University Press, 1964.

———. *The Visible and the Invisible*. Evanston: Northwestern University Press, 1968.

Shildrick, Margrit. "Posthumanism and the Monstrous Body". In *Body and Society*, 2, 1 (1996): 1–15.

— — —. *Leaky Bodies and Boundaries· Feminism, Postmodernism and (Bio)ethics*. London: Routledge, 1997.

— — —. "This Body Which Is Not One Dealing with Differences" in *Body & Society*, 5, 2(1999): 77–92

————. *Embodying the Monster Encounters with the Vulnerable Self* London: Sage, 2002.

Thijssen, J. M. "Twins as Monsters: Albertus Magnus's Theory of the Generation of Twins and Its Philosophical Context " In *Bulletin of the History of Medicine* 61 (1987): 237–246.

Vasseleu, Cathryn. *Textures of Light Vision and Touch In Irigaray, Levinas and Merleau-Ponty* London: Routledge, 1998.

Yorkshire Television. *Katie and Eilish Siamese Twins*. 1993.

————. *Eilish. Life without Katie* 1995

Chapter 4

Ontology and Feminism

Käthe Trettin

I propose a solution of two notorious problems of feminism by applying a specific ontological theory, namely, the Ontology of Tropes. The Individuality Problem (how can general properties or generic concepts account for individual features, e.g., individual womennesses?) is solved by construing properties as particulars; the Generality Problem (what is the reference of the generic term "woman" and the plural term "women"?) is solved by proposing that the terms in question refer to a resemblance class. After some introductory remarks on widespread confusions concerning the notions of "essentialism" and "ontology," I present a brief account of trope structure and then discuss a solution of the Generality Problem which has been suggested by Natalie Stoljar. I argue that Stoljar's Resemblance Nominalism can be improved by accepting tropes as the constituents of resemblance classes. On the whole, I present a particularist and realist ontological theory which supplies a general explication of gender differences and gender similarities.

Introduction

The current debate within feminist philosophy is deeply influenced by the presupposition that ontological and metaphysical investigations in general are at best out of date. Where the structure of gendered beings is concerned, ontology is often taken to be the main source of antifeminist thinking. This skeptical attitude has manifested itself most clearly by the widely accepted doctrines of anti-essentialism and antibiologism, as well as by the assumption that gender is a social and cultural construction. Endorsing constructionism and rejecting essences, especially those of a natural kind, has led to the conclusion that all has been said and nothing is left concerning the relationship between feminist philosophy and ontology.[1]

This conclusion, however, is false. For one, anti-essentialism is itself an ontological assumption, albeit a negative one. To say that there are no female essences or that there is no natural womanness is an ontological statement and is therefore open for some more ontological debate. So, what is wrong is the implicit equation of essentialism with ontology as such or, to put it another way, from anti-essentialism a general anti-ontologism does not follow. Secondly, social or cultural constructionism, although quite often obviously conceived of this way, is not a magic weapon against ontological considerations. What are social facts, after all? Nobody can deny, for instance, the social fact about women that, on average, they work harder and earn less than men, but is this fact less real in virtue of being "only" socially constructed? Or, is, for example, the Muslimian or Mormonic procedure of marrying young girls to men they don't even know or don't like not a brute fact, even if it depends on a specific cultural construction of gender? Hence, gender constructionism while concentrating on rejecting essentialism tends to play down the contingent reality of social and cultural facts.[2]

After this introductory remark which—admittedly—has turned out a bit programmatic, nobody will be surprised that I shall advocate ontological research as one important field of philosophy in order to meet feminist requirements. More precisely, I attempt to show the solution of two notorious problems of feminism by applying a specific ontological theory, namely, the Ontology of Tropes.

The first problem I shall call the Individuality Problem. If we acknowledge that individual persons differ in various respects from each other and that each of them will show different features at different times of their personal life-history as well as relative to the diverse situations each of them lives in, how can general properties or generic concepts account for these individual features? In other words, how can the general property of womanness, expressed in English normally by the predicate "is a woman," account for the individual womannesses of, let's say, Golda Meir, Indira Gandhi, Gertrude Stein, and Madame Curie? So, the Individuality Problem opens up a line of reasoning that challenges the assumption of universals, in our case, the assumption of gender universals. Taking individuality and diversity seriously will therefore lead most naturally to particularism with regard to properties.

The second problem I shall call, accordingly, the Generality Problem. We are confronted with that one, the minute we leave the Individuality Problem. For, suppose we have solved this problem, and everybody has her particular personal gender, how can we conceive of some general notion of woman? Is there nothing real left which Golda Meir, Indira Gandhi, Gertrude Stein and Madame Curie have in common? Should we answer Simone de Beauvoir's classical question "Are there women, really?"[3] with a brief "No, there aren't," just for fear that otherwise we would have to acknowledge some general feature shared by those people we refer to as women? The answer I propose is "Yes, there are women, really," but the existence of women or the reference of the plural term "women" does not presuppose a universal quality of womanness. The solution of the Generality Problem, or so I shall argue, will be provided by the similarity the particular genders may exhibit. What the generic term "woman" and the plural term "women" refer to is a resemblance class: the class of particular female qualities.

Hence, what I am going to propose is a particularist and realist theory which supplies a general explication of gender differences and gender similarities. This theory I call an Ontology of Individual Qualities which is a specific version of Trope Theory. The somewhat exotic name "trope," although by now quite familiar within ontological debate, has been introduced by the Harvard philosopher Donald C. Williams in his essay "On the Elements of Being" (1953) and revived by the Australian philosopher Keith Campbell in his book *Abstract Particulars* (1990). An essential feature of Trope Ontology is that properties (accidents, attributes) are not construed as universals, but as particular or individual qualities. This means a revision of the classical conception on which properties taken as universals have to be individuated or exemplified by presupposed singular objects or substances. On the trope view, by contrast, one can do without a basic category of substance or thing or object. Instead, one reconstructs particular objects as coherent complexes or bundles of coexisting particular qualities. Perhaps I should mention that a true ontological theory cannot restrict itself to just replacing one or two categories by a different one. The interesting point of such a theory will only show up, if one tries to reconstruct the whole of what there is and possibly can be from its basic categories. In doing so it will eventually provide an explication of our experiential and intellectual intuitions about reality or of what Husserl called the "natural ontological attitude."[4]   As it belongs to one of our deepest pre-theoretical intuitions that there are such things as women and men, any good ontology has to provide a general framework of explicating this state of affairs. In order to show that trope theory is apt to provide such a framework, I shall first present a brief account of trope structure in five points and then discuss a very interesting solution of the above mentioned Generality Problem which has been suggested by Natalie Stoljar. On her account, "woman" is to be construed as a "cluster term" referring to a resemblance class. As trope theory relies on resemblance classes as well, I shall argue that Stoljar's theory can be improved by accepting tropes as the constituents of that cluster.

Trope Structure

1 Tropes as Basic Individuals

A trope is an individual quality. It is individual in that it is simple and unique, although it will have various degrees of similarity to other individuals. What a trope conveys is a particular quality. Thus, a trope of redness resembles another trope of redness, because each of them respectively is the individual redness it is. In accordance with K. Campbell, I propose that the individuality of tropes is basic and unanalyzable.[5]

2 Tropes as Basic Constituents

Tropes are taken to be the basic constituents of what there is and possibly can be. This claim may be described in a general way as follows:

(i) Tropes constitute the realm of reality. If tropes exist, then a real world exists. Therefore existent tropes may be called the realizers of a world.

(ii) Tropes constitute the realm of possibility. The constitution of the realm of possibility is derivative on what is realized. If tropes exist and thereby constitute a real world, they constitute by the same token (a) a possible world that is realized and (b) unrealized possibilities of the realized world, i.e., possible worlds.

Therefore existent tropes are not only realizers but possibilisers as well. Hence, tropes constitute a maximal realm of being.

3 Existence of Tropes

The first relatedness a trope exhibits merely spells out what it means to say that tropes are the constituents of what there is and possibly can be. They have to be somewhere. If we take "somewhere" to be a possible world, we can say: any trope t bears a relation R_E to world w; i.e., it exists in that world. The Existence Relation, as we may call it, can be clarified in terms of world-overlap. Any trope t exists, if and only if t overlaps a world w.

4 Coexistence of Tropes

The second relation of a trope is such that it may coincide, concur or coexist with some other tropes. Stating the formal features of concurrence[7] is the easy part of the analysis: with concurrence or compresence of tropes x, y, and z we get reflexivity, symmetry, and transitivity, i.e., an equivalence relation. But there is a lot more to say about concurring tropes. If we start with trope existence as described in (3), concurrent tropes are those tropes which overlap the same world or which occupy the same region. But surely not every trope will concur with any next best trope. One way to account for the diversity and distinctness of trope complexes is the introduction of the Principle of Compossibility. It says that qualities are compossible, if there is no contradiction involved. Take, for example, a trope of roundness and a trope of squareness. Each of them is a possible and even real trope, but they do not obey the Principle of Compossibility and hence cannot concur. But this principle only supplies a necessary condition for tropes to concur, thereby excluding the fusion of incompatible tropes, but it does not supply a sufficient condition to constitute a trope complex. Take, for example, a trope of redness and a trope of roundness. Surely they are compossible, as any red ball will demonstrate. But, of course, a trope of redness may concur with a trope of squareness, and a trope of roundness with a trope of blue. Hence a pressing question arises: What is it that unifies compossible tropes? What supplies a sufficient reason for tropes to really combine, fuse, or merge and thereby build a complex? As we have, on our assumption, only tropes (= individual qualities) to operate with, a Principle of Unification has to be spelled out within the scope of tropes. On my account the

Principle of Unification is something like the following: Compossible tropes a, b, and c build a trope complex, if and only if there is at least a trope f belonging to a similarity set A, and f causes a, b, and c to unite. What the principle presupposes is a causal interaction of tropes. It depends on the individual qualities acted upon as well as on the individual quality acting as a cause. Although nothing can be a cause without exerting an individual quality, not every individual quality will effect a unification of tropes. Unification, then, is based on causal interaction of tropes, and the latter might be understood as obeying the more general principle of Ontological Dependence.[8]

We may summarize concurrence of existent tropes as being a (reflexive, symmetric, and transitive) relation C, holding for any tropes x, y, and z, if and only if (i) they are compossible and (ii) obey a Principle of Unification by constituting a more or less tight complex or bundle of individual qualities. Hence, the relation of concurrence is the main structure-building feature with respect to the combinatorial varieties within the real world, for instance, specific things and particular persons.

5 Similarity of Tropes

The third constitutive relation of tropes is that of similarity or resemblance. Any trope t_i may resemble a trope t_j. Similarity or resemblance, deriving from the unique qualities that tropes are, is an inherent (reflexive, symmetric) relation. For example, if there are some tropes of wisdom, let's say, Socrates's wisdom, Plato's wisdom, and Hypatia's wisdom, there will be instantly a similarity relation holding between the three tropes such that these individual wisdoms yield a similarity complex of wisdom-in-general. Whether the similarity relation is transitive or not is still a controversial issue. On the assumption that similarity is not sameness or strict likeness, it will probably be adequate to construe it as transitive. Belonging to a resemblance class—and all possible and real tropes belong to some such set or class, with the exception of singleton tropes, if there are any—yields the classical category of universals. Any universal is reconstructed as a class of similar tropes. With similarity of individual qualities we gain general qualities.

There has been much debate on the question whether or not similarity of tropes involves a vicious regress.[9] As I cannot discuss this matter in detail here, I shall restrict myself to just a few remarks.

(i) There is no regress. For one, a red-trope's being similar to another red-trope does not yield an additional trope, something like a "similarity trope." If tropes resemble one another they do so in virtue of their respective individual qualities, and nothing whatsoever has to be supplemented to this fact. In other words, similarity of tropes is a structure which is immediately given by the tropes themselves. Therefore one might say that similarity supervenes on tropes. If there ever has been an occasion to put the magic formula of supervenience into operation, this would be one. But on my exposition of trope structure, I can do equally well without it. Because the similarity relation is not construed as equivalent with "strict likeness." Consider, for example, six tropes: a trope of mauve, a trope of night blue, a black-trope, a trope of canary yellow, a trope of orange, and a trope of rosé. Most people asked to classify these tropes by criteria of similarity will come up with the following result: the first three tropes are the dark ones, the rest belong to the class of light tropes. This is a rough but perfectly adequate partitioning of tropes into resemblance classes. Note, however, that the dark and light qualities of these tropes are not additional qualities. Consider the tropes of mauve and of rosé, each belonging so far to different similarity classes. Surely they constitute another resemblance class which might be labeled the class of lilac-tropes. And neither a canary-trope nor a black-trope would get a ticket to join the lilac club.

(ii) Just one remark concerning the objection that trope theorists would inevitably stumble into the next disaster, namely that of having to acknowledge universals as basic by the very talk of "relations," if they managed at all to rescue themselves from the pitfall of vicious regress: *Prima facie* this objection has some plausibility, but it can be refuted. There is no need for a connecting or relating entity, at least in my version of trope ontology. Relations, be they construed as universals or as particulars, simply have no ontological work to do. Tropes "relate" internally to each other in virtue of the particular qualities that they are without the help of genuine relating entities. Therefore relations are categorically dispensable.

On Resemblance

So, what the trope view suggests is that all there is and possibly can be is reconstructable from individual qualities. While compresence accounts for objects and persons, similarity accounts for general qualities. Accordingly, a person, for instance, Gertrude Stein, is a highly complex structure of different tropes. If we adopt a widespread feminist scheme of attribution, Gertrude Stein would probably be said to have exemplified or instantiated the categories of being Woman, White, Middle Class, Professional, and Lesbian. One wonders, however, what Gertrude Stein may have been in herself and how she has managed to do all that instantiation or exemplification. Moreover, one might be puzzled of how to construe her as the real person she obviously was, in case the categories express merely nominals, i.e., nothing real. On the trope view, by contrast, these puzzles can be solved. Gertrude Stein's being a writer, a woman and a lesbian, to pick out just a few of the attributes, may be reconstructed in two steps.

Step 1: A certain trope complex, namely, Gertrude Stein, includes, besides many others, at least a trope of writing prose, a trope of writing poetry, a trope of XX chromosome, a trope of wearing huge dresses, a trope of being educated in Radcliffe College, and last, but not least, a trope of a loving feel for women, especially for Alice B. Toklas.

Step 2: All these overlapping and compresent tropes, which partly constitute the person Gertrude Stein, are each members of different resemblance classes. The class of writing will comprise an Ernest-Hemingway-writing-trope and a Virginia-Wolff-writing-trope as well as many others. More difficult is the class of womanness. On my example, three tropes are mentioned, one biological, one social, one cultural. Do they really gather in a resemblance class? Why should, for example, the individual feature of wearing huge dresses, be a trope of womanness? Aren't there women who wear no dresses at all, even not tiny ones, whereas some men in India or North-Africa as well as Catholic priests wear even huger dresses? And what about the supposed similarity between a trope of XX chromosome and a trope of studying in Radcliffe College?

I shall postpone discussion of this matter for a minute in order to get clear about Gertrude Stein's love tropes. Her particular property of loving women surely belongs to a resemblance class which is normally called lesbian. Now, Picasso, just like Stein, has also been a great friend of women, but it would at least sound odd to categorize Picasso's loving feelings for women as lesbian. So, can we do with just one resemblance class of love tropes? My proposal is that one has to admit at least four subclasses, three of which will be classes of sexual love tropes, namely, a heterosexual, a homosexual, and a lesbian, as well as a nonsexual and gender-neutral subclass collecting such loving feelings as someone may have for her child, his grandmother, the cat Tibbles, or even for God or a Goddess. On my assumption, the love tropes of Gertrude Stein would predominantly assemble in the two similarity classes of lesbian and of gender-neutral tropes, respectively, while both are members of the entire love trope class. This reconstruction, however, obviously presupposes a good answer to the questions: What makes a trope complex, such as Gertrude Stein, a woman? Or, what makes a trope complex, such as Pablo Picasso, a man?

Recurring to the discussion of gender resemblance classes, I should like to refer to a proposal which Natalie Stoljar has recently offered.[10] Her account of "woman" has two elements: First, the concept of woman is a "cluster term"; i e., there is a cluster of different features in our concept of woman and in order for an individual to satisfy the concept, it is sufficient to satisfy enough of, rather than all and only, the features in the cluster. Secondly, the type "woman" is a type in virtue of the resemblance structure which obtains among individual members of the type.[11]

This proposal which she calls herself "resemblance nominalism" shall provide a middle avenue between the too strong appeal to nominal essence and a too weak predicate nominalism. The concept "woman" on her account clusters together four elements: First, womanness is attributed on the basis of female sex (XX chromosome); secondly, it is based on phenomenal features (of what it feels like to be a woman) based on physical feelings (for instance, menstrual cramps, childbirth, etc.); thirdly, social roles such as habits and dress; and finally, self-attributions like calling oneself a woman and being called a woman.[12]

On Stoljar's account "an exemplar must satisfy at least three of the dimensions in the concept of woman in order to count as a woman."[13] So, for instance, having an XX chromosome is not necessary for being an individual woman.

I am very much in favour of Natalie Stoljar's approach. Nonetheless, I am not sure, if her nominalism, even if defined by resemblance and not by identity, will account for the fact that there are women, really. The reason is that Stoljar, like any other nominalist, simply presupposes the individual person instead of reconstructing her from particular properties or individual qualities. So, I wonder where she gets all these "dimensions" from that an "exemplar" has to satisfy in order to count as a woman. On the trope view, the exemplars as well as the dimensions of resemblance are reconstructed from individual qualities. If certain tropes exist, they will eventually yield such wonderful "exemplars" as the trope configuration named "Gertrude Stein" and thereby generating quite a lot of resemblance classes, some of which are gender classes with their partly overlapping subclasses.

It should go without saying by now that being a trope realist does not imply being an essentialist. The very interesting question of essential and accidental tropes within a trope complex is a second-order-question. I think it is essential for a human being and for many other living beings to include some sexual tropes. But it is not essential that they be female or male.

Notes

1. Charlotte Witt called this the "core argument" of feminist anti-essentialism. See Witt, (1995), section I.

2. For a critical discussion of different types of social construction, see Haslanger, (1995)

3. Beauvoir (1949) 1993, 11.

4. Ideen zu einer reinen Phenomenologie I, 2. Abschnitt, Kapitel 1.

5 For a more detailed account see my "Tropes and Things" (Trettin, 2000).

6. Campbell (1990), 69.

7. In the following, I shall mainly stick to the term "concurrence" as introduced by D. C. Williams (1953), but nothing much hangs on terminology here. I could have adopted "compresence " (introduced by Leibniz and Russell) as well, and normally both terms are used synonymously.

8. For more details concerning Existential or Ontological Dependence, see Mulligan (1998) and Trettin, (2001).

9. See, for instance, G. Küng's (1967) regress argument and K. Campbell's (1990) refutation thereof, as well as more recent objections against trope similarity of H. Hochberg, (1992) and C. Daly, (1994), the latter explicitly criticises Campbell, (1990).

10. Stoljar (1995).

11. Stoljar (1995), 282f.

12. Stoljar (1995), 283f.

13. Stoljar (1995), 284.

Bibliography

Beauvoir, Simone de. *Le Deuxième Sexe I· Les Faits et les Mythes* Paris: Gallimard, 1949
————*The second sex.* Translated and edited by H. M Parshley. New York: Penguin, 1993.
Campbell, Keith. *Abstract Particulars.* Oxford: Blackwell, 1990
Daly, Chris. "Tropes." *Proceedings of the Aristotelian Society, (*In 94, Part I) 253–261.

Haslanger, Sally. "Ontology and Social Construction." *Philosophical Topics* 23 (1995): 95–125

Hochberg, Herbert. "Troubles with Tropes," *Philosophical Studies* 67 (1992): 193–195

Husserl, Edmund. *Ideen zu einer reinen Phänomenologie und phänomenologischen Philosophie I Husserliana, Band III/1*. Den Haag: Martinus Nijhoff., (1922) 1976

Küng, Guido *Ontology and the Logistic Analysis of Language,* revised edition Dordrecht: Reidel, 1967.

Mulligan, Kevin "Relations—Through Thick and Thin," *Erkenntnis* 48 (1998): 325–353.

Stoljar, Natalie "Essence, Identity, and the Concept of Woman," *Philosophical Topics* 23 (1995): 261–293.

Trettin, Käthe. "Tropes and Things." Pp. 279–303 in *Things, Facts, and Events*, edited by J Faye, U. Scheffler, and M. Urchs. Amsterdam/Atlanta: Rodopi, 2000.

———— "Ontologische Abhängigkeit in der Tropentheorie." *Metaphysica* 2, No 1 (2001): 23–54

Williams, Donald C. "On the Elements of Being," *Review of Metaphysics* 7 (1953): 3–18, 171–192 Reprinted in D. C. Williams, ed. , *Principles of Empirical Realism*, Pp. 74–109 Springfield, Illinois: C. Thomas Publishers, 1966.

Witt, Charlotte, "Anti-essentialism in Feminist Theory," *Philosophical Topics* 23 (1995): 321–344.

Chapter 5

Diotima, Wittgenstein, and A Language for Liberation

Deborah Orr

Introduction

It has become a commonplace in feminist philosophy and theory that the language in which we think, speak, and construct our world is male, patriarchal, and oppressive. According to the major body of theory expounding and elaborating upon this understanding of language—theory founded in the work of Saussure; developed by Lacan, Derrida, and numerous poststructuralists; and challenged but sometimes left in place, often unwittingly, as the bedrock of their own linguistic practices by many feminists—language is not simply the product of a patriarchal culture which could, with whatever difficulty, be reformed. It is at its core masculine, structured around the phallus and the Name of the Father. According to this theoretical stance language is a unitary system of meaning, dualistic and hierarchal, in which women can only be represented by absence and lack. Thus even to speak our name becomes problematic for women. And outside of this language there is no possibility of meaning. The "body" and the material world lie there, but not the distinctly human world of "discourse", of shared meaning, of knowledge, of understanding, and of all that these make possible. On this view of language the options for women concerned to contest and subvert patriarchal oppression are distinctly limited: the formulation of new words which seem to do little more than replace the old ones in inevitably masculinist structures of meaning (the development of "Feminese" one might call it), the play of deconstruction and *écriture féminine*, or the wary use of patriarchal language in conscious awareness of its limitations and dangers seem to exhaust the possibilities.

In the bleak atmosphere of this situation Andrea Nye has written a series of papers on the philosophy of the woman who, if Nye is correct, may well be considered the first woman philosopher to contest the nascent patriarchal order, Diotima of Mantinea. All we know of Diotima's philosophical work appears in Plato's *Symposium* and, from antiquity through to the present, she has been understood as a fictional creation of Plato's, developed to, in the words of David Halperin (1990), propound to Socrates "an ethic of 'correct paederasty'" and to introduce the Theory of Forms. But Nye argues for Diotima's historical existence and holds that she articulated a pre-Socratic worldview, one that was rapidly being marginalized by masculinist Greek thought. At the heart of Nye's work is the contention that Diotima employed a language and a logic that was neither Platonic nor the hegemonic "discourse" of poststructuralist theory. It was not only *through* but also *because of* her linguistic usage, rooted in that pre-Socratic worldview to which Nye points, that Diotima was able to convey an understanding of the self in loving and generative relationship with others who, because of their grounding in that relationship, could produce cultural and social forms dedicated to human flourishing.

In a series of papers Nye (1988, 1989, 1990a) has argued that the dialogue of the *Symposium* was produced during an historical moment of cultural conflict and suppression when a dichotomous masculinist logic—structured by the laws of noncontradiction and excluded middle, "grandfathered" by Parmenides, fathered and codified by Plato—contended with and ultimately marginalized the nondualistic, nonhierarchical, and, on Parmenides' and Plato's terms, illogical "philosophy of mortal opinion" (Nye, 1988). Today, so deeply rooted in our consciousness are this now-dominant patriarchal culture's assumptions governing gender and logic that even so radical and astute a critic of patriarchy as Luce Irigaray is unable to entirely uproot them. Nye contends that Irigaray responds to, but also through, Plato, the philosophy, and the world he engendered by reading Diotima as "a lapsed French feminist struggling to maintain the 'correct method' against philosophical orthodoxy" (Nye, 1989, 47). In consequence Irigaray reads Diotima not as a philosopher who presented a powerful alternative to Plato's world and philosophy, one that could be usefully appropriated by contemporary feminists, but as a crypto-Platonist and player of his philosophical game. This reading leaves Irigaray herself only one way out of the prison of patriarchal discourse, the way through deconstruction, *jouissance*, and *ecriture feminine*, a way which is no way out at all tied as it is to the assumptions of the views she seeks to subvert.

But in Nye's view Diotima was far less a prisoner of patriarchy than Irigaray believes. She argues that Diotima speaks not from, but from outside of, the Platonic patriarchy and against its cultural formations, whether ancient, modern, or postmodern. On Nye's reading Diotima speaks in the voice of "mortal opinion," articulating the world-view of pre-Greek Mediterranean culture (Nye, 1988), and on behalf of a deity that is the "generative principle at the heart of natural existence" (Nye, 1990a, 150). Nye's work shows that taken together Diotima's logic, her epistemology, her concept of human identity, and her understanding of the nature and role of love in human life form a picture of Diotimean lovers engaged in a "loving conversation" which issues in the creation of "new forms of life" that encompass the full range of human creativity: families, practices, institutions, sciences, sentiments, and ideas (see Plato, 92–3).

The primary hurdle in approaching Diotima's philosophy is just the question Nye and Irigaray consider; how we are to understand her? How can her words possibly have sense and meaning for us? How can she be read as other than a Platonist, a woman who, while she may be made to appear on the surface to be presenting a challenge to male hegemony, on deeper analysis is revealed to be speaking its language and extending its power? As Audre Lorde has reminded us in a different but related context, "the master's tools will never dismantle the master's house" (Lorde, 1984), and so if language and logic are the master's tools, surely the best we can hope to do with them is to build a more comfortable prison. While I am unable in this short work to engage with either Platonic or poststructuralist theory in full detail, in this paper I will argue that there is another way of understanding Diotima, a way that is open to all of us. We do not have to, somehow, throw ourselves conceptually back into the pre-Socratic world to do so, nor do we need a graduate degree in French feminism.

I argue in this paper that Wittgenstein, through bringing to our attention the ways in which pretheoretical language functions in language-games, can show how Diotima can be understood on her own terms. Let me succinctly encapsulate some salient points of his mature work that I expand upon in what follows: Wittgenstein argues against both essentialist and nominalist theories of language. In place of these theories he locates the sense of language in the conceptual grammar of language-games. Conceptual grammar "describes . . . the use of signs" (PI, 496) in the context of human life; it examines the multitude of ways in which language is woven into the lives and activities of human beings. While those lives are inscribed at a very deep level by culture, any accurate picture of the human must include what is "animal" (OC, 475), i.e., extra- and prelinguistic, in our inheritance. This latter includes possibilities of growth, development, and maturation which are logically necessary for the acquisition of the language-games of a mature woman's or man's love such as Diotima had in mind. Language-games, even highly abstract language-games, are "extensions" of "natural, instinctive" behaviors (Z, 545) and thus conceptual grammar requires the foregrounding of human "natural history" (PI 25, 415). Two powerful contributions emerge from Wittgenstein's approach that are important to my argument. The first emerges from the metaphor of language "woven into" human life, and thus not only nuancing existing patterns but also creating new patterns in human life. I stress the point that, while human being is continuous with the natural world, it cannot be understood on the materialistic model of matter-in-motion conjoined with language, the preferred account of nominalist theories; nor, in light of Wittgenstein's refutation of the correspondence theory of meaning, the theory of autonomous rules, and mentalism, can a Cartesian dualism be made to hold. The metaphor of weaving foregrounds the sentience and intersubjectivity of the human form of life as the warp into which the weft of language is woven to produce the language-games which pattern our lives. I will elaborate on these points in what follows. The second contribution of Wittgenstein's approach is to support the argument that Diotima's speech can not simply *best*, but *only*, be understood on a language-games account and so as delivering a message which is as relevant today as it was twenty-five hundred years ago. The Procrustean nipping and tucking that is required to fit her words to the Theory of Forms kills them and so they cannot be impressed into the service of Platonism. If this argument is valid, then Diotima speaks a language that we can use to further feminist libratory projects and her message, when properly understood, can guide us on our way.

I would suggest that, if Parmenides was the "grandfather" of the patriarchal philosophical tradition, then Diotima, in her honoring of the human form of life and her reliance on natural, pretheoretical language, was the grandmother of its most incisive contemporary critic, Ludwig Wittgenstein. In the rest of the space available to me I would like to draw out some of the affinities between the work of Diotima and that of Wittgenstein's mature period. I wish to begin to establish that there is a family relationship to be discerned in the work of these two great teachers although one which, as is so often the case in families, was unknown to either of them. I suggest in what follows, and space will allow me to do little more than suggest, that the family resemblance is striking and undeniable once Diotima and Wittgenstein are placed side by side.

Reading Diotima

I have indicated above, in the same critical tone employed by Nye, that it was a failure on Irigaray's part not to have stepped outside of patriarchal discourse, not to have taken a different path, in her reading of Diotima's speech. Nye has said of Irigaray's feminist strategy that Irigaray, as feminist critic of Western philosophy, "adopts a textual practice, a *travail du langage*. She has no naive notion of refuting male philosophers in their own terms. Instead, she approaches them as texts, that is, as internally generated, more or less ordered systems of meaning whose logical order and pretended truth must be deconstructed. The reader of a text must avoid being taken in both by an establishment of authoritative truth or by the temptation to establish a rival thesis" (Nye, 1989, 49).

But "being taken in by an establishment of authoritative truth" or capitulating to "the temptation to establish a rival thesis" do not exhaust the philosopher's options, a fact of which I believe Diotima was well aware for we do not see her doing either of these things in the speech Socrates reports in the *Symposium*. By dropping both the assumptions of patriarchal philosophy and also those of feminist deconstruction, we can read in Diotima a message that eludes patriarchal thought and provides a potent challenge to it (Orr, 2002b). What I believe Diotima was doing was using a non-technical natural language to remind an already philosophically confused young man, her student Socrates, of a few commonplaces of human existence which he appears to have forgotten. Specifically, but to greatly compress her points, she wants to remind him that we are all creatures of the natural world who are born, grow, develop, and die; who live and talk together; who love and call beautiful that which makes us happy; and that the process of human maturation involves moving past an adolescent sexual fixation on beautiful bodies to "reckon beauty of soul more valuable than beauty of body" (Plato, 92). Our love of beauty is our inspiration to create, to give birth to, the conditions of family, society, and culture in which that which we love can flourish. Further, as our understanding deepens and matures, we may come to apprehend "a beauty which is worthy of our reverence," which is, in Nye's words, "the generative principle at the heart of natural existence" (Nye, 1990a, 150).

At this point it may be objected that I have overlooked a hermeneutic problem of my own, that I am begging the question in assuming that Diotima's speech is that of a woman and not that of a male philosopher developing his own metaphysical positions. In this regard Andrea Nye has argued that, while a rereading of Diotima is a "speculative project" (Nye, 1988, 262), it is reasonable to ground it in what we know and can deduce about pre-Greek culture, just as the canon of pre-Socratic *male* philosophers has been reconstructed in the absence of original sources (Nye, 1988, 262). In addition, she holds that there is no good reason to believe that Plato broke in the *Symposium* with his otherwise consistent practice of using actual historical figures in his dialogues (Nye, 1989, 46). Further, Nye maintains, there are good reasons to believe that Diotima was an historical character, a priestess/prophetess from Mantinea who spoke with the authority of her position (Nye, 1989, 53–54).

These points are bound to remain contentious but we do not have to rely on them in order to hear in Diotima's speech a message useful to feminists today. In fact, I would propose that even if it could be conclusively shown that Plato *did* fabricate Diotima, this would only provide a delicious, but at the same time for Plato deadly, irony and in no way detract from the argument I make below. My grounds for this proposal are Wittgensteinian. As I have already noted, at the center of Wittgenstein's mature work is the argument that language only has sense in the context of the language-games in which it is actually used, that is, in the context of the activities and practices of human beings, in the flow of human life. Metaphysicians make the fundamental grammatical error of ripping words from those language-games, which are their source of sense, laboring under the delusion that these words either carry that sense with them into the pseudo-games they then construct, or even that they can give them a new sense, a refinement of their ordinary usages, by fiat. But, Wittgenstein argues, "[w]hen philosophers use a word—"knowledge", "being", "object", "I", "proposition", "name"—and try to grasp the *essence* of the thing, one must always ask oneself: is the word ever actually used in this way in the language-game which is its original home?—What *we* do is to bring words back from their metaphysical to their everyday use" (PI, 116, italics in original, see also 120, 134). Shorn of their everyday uses, as Diotima's words must be in order to read into them the Theory of Forms, these words become senseless, they say nothing at all.

A second point in support of reading Diotima's language as non-metaphysical is that her words make perfectly good sense when read and understood in an everyday fashion, in the context of the language-games which give them life. Further, what they say is something simple and uncontroversial both in her world and in our world today for they speak of fundamental aspects of the human condition that have not changed from her time to our own. In Wittgensteinian terms, an important part of what she is doing in the speech reported by Plato is reminding Socrates of some of the features of their shared "world-picture." Wittgenstein argues that a linguistic community's "world-picture" emerges as much from human lived experience as from the words that comprise their language-games. Language-games are a synthesis of "language and the actions into which it is woven" (PI, 7), and here "action" is broadly understood to include subjective (physical, cognitive, and emotional) as well as natural and social experience. While much of the world-picture may remain unarticulated, it serves as the "matter of course foundation" for our lives together (OC, 167 and passim). Thus to change or deny the aspects of that part of the picture of the human that Diotima highlights for Socrates would be to fundamentally alter our concept of the human.[1]

So while there may well be hermeneutical issues in reading Diotima's speech in twenty-first century English, I propose that the heart of her message comes through to us. In what follows I will listen to it by hearing her words as simple, everyday speech spoken by a wise woman to a student who she feared might, nevertheless, be incapable of understanding it. In other words, I am proposing that "mortal opinion" lives on in the embodied experience of every human being. This "mortal opinion," which Parmenides disparaged and which Nye attributes to Diotima (Nye, 1988), structures the logically primitive level of a common world-picture, one that the contemporary Western linguistic community shares with Diotima. It is expressed through the natural language-games of everyday life that Wittgenstein investigated in his later work.[2]

Although we have very little of the work of Diotima available to us, the degree to which the formal aspects of her philosophy parallel the much more elaborately worked positions of the later Wittgenstein is, to me, astounding once it is seen. I will explore several points of resemblance they share. While each of these points interlocks with and supports the others, I will separate out for examination some of the major areas of agreement in their (1) methodology, (2) rejection of binaries and hierarchy, (3) human ontology and linguistic practice, (4) personal identity and epistemology, and (5) the ethico-religious use of philosophy.

Philosophical Methodology

First, Diotima and Wittgenstein shared a philosophical methodology. Both philosophized not by advancing theses (PI, 109, 128) but by "assembling reminders for a particular purpose" (PI, 127). These reminders concerned the uses of language and the linguistic community's shared world-view. Wittgenstein called this world-view its "world-picture" in order to foreground the participation of embodied experience in its formation (OC, 93–97, 148, 150–155, 472–475, 478, and passim). The "particular purpose" of issuing these reminders was, in Diotima's words, to redirect the feet of the pilgrim who has strayed from the right path (Plato, 92); in Wittgenstein's words, it was to give the philosopher peace (PI, 133) by showing her or him the way out of the fly bottle of philosophical confusion in which s/he is trapped (PI, 309). This fly bottle is a prison created by misunderstanding how language functions. For instance, Platonists believe that language functions by picking out and naming the thing which all instances of a concept has in common, its Form or essence. But Plato's student, Aristotle, reminded him that it is difficult to see, for example, how the hypothetical Form of the Good bears any relevance to the particular goods that shoemakers or carpenters or doctors seek, let alone to the good which brings happiness to humans (Aristotle, 1947, 313–322). However, it was not until the work of Wittgenstein's mature period that a philosopher produced a large-scale study of the family resemblance character of concepts. For instance, there is a web of similarities and differences in the uses of the word "good" in a range of language-games (PI, 65–67) that give it its sense. No one use can be picked out as paradigmatic and so essentialism is avoided, and, because the conceptual grammar of each use contextualizes it in human life and praxis, nominalism cannot get a foothold.

Thus throughout their works we find both Diotima and Wittgenstein issuing reminders of how words are used in order to foreground that which is both simple and familiar (PI, 129), but which has been forgotten by the philosopher, obscured from view by the "houses of cards" (PI, 118) built out of misused language. Very often that is the context of words in specific language-games and, when this is missed, so is the relationship of that language to human life. To cite just a few examples, throughout her discourse Diotima reminds Socrates of the uses of the word 'love' and how it relates to the use of "beauty"; how different types of love are conceptually distinguished; how we can call someone "the same person" although they change over time (Plato, 88–89; and what we call wisdom.[3] Both Diotima and Wittgenstein philosophized in their natural language, avoiding jargon and theory, and both used their language to undermine patriarchal philosophy, although neither of them would have been likely to use that particular name for their target. Most importantly, both practiced their form of philosophical therapy in an attempt to return their students to health, to a clearheaded understanding of their lives that would open the way for them to live more fully and productively.

Binaristic and Hierarchic Thinking

Second, neither Diotima nor Wittgenstein employed a dichotomous, hierarchical language, nor were they entrapped by the "laws of logic" of that language. Much of Wittgenstein's mature work is devoted to showing how radically at odds the use of natural language is with the "crystalline purity" (PI, 107) which formal logic sought to read into it. These formalized systems are not, Wittgenstein argued, the articulation of deep structures underlying all legitimate language, rather they are the creations of philosophers who have left the world of human talk and daily life far behind. The founding move in the construction of these systems lies outside of language: "The philosopher has determined that he will not see and will not hear, and so will not understand what others say, a refusal that gives him license to substitute his words for theirs" (Nye, 1987, 95).

At one point Wittgenstein used the metaphor of a city to depict the way in which the multitude of language-games we play are grouped together in our lives: "Our language can be seen as an ancient city: a maze of little streets and squares, of old and new houses, and of houses with additions from various periods: and this surrounded by a multitude of new boroughs with straight regular streets and uniform houses" (PI, 18). Certainly some people sometimes play games in the new buildings of the city that more or less "fit" with the requirements of formal logic; but we all also play the old games with the language upon which these new ones are parasitic. It is in this logically primary and old language, spoken at the heart of the old city, our birthplace, which is our mother tongue. We live out much of our lives there, in ways that Diotima tried to remind a student of who was already infected by a philosophy that wanted to deny or evade its past. Nye has argued persuasively for the existence of a "pre-Hellenic philosophy of mortal opinion," a way of thinking employed by Diotima that was innocent not only of the gendered ordering of patriarchal thought but that also avoided dichotomous thinking grounded in the laws of noncontradiction and excluded middle, in favor of a multitermed natural logic better able to express and explore the complexity of human experience. "Do you really think that if something isn't beautiful, then it is ugly . . . and if someone is not wise he or she is ignorant: Have you never heard of something between knowledge and ignorance . . . ," argues Diotima (Plato quoted in Nye, 1988, 266; cf. Nye 1990b, esp. Chaps. 1 and 2). Diotima's words, articulating mortal opinion in the language spoken in the heart of the old city, defy the logic of Parmenides. Because this language grounds one firmly in the body and daily life, he branded "mortal opinion" illogical and fled its milieu.

Human Ontology and Linguistic Use

At a third point of intersection in their work Diotima and Wittgenstein share a strikingly similar concept of the human ontology and the human condition. As well, their views of the role of language in personal development share major points of affinity. In this section I will foreground some of the features of these aspects of their shared understanding. Most importantly, and in contrast to the dualism which grounds Irigaray's critique of Diotima, while both Diotima and Wittgenstein understand human being as overlapping the category of *animal*, neither inscribes in their view the radical dualism which would render human sexual behavior merely "causal" with the implication that this animal's "love" could only be raised to human status through the use of a rational faculty (see Irigaray, 27). I develop these points below.

In Plato's *Symposium* Diotima reminds Socrates that to be human is to desire the physical beauty of others, and to desire to procreate with them. It is from this humanized, but still animal, function that we mature to desire and create other types of progeny, children of the spirit that will bring other types of beauty into the world. In her speech it is the process of human maturation, not the philosophical discovery of the realm of the Forms, which enables the development of these logically secondary, loving language-games. I propose that the nature of the maturation process Diotima has in mind here is *not* to take a quantum leap from purely instinctual—in Irigaray's word "causal" (27)—behavior to behavior grounded in rational processes. Indeed, if one does not come to this text with a predisposition to read Diotima as a Platonist, one is hard pressed to find textual evidence for such a theory in her recorded words. On the contrary, what she is pointing to is the growth of an individual's care and concern from the narrow focus on a particular individual—lover and/or child—to care and concern for the broader social group and its institutions. Diotima tailored her speech to her audience, in the first instance Socrates, and so referenced the forms of love—importantly that of boys—and care—for the polis and for ideas—which were of concern to that audience. I suspect that, had she been speaking to a woman of this culture, she might have shifted focus to the love between mother and child and its formative role in the child's development of more mature forms of love. Although I cannot develop this point here, Diotima's argument resonates in interesting ways with the moral maturation process Carol Gilligan (1982) has empirically observed in girls and women and, other research has found, is available to boys as well (Johnston, 1998).[5]

In a similar vein Wittgenstein repeatedly returns in his work to the ways in which language-games grow out of our "primitive", "instinctive", "animal experience" (Z, 540, 541, 545; OC, 475) to mature and take forms not available at earlier stages of personal development, and certainly not available to non-human forms of life. One well-known example will help demonstrate this.

In his critique of Cartesian models of mind in which words name logically private experience, Wittgenstein set an alternative picture by investigating the logic of a child's language acquisition and exploring the conceptual grammar of first person experiential predicates:

> how does a human being learn the meaning of the names of sensations?—of the word "pain" for example Here is one possibility: words are connected with the primitive, the natural, expressions of the sensation and used in their place. A child has hurt himself and he cries; and then adults talk to him and teach him exclamations, and, later, sentences They teach the child new pain-behaviour. "So you are saying that the word 'pain' really means crying?" On the contrary: the verbal expression of pain replaces crying and does not describe it. (PI, sec. 244)

He also writes:

> It is a help here to remember that it is a primitive reaction to tend, to treat, the part that hurts when someone else is in pain; and not merely when oneself is—and so to pay attention to other people's pain-behaviour, as one does *not* pay attention to one's own pain behaviour.
> But what is the word "primitive" meant to say here? Presumably that this sort of behaviour is *pre-linguistic*· that a language-game is based *on* it, that it is the prototype of a way of thinking and not the result of thought. (Z, sec. 540–541)

In these and a multitude of other passages in *Philosophical Investigations* and his other published writings Wittgenstein attacks Western culture's dominant models of mind, language, and logic both by showing their incoherence when subjected to minute scrutiny, and by proposing an alternative way of understanding language; as language-games rooted in the human form of life which is a part of the natural world, which is animal. In these games the logical relationship between, e.g., the word "pain" and the experience of pain, what he called its conceptual grammar, is internal, not merely contingent (ROC, 1). It is this logically necessary interface between language and human experience that gives the use of the word "pain" sense. As these passages show, language acquisition is possible because adults understand the child's expressions of experiences such as pain, and also it's experiences of pleasure, love, and much else. What the word "understand" means here is that adults *respond* to the child's prelinguistic behavior in appropriate ways. Wittgenstein frequently uses the word "instinctive" (e.g., Z, 545) to characterize the naturalness of these responses. By this he does not reduce these responses to a form of materialistic causality, but rather indicates the naturalness, the spontaneousness, of many human responses, i.e., the fact that they are not based on ratiocination. "My relation to the appearance [e.g., of pain in another person] is part of my concept" (Z, 543). In the course of these interactions with other persons a child learns to weave language into its experiences, it learns language-games. It is on the basis of learning to play these primitive games we are able to progress to more complex and sophisticated ones as well as to manipulate our experience in a variety of ways.[6] Throughout the work of his mature period Wittgenstein argued against both essentialism and against theories, such as the one he held in his *Tractatus* period, that language functions on the model of an abstract system of rules which, *per impossible*, govern its application in human life.[7]

Contemporary structuralist and poststructuralist theories have attempted to loosen up the static structures of old-style essentialist thinking and the referential theories of meaning which went with it, but frequently re-inscribe its founding assumptions. Dualistic thinking and the reification of language into an abstract system of self-governing rules lies at the foundation of Saussure's structuralism and infects his heirs, structuralist and post-structuralist, despite the variations they have worked on his theme. It manifests in Irigaray's reading of Diotima's speech in her assumption of a radical distinction between body and soul, an assumption that she erroneously attributes to Diotima. Diotima's method "miscarries," she argues, because she understands physical love causally, as something animal (Irigaray, 25–27), and thus different in kind from love of the soul, which is properly concerned with wisdom and immortality. In consequence, Irigaray understands Diotima to be saying that "Beauty of body and of soul are hierarchized, and love of women becomes the lot of those who, incapable of being creators in soul, are fecund of body . . . " (Irigaray, 29). "Carnal procreation is subordinated to the engendering of beautiful and good things. Immortal things" (31). But this reading of Diotima is a mistake that rests on Irigaray's own philosophical commitments, her own struggle with mind/body dualism, and the belief that difference must entail hierarchy. The aim of Diotima's speech is not to engage in such philosophizing, but rather to argue that the "cause" of all forms of love and creativity, of the body and of the soul, of poetry and crafts, of families and states, is a creative impulse, a generative force at the center of all of life, which inspires us to go beyond simple existence and create that which is beautiful. This is the way in which we achieve immortality. In this I believe that it is more in keeping with the spirit of Diotima's speech to understand that animals have a share in what is divine through their creative activity, rather than that physical love is being reduced to "mere causality", a lower order of activity which is not bound up with human values, purposes and understanding.

Wittgenstein's work alerts us to the boundaries which exist between what is possible for humans and for nonhumans—e.g., a dog cannot hope (PI, 174)—and foregrounds the role of maturation and development in the acquisition of language-games—neither can we hope until we have reached a certain level of both maturity and language acquisition. Similarly, although the word love is used across a range of human experiences which are tied together by family resemblances, the sense it has for a child who loves her mother is vastly different from that which it has when used in the language-games of a mature and wise woman such as Diotima. When Irigaray reads Diotima's discussion of physical love causally, she reads into it a determinism that is foreign to both Diotima's and Wittgenstein's thought. While Wittgenstein viewed language-games as an outgrowth from what is humanly pre- and non-linguistic, his view here was no more causal or "merely" biologistic than Diotima's. Rather, humans have a range of potentials that can be shaped and formed, or even suppressed, through the acquisition of language-games. Notoriously, glaring examples of the possibilities for manipulation and suppression are found if we consider the language-games involved in the formation of gender, in the ways, for instance, in which boys are encouraged to develop the language-games of science and mathematics while girls are encouraged to develop empathy, caring, and nurturance. What emerges from Wittgenstein's philosophy is the understanding that both mathematics and nurturance are *human* possibilities and that these all-to-real clichés of gender have their source in history and culture, not biology.

An important outcome of Wittgenstein's work on the interrelated themes of language and philosophy of mind, one that resonates with Diotima's work, is the uncovering of the natural-language concept of the human and the demonstration that it falls neither into materialism nor Cartesianism. "The human body is the best picture of the human soul" (PI, 178) brings out the point that on a logically primitive level our concepts of body and soul/mind[8] are not, indeed cannot, be separated from each other. The separated concepts of the human body and the human soul/mind are logically later developments that are, in Wittgenstein's word, parasitic on an holistic concept of a human being and on the more logically primitive language-games we play with others. As Wittgenstein points out, "My attitude toward him is an attitude towards a soul. I am not of the *opinion* he has a soul" (PI, 178), i.e., this is not something about which I may be mistaken if dualism turns out to be untenable. This is a point of conceptual grammar, not an autobiographical remark, which brings out the logical relationship between the language user's lived relationships with other human beings which are grounded in prelinguistic, primitive, and natural behaviors, and the language of interpersonal relationship. Thus the ontologically rigid distinction between the human body and the human soul/mind[8] is a product of philosophical confusion, the mistaking of a grammatical distinction for a difference in kinds of things; the ontologist "predicate[s] of the thing what lies in the method of representing it" (PI, 104).

Across a range of language uses, from the most concrete to the most abstract, Wittgenstein has rooted those uses firmly in embodied, nonlinguistic human experience, in natural behaviors, in reactions to others, in sensations, and in a multitude of other human commonalities. In this he both aligns his understanding with Diotima's emphasis on embodiment and, through focusing closely on conceptual grammar, develops her position in useful ways. In delineating a developmental picture in which human being is shaped through the interplay of natural maturation processes and the acquisition of language-games, they have provided a third way of responding to patriarchal philosophy—one which is neither playing its game nor that of the feminist deconstructionist—a way which Irigaray has missed.

Personal Identity and Epistemology

In a fourth point Diotima and Wittgenstein also agree in their understanding of the nature of human identity, of epistemology, and of the interrelationship of these two. Andrea Nye quotes a longish section of Diotima's speech to explore these topics (Nye, 1988, 267). I reproduce it here in a slightly different translation:

> Even during the period for which any living being is said to live and retain his identity—as a man, for example, is called the same man from boyhood to old age—he does not in fact retain the same attributes, although he is called the same person; he is always becoming a new being and undergoing a process of loss and reparation, which affects his hair, his flesh, his bones, his blood, and his whole body. And not only his body, but his soul as well. No man's character, habits, opinions, desires, pleasures, pains, and fears remain always the same; new ones come into existence and old ones disappear. What happens with pieces of knowledge is even more remarkable; it is not merely that some appear and others disappear, so that we no more retain our identity with regard to knowledge than with regard to the other things I have mentioned, but that each individual piece of knowledge is subject to the same process as we are ourselves. When we use the word recollection we imply by using it that knowledge departs from us; forgetting is the departure of knowledge, and recollection, by implanting a new impression in the place of that which is lost, preserves it, and gives it a spurious appearance of uninterrupted identity (Plato, 88–89)

Here Diotima presents a picture of personal identity that is fluid, open to change and development over time. She suggests not only that there is no unitary and enduring essence of human being but also, by the close connection of her depiction of a fluid soul with the doctrine of ever-changing knowledge, alerts us that there is some connection here to be explored. In explicating this Nye explains that for Diotima, "The very stuff of the body thinks; flesh is not dead material but has the ability to be conscious of conflicting impulses and move toward a resolution. Thought leads to satisfaction (literally fullness . . .) but that satisfaction can never be only an intellectual resolution, because we think with, and not outside or inside, our body" (Nye, 1988, 265). Nye's gloss of Diotima resonates deeply with Wittgenstein's work in the foregrounding of the crucial role of embodied behavior in "thinking" language-games, in those games which have been sited in "the mind" by much of patriarchal theorizing, and in the play of signifiers alienated from embodied experience in much post-modernist theorizing. In contrast, for Diotima and Wittgenstein humans change not only in their physical aspect, they change in their souls as well and this change is a function of changes in their "knowledge," in the language-games they play.

Likewise, Wittgenstein's rejection of behaviorism and Cartesianism is the rejection of an essentialized self: "'I' is not the name of a person" (PI, 410) but a concept that's various uses are held together by numerous "family resemblances" (PI, 67). The concept of personal identity that emerges from his work is constituted as a composite of the language-games we have learned to play. However, recalling how firmly rooted language-games are in corporeal experience, this is clearly not the alienated self of poststructuralist theorizing. Thinking, believing, knowing, understanding, feeling, and related mental predicates are things done by human beings, but not in some incorporeal, ghostly part of themselves, nor through the mechanical movements of complex living automata, nor is it the function of the play of signifiers. To reinforce this point with a famous example from Wittgenstein's *Philosophical Investigations*, a person's understanding of "bring me five red apples" comes out in how she responds to that request, in what she does (PI, 1). Understanding is not a product of mental acts, nor the performance of a merely material "body". On the contrary, the criterion of understanding is the action of a living human being.

Through a multitude of examples in his mature work, Wittgenstein connected the predicates of mentation with how a person acts, with typical learner's reactions, with being able to do something, with being able to go on producing a series, with appropriate behavior, etc., etc. In short, while not denying that we do such things as make a mental calculation or keep our thoughts to ourselves, for Wittgenstein as well as for Diotima, we think with the body. For both Diotima and Wittgenstein personal identity was fluid and ever-changing and this is intimately bound up with an epistemology centered in the body. In a very real sense, we are what we know, or better, we are the language-games we play.

Philosophy as an Ethico-Religious[9] Therapy

A fifth and final point of affinity between the work of Diotima and Wittgenstein that I would like to draw out here lies in the ethico-religious nature of their philosophizing. Like Diotima, Wittgenstein believed that we had lost our way, bewitched and lured off the path by the seductions of language wrongly understood and wrongly used. The consequences of this have been devastating: millennia of cultural development which, while promising the good life, have done everything to militate against that goal, and personal lives distorted, even destroyed, by a diseased understanding. In diagnosing the malaise of modern culture, the etiological roots of which lie in the nascent culture that Diotima challenged, and in prescribing its treatment, Wittgenstein has said that, "The sickness of a time is cured by an alteration in the mode of life of human beings, and it was possible for the sickness of philosophical problems to get cured only through a changed mode of thought and of life, not through a medicine invented by an individual" (RFM, Pt. II, 4).

Because language only has sense in the context of human lives and purposes—that is, as language-games—language and those lives and purposes must change together. Wittgenstein said of his methodology that "The work of the philosopher consists in assembling reminders . . ."(PI, 127, cf. 89), it is not a matter of "advancing *theses*" (PI, 128, italics in original). If we resist the temptation to see Diotima engaging in the linguistic contortions necessary to produce the Theory of Forms, it becomes not only a plausible but an obvious reading to find a methodology closely akin to Wittgenstein's in her work. Like Wittgenstein, she repeatedly reminds Socrates of how language is used: "we call a man 'the same' although he changes over his life-span" is a comment on the conceptual grammar of "the same"; "The generic concept [of love] embraces every desire for good and for happiness" (Plato, 85) is likewise. Her speech is full of such grammatical remarks. Also like Wittgenstein, Diotima does not "advance theses" but reminds Socrates of simple and obvious matters which he had neglected. To quote Wittgenstein again, "The aspects of things that are most important for us are hidden because of their simplicity and familiarity. . . . We fail to be struck by what, once seen, is most striking and most powerful" (PI, 129). Thus Diotima reminds Socrates of the typical process of human growth, from love of beautiful bodies through to the development of an understanding of beauty that enables the creation of "true goodness" (Plato, 95) in the world. By her own statement she is reminding Socrates of these things because he is in danger of "going astray" (92) and she, in her capacity as his teacher, believes these reminders may help him in his development.

Both Diotima and Wittgenstein, then, practiced a form of philosophical therapy that aimed to clear up confusions of the understanding, confusions that, it must be stressed, manifest in how one lives one's life. They did not do this by advancing theses or theories. Indeed, if one accepts Diotima's understanding of human embodiment and growth, the very thought of anyone's life being improved by acceptance of the Theory of Forms is an odd one. Philosophy is "what is possible *before* all new discoveries and inventions" (PI, 126, italics in original); its methodology is to provide reminders of how language is used and of simple facts of the human form of life that provide the context for that use. The hoped-for outcome of their therapies on those who underwent them was a less confused and deluded understanding. Only then will humans be able to talk together in an intercourse which will be productive of more fully human, that is, of more ethically and spiritually fulfilling, ways of life. Embedded in both the life and the philosophy of Wittgenstein is a fundamentally ethical intent and, because his aim was to created the conditions for human souls to improve themselves, we can call his work spiritual as well. Diotima also, in her philosophical practice, sought to lead the straying pilgrim to "the region where a man's life should be spent, in the contemplation of absolute beauty" (Plato, 94). In a passage misconstrued from the time of Plato to that of modern commentators as the articulation of a "correct paederasty" and an introduction to the Theory of the Forms, Diotima maps the path (*mutatis mutandis* re: sex) we all, male and female and whatever our sexuality, must follow:

> When a man, starting from this sensible world and making his way upward by a right use of his feeling of love for boys, begins to catch sight of that beauty, he is very near his goal. This is the right way of approaching or being initiated into the mysteries of love, to begin with examples of beauty in this world, and using them as steps to ascend continually with that absolute beauty as one's aim, from one instance of physical beauty to two and from two to all, then from physical beauty to moral beauty, and from moral beauty to the beauty of knowledge, until from knowledge of various kinds one arrives at the supreme knowledge whose sole object is that absolute beauty, and knows at last what absolute beauty is. (Plato, 94)

With the help of Nye and Wittgenstein we can now understand this teaching of Diotima's not as a description of the soul's flight from the body and physical love and into the rarefied atmosphere of the Forms but as what Nye has described as a "lateral" progress "from narrow sexual relations and exclusive concern with one's own family, to 'better' (not 'higher'), more inclusive relationships" (Nye, 1989, 48), to the love of souls rather than simply the love of bodies, until finally the Diotimean lover gains an understanding, a vision if you will, of that "absolute beauty," not a Platonic Form but "an inner generative impulse at the heart of life" (Nye, 1989, 48) which is worthy of our reverence. That "inner generative impulse" is at the heart of one's own life and thus we can understand "the supreme knowledge whose sole object is that absolute beauty" as self knowledge.

It is a temptation, weaned as we are on Platonic philosophy, to reify the "absolute beauty" of which Diotima speaks, to think it must be some one thing for all who find it. The model here, of course, is Plato's Form of the Good. Whether it is Plato or you or I who find it, we all find the same thing. It may be a help here to remember the many leaders, creators, and teachers of whom one would not hesitate to say, "they had a vision of the good, of absolute beauty": Siddhartha Gautama, Jesus, Mohammad, Beethoven, Michelangelo, Mother Teresa, Martin Luther King, Jr., a teacher not known to the world but important in one's life, the list could go on and on. None of these great creators deserted the world, they all had a vision of supreme beauty sourced in their own being, and their actions in bringing that vision to being in the world were loving and generative. The beauty and good which each brought into the world was as varied as was their lives and their circumstances, a unique and distinct contribution to the rich tapestry of life.

Conclusion

I have brought Diotima and Wittgenstein together in this paper because I believe there clearly is, in his term, a strong family resemblance between their works. Both practice a similar philosophical method: the arrangement of reminders for the purpose of clearing up confusions that mislead and harm us. Both understand their work to have the aim of ethical and spiritual growth as well as cultural reform. Both present deep challenges to patriarchal philosophy and culture through their affirmation and use of natural language, a way of speaking which does not share in the assumptions of dualism, hierarchy, gender, or proper formalized logic of that culture. Wittgenstein has argued, as Diotima may well have also, that the linguistic and logical practices of the now dominant culture are parasitic upon natural language, could not exist without it, and continue to depend, however covertly, on the facts of "our natural history" (PI, 25) in which its host is rooted. Both Diotima and Wittgenstein propose a picture of human being which highlights corporality and continuity with the rest of nature; which stresses the interconnectedness of epistemology, the body and personal identity; and which sees change and even aging and decay as necessary and desirable. Both had faith in a "generative principle at the heart of all natural existence," although neither used precisely that term, and they believed that, with a proper use of language, we could talk with each other and in so doing foster the development of that principle in uniquely human ways; but both expressed some pessimism with regard to our inclination to do so. Diotima brings to philosophy a distinctly female perspective as well as a cultural experience which enabled her to see and articulate the importance of generativity in ways which Wittgenstein did not, and which gives her voice an accent welcome to the female ear; Wittgenstein, perhaps simply because we have so much more of his work, brings a much more fully developed exploration of the nature and workings of language-games with which we can contest patriarchal culture by reclaiming the language which is rightfully ours.

Notes

1. This would certainly be overstated if it were taken to mean that the entirety of a contemporary Western woman's world-picture were isomorphic with Diotima's. This is not what I wish to imply. I am arguing that the picture of the human and the conceptual grammar of linguistically primary language-games are what they share. I acknowledge that I am painting in very broad strokes when I allude to "the contemporary Western linguistic community," however I believe that an examination of the depth grammar of the major languages of what is generally referred to as "Western culture" will show far more primitive world-picture similarities than differences

2. A number of feminist philosophers have recently explored aspects of Diotima's speech and her life. I have found the work of Anne-Marie Bowery (1996) and Shannon Bell (1994, 1992) especially stimulating. In my essay the focus is narrowly centered on Diotima's logic and language and so much of the current scholarship must be ignored

3. This statement may seem question begging since we have not yet established that Diotima was not pointing out Platonic entities. The points that follow will provide support for my non-Platonic and de-essentialized reading.

4. I am arguing in this paper that both Diotima and Wittgenstein shared the belief that incorrect uses of language create "diseases of the understanding " Because, as the concept of language-games makes us aware, the use of language implicates all aspects of our being, such a diseased understanding will not be confined to cognitive processes, but may contaminate all aspects of our lives. Wittgenstein was explicit that such disease might require more that one kind of treatment (PI 133), but both he and Diotima confined their therapies to direct treatment of how we think. Other thinkers in other traditions, most notably Eastern Hindu and Buddhist philosophers, have greatly enlarged the therapeutic modalities with yogic and meditation techniques which are designed to engage not only mind but body and soul. The Buddhist philosopher Nagarjuna's (1995) work is of particular interest both for the powerful arguments he developed against essentialist and nihilist view and for the therapeutic purpose of his writings. Western scholars and researchers are beginning to explore the rich potential these techniques hold out for pedagogy (Miller, 2005) and especially anti-oppressive pedagogy (Forbes, 2005, 2003; Orr, 2005, 2004).

5. Zora Neale Hurston's, *Their Eyes Were Watching God* (1978) provides a fictional treatment of the maturation of the soul which is the subject of Diotima's speech. (see Orr, 2002a).

6. Gender acquisition can be understood in terms of the possibility of manipulating and shaping experience through the acquisition of culturally constructed language-games. For instance, to illustrate this point in very simplistic and stereotypic terms, in contemporary North American culture girls are still encouraged to learn much more finely nuanced games of emotion than boys, boys to develop human abilities such as math proficiency which are discouraged in girls. I have argued elsewhere (1995) that this gender shaping in turns leads to the development of what Carol Gilligan has identified as differential, gender-linked "moral voices" (1982).

7. More formalized and abstract games are also developed which do not have such clear developmental connections with bodily experience but which are no less dependent upon human pre- and nonlinguistic actions, reactions and consistencies of behavior. A well-known example of this is shown in the series of passages in *Philosophical Investigations* on rule following in mathematics that were so famously misconstrued by Saul Kripke (1982). I wish to dwell on this for a moment because it will help to illuminate the crux of the problem in Saussure's linguistics which reappears to infect the work of Luce Irigaray and consequently her (mis)reading of Diotima's speech. It will also further elaborate on the notion of language-games as words woven into human life that achieve much of their regularity not by the imposition of "rules" but from the patterns to be found in our lives as well as in the customs and institutions we create.

For Saussure language is a rule governed system of signs which have meaning through their relationships with other signs, and which consists of signifier (sound patterns) and signified (concepts), both of which are mental—the *Course in General Linguistics* even includes a little diagram showing thought being transferred from the brain of one person to that of another (Saussure, 11) This, of course, is the kernel of Irigaray's assumption that Diotima's speech must be understood as a "text" in the sense of an "internally generated, more or less ordered system of meaning". In a telling analogy Saussure compared language with chess in order to make the distinction between what is —essential and what inessential to the system:

If I use ivory chessmen instead of wooden ones, the change has no effect on the system; but if I decrease or increase the number of chessmen, this change has a profound effect on the "grammar" of the game. One must always distinguish between what is internal and what is external. In each instance one can determine the nature of the phenomenon by applying this rule: everything that changes the system in any way is internal (Saussure, 22–23)

Thus for Saussure what is essential to language, what is internal and determines the grammar of the system, is signs, i.e., signifiers and signifieds. All else is external, contingent. But Wittgenstein has shown, I argue, that this statement of Saussure's theory of language contains its major philosophical problems: its sundering of language from the rest of human experience, i.e., his failure to understand language as language-games; his sequestering of an essential component of language in the "mind", i.e., the creation of a logically private language; and his consequent reliance on rules to govern use and create meaning. Wittgenstein's complex work on this model of language takes the form of an extended *reduction ad absurdum* to show that it issues in solipsism and, in the last analysis, the reduction of language to nonsense. The "inner object", be that a thought, feeling, or "signified", is like a beetle in a box: each person has their own, no one can see anyone else's and thus, "one can 'divide through' by the thing in the box; it cancels out, whatever it is." (PI, 293). Useful introductions to this aspect of his work have been developed by Malcolm (1963a, 9163b, and 1977. See also his 1986).

Also considering a game of chess, Wittgenstein asks us to imagine two people yelling and stamping their feet "in such a way that their procedure is translatable by suitable rules into a game of chess" (PI, 200). Would we be inclined to say they were playing chess, he asks, and by what right? For Saussure the answer to this would be a simple yes, because what they are doing *can* be translated, by rules, into a game of chess i.e., this performance has the internal structure of chess. But Wittgenstein does not see the matter so simply: He begins the next section with, "This was our paradox: no course of action could be determined by a rule, because every course of action can be made out to accord with the rule. The answer was: if everything can be made out to accord with the rule, then it can also be made out to conflict with it. And so there would be neither accord nor conflict here" (PI, 201).

Here, according to Saul Kripke, Wittgenstein states the form of philosophical skepticism that arises from the model of language as a system of rule-governed signs. Kripke argues that, for example, "in learning to add I grasp a rule" (Kripke, 8) but, since rules can be variously interpreted, "the sceptic holds that no fact about my past history— nothing that was ever in my mind, or in my external behavior—establishes that I meant plus rather than quus [to indicate an alternative meaning for '+']" (Kripke, 13). Thus language conceived on the model advanced by Saussure and appropriated by his philosophical and psychoanalytically oriented heirs issues in a universal and vicious skepticism: There is no way to guarantee the connection between any signifier and any signified and thus there can be no consistency in our use of signs. Not only can we not successfully transfer thought from A's head into B's head, as per the little diagram in the *Course*, we cannot guarantee within our own heads what we mean from time to time, i.e., that we are correctly applying the rule. Language, Wittgenstein would say, has been reduced to nonsense.

Although Kripke attributed this form of skepticism to Wittgenstein, Wittgenstein not only did not fall into it, he identified its source and argued extensively to dissolve this pseudo-problem. The rest of PI, 201, which Kripke does not quote in setting up this problem, reads as follows:

It can be seen that there is a misunderstanding here from the mere fact that in the course of our argument we give one interpretation after another, as if each one contented us at least for a moment, until we thought of yet another standing behind it. What this shews is that there is a way of grasping a rule which is *not* an *interpretation*, but which is exhibited in what we call "obeying the rule" and "going against it" in actual cases Hence there is an inclination to say: every action according to the rule is an interpretation But we ought to restrict the term "interpretation" to the substitution of one expression of the rule for another

Wittgenstein's argument here is that what we call grasping a rule, understanding and using language correctly, comes out in what we *do* in particular cases. One understands the rule if one plays the game correctly, i.e., makes the right linguistic move in the broader context of human experiences and purposes. "'Obeying a rule' is a practice" (PI, 202), something we do, activity of a person. This point is part of the importance for Wittgenstein of understanding language-games on analogy with the use of tools (PI, 23), to further human purposes which very often lie outside of language and which do not stand in need of further justification by appeal to rules.

Wittgenstein argues that, "[w]hen I obey a rule, I do not choose. I obey the rule *blindly*" (PI, 219) and consequently obeying a rule cannot be read as an act of interpretation In part Kripke's confusion comes of understanding rules as, in every case, things which exist separately from human practices and which get applied from case to case to guide those practices. From this assumption arises the question of how we know we are applying the rule correctly and thus the "skeptical paradox" is generated. Instead Wittgenstein encourages us to look for consistencies and patterns in human activities, and to understand "rules" as derivatives from those practices, as something we read off of, or into, the practice (PI, 54; see also PI, 244). Just as a child does not need a rule to tell her to cry when she hurts herself, so she does not appeal to a rule in order to say "I am in pain." To think otherwise is to "sublime" rules.

The purpose of Wittgenstein's philosophical therapy is to turn our attention away from this delusion, this crystal pure dream of a sublimed language, whether that dream takes the form of a rigid mechanism, such as is found in the Early Greeks and his own *Tractatus*, or the more fluid form of poststructuralist theories. His strategy was, on the negative side, to show, in far greater detail that I have been able to indicate here, the incoherence of these theories and, on the positive side, to encourage us to pay attention instead to the ebb and flow of human life and activities and the role language plays in these. In doing so we can see that the acquisition and use of language is the outgrowth of the possibilities that inhere in humans, including their intellectual and spiritual growth. In conclusion, those yelling and stomping individuals in his example need to be understood on their own terms, not on the terms that we bring to our observation of them, not in accord with rules that we might read into their practice. On the same grounds we ought to grant Diotima her own voice

8. I have conjoined these two terms owing to their conflation in much patriarchal philosophy. For instance Descartes regularly and deliberately used them interchangeably, not a surprising practice given the derivation of Descartes' thought from Plato via Augustine.

9. My use of 'religious' here is more a matter of convenience than of accuracy (see Smith, 1998). The aim of the work of both Diotima and Wittgenstein was, I believe, to effect spiritual growth and development and cannot easily be situated within the purview of a religion.

Bibliography

(N.B.: I have followed the convention of citing Wittgenstein by title abbreviation followed by section number If a page is referred to, that is indicated. Standard abbreviations of Wittgenstein's texts are given after their citation in the Bibliography.)

Alcoff, Linda. "Cultural Feminism Versus Post-Structuralism: The Identity Crisis in Feminist Theory." *Signs A Journal of Women in Culture and Society* 13, no. 3 (1988): 405–436.

Aristotle. *Nichomachean Ethics* Pp 298–543 in *Introduction to Aristotle*, edited by Richard McKeon. New York: The Modern Library, 1947.

Bell, Shannon. *Reading, Writing and Rewriting the Prostitute Body*. Bloomington and Indianapolis: Indiana University Press, 1994.

———. "Tomb of the Sacred Prostitute: The *Symposium* " Pp. 198—210 in *Shadow of Spirit. Postmodernism and Religion*, edited by Philippa Berry and Andrew Wernick. London and New York: Routledge, 1992.

Bowery, Anne-Marie. "Diotima Tells Socrates a Story: A Narrative Analysis of Plato's *Symposium* " Pp. 175–194 in *Feminism and Ancient Philosophy*, edited by Julia K. Ward. New York and London: Routledge, 1996.

Forbes, David. "Turn the Wheel. Integral School Counseling for Male Adolescents." *Journal of Counseling and Development* 81 (Spring 2003): 142–149.

———. "In Da Zone: Meditation, Masculinity, and a Meaningful Life." Pp. 153–160 in *Holistic Learning and Spirituality in Education· Breaking New Ground*, edited by Jack Miller, Selia Karsten, Diana Denton, Deborah Orr, Isabella Kates. New York: SUNY, 2005.

Fuss, Diana. *Essentially Speaking: Feminism, Nature and Difference*. New York and London: Routledge, 1989.

Gilligan, Carol. *In a Different Voice. Psychological Theory and Women's Development* Cambridge, Massachusetts, and London, England: Harvard University Press, 1982.

Halperin, David M. "Why is Diotima a Woman?" Pp. 113–151 in *One Hundred Years of Homosexuality and Other Essays on Greek Love*. New York, London: Routledge, 1990

Hurston, Zora Neale. *Their Eyes Were Watching God*. Urbana and Chicago: University of Illinois Press, 1978.

Irigaray, Luce "Sorcerer Love A Reading of Plato, *Symposium*, 'Diotima's Speech'" Pp 20—33 in *An Ethics of Sexual Difference,* translated by Carolyn Burke and Gillian C. Gill. Ithaca, N. Y.: Cornell University Press, 1993.

Johnston, D. Kay, "Adolescents' Solutions to Dilemmas in Fables: Two Moral Orientations—Two Problem Solving Strategies." Pp. 49–71 in *Mapping the Moral Domain· A Contribution of Women's Thinking to Psychological Theory and Education*, edited by Carol Gilligan, Janie Victoria Ward, and Jill McLean Taylor with Betty Bardige. Cambridge, Massachusetts: Center for the Study of Gender, Education and Human Development, Harvard University Graduate School of Education, 1988.

Kripke, Saul A. *Wittgenstein on Rules and Private Language: An Elementary Exposition* Cambridge, Mass.: Harvard University Press, 1982.

Lorde, Audre. "The Master's Tools Will Never Dismantle the Master's House." In *Sister Outsider· Essays and Speeches*. Freedom, C : The Crossing Press, 1984.

Malcolm, Norman *Nothing is Hidden. Wittgenstein's Criticism of His Early Thought.* Oxford: Basil Blackwell, 1986.

————. "The Privacy of Experience." Pp. 104–132 in *Thought and Knowledge. Essays by Norman Malcolm* Ithaca and London: Cornell University Press, 1977.

————. "Knowledge of Other Minds." Pp. 130–140 in *Knowledge and Certainty Essays and Lectures* Ithaca and London: Cornell University Press, 1963a.

————. "Wittgenstein's *Philosophical Investigations* " Pp. 96–129 In *Knowledge and Certainty· Essays and Lectures* Ithaca and London: Cornell University Press, 1963b.

Miller, Jack, Selia Karsten, Diana Denton, Deborah Orr, Isabella Kates, eds. *Holistic Learning and Spirituality in Education· Breaking New Ground.* New York: SUNY, 2005.

Nagarjuna, *Mulamadhyamakakarika (The Fundamental Wisdom of the Middle Way).* Translated and Commentary by Jay L. Garfield. New York and Oxford: Oxford University Press, 1995

Nye, Andrea. "The Subject of Love Diotima and Her Critics." *The Journal of Value Inquiry* 24, (1990a): 135–153.

————. *Words of Power· A Feminist Reading of the History of Logic.* New York and London: Routledge, 1990b.

————. "The Hidden Host: Irigaray and Diotima at Plato's *Symposium.*" *Hypatia* 3, no.3 (1989): 45–61

————. "Rethinking Male and Female: The   Pre-Hellenic Philosophy of   Mortal Opinion." *History of European Ideas* 9, no.3 (1988): 261–280.

————. "The Unity of Language." *Hypatia* 2, no. 2 (1987): 95–111.

Orr, Deborah. "Minding the Soul in Education: Conceptualizing and Teaching to the Whole Person." Pp. 87–100 in *Holistic Learning and Spirituality in Education· Breaking New Ground,* edited by Jack Miller, Selia Karsten, Diana Denton, Deborah Orr, Isabella Kates. New York: SUNY, 2005

————."The Uses of Mindfulness in Feminist Anti-Oppressive Pedagogies: Philosophy and Praxis." *Canadian Journal of Education* 27, no. 4 (2004): 477–88.

————. "The Crone as Lover and Teacher. A Philosophical Reading of Zora Neale Hurstons' *Their Eyes Were Watching God.* " *Journal of Feminist Studies in Religion* 18, no. 1 (2002a): 25—50.

————. "Developing Wittgenstein's Picture of the Soul: Toward a Feminist Spiritual Erotics." Pp. 322–343 in *Feminist Interpretations of Wittgenstein,* edited by Naomi Scheman and Peg O'Connor, *Re-Reading the Canon,* series edited by Nancy Tuana. University Park, Pennsylvania: The Pennsylvania State Press, 2002.

————. "On Logic and Moral Voice." *Informal Logic* 17, no.3 (1995.) 347–363.

Plato. *The Symposium* Translated by Walter Hamilton. Harmondsworth, Middlesex, England: Penguin Books, 1981

Saussure, Ferdinand de. *Course in General Linguistics* Edited by Charles Bally and Albert Sechehaye, translated by Wade Baskin. New York: Philosophical Library, 1959.

Scheman, Naomi and Peg O'Connor, eds. *Feminist Interpretations of Wittgenstein, Re-Reading the Canon,* series editor Nancy Tuana. University Park, Pennsylvania: The Pennsylvania State University Press, 2002.

Smith, Jonathan Z., "Religion, Religions, Religious." Pp 269–284 in *Critical Terms for Religious Studies,* edited by Mark C Taylor Chicago & London, The University of Chicago Press. 1998

Wittgenstein, Ludwig. *Remarks on Colour* Edited by G E. M. Anscombe, translated by Linda L. McAlister and Margarete Schattle Oxford: Basil Blackwell, 1978. [ROC]

———. *Remarks on the Foundations of Mathematics* Ed. by G.H. Von Wright, R. Rhees, G.E.M. Anscombe, trans. by G.E.M. Anscombe. Cambridge, Mass. and London, England: The M.I.T. Press, 1975 [RFM]

———. *Zettel.* Edited by G. E. M. Anscombe, G H. Von Wright, translated by G. E. M. Anscombe. Berkeley and Los Angles: University of California Press, 1975. [Z]

———. *On Certainty.* Edited by G. E. M. Anscombe and G. H. Von Wright, translated by Denis Paul and G. E. M. Anscombe. New York, Evanston, San Fransciso, London: Harper & Row, Publishers, 1972. [OC]

———. *Philosophical Investigations* Translated by G E. M Anscombe. Oxford: Basil Blackwell, 1968. [PI]

Chapter 6

Re-situating the *Feminine* in Contemporary French Philosophy

Louise Burchill

Whether taxed as essentialist or hailed as ontologically undecidable, construed as a reification of women's relegation to a presymbolic sphere within the patriarchal social order or cast, on the contrary, as a nonrepresentable "outside" exceeding—and, as such, intrinsically destabilizing—the hierarchizing dichotomies classically structuring phallogocentric discourse, the category of "the feminine" has, since its reception in Anglo-American thought some thirty years ago, been resolutely read with reference to the problematic of sexual difference. This is not to say that this category has been uniformly indexed to a sexual specificity, as the bearer of a rigorous referential relationship to "women" (accredited or discredited, for their part, as the "subject" of feminism), but, rather, that it is precisely the question of whether, and to what effect, such a referential relationship holds or not that has consistently framed the terms in which "the feminine" has been discussed. Indeed, while "the feminine" has been variously acclaimed or disclaimed as a notion purporting to bespeak something of a repressed and repudiated female alterity unable to find expression in an economy founded upon its exclusion, it has no less been decried, quite to the contrary, as having little or nothing to do with a female specificity—with proponents of this position often claiming that it displaces the question of such a specificity to that of a broad-ranging differentiation implied in all psycho-sexual constitution,[1] when they do not more boldly accuse it of being a surreptitious subterfuge by which (male) philosophers aim to refashion and invigorate their "auto-affection."[2] My intention in what follows is not to take up a stance within this debate as such but to shift ground retroactively as it were, by going back to an interrogation that, whilst raised upon the reception of "the feminine" within Anglo-American thought, seemed very quickly to cede its object of inquiry to the prevalent problematic of sexual difference, such that this category was to be monopolized by studies searching to explore what "meaning" and "value" it might hold for feminism.[3] Moreover, the responses that were proffered at the time to the interrogation to which I'm referring—focusing on the specific operation performed by "the feminine" within the philosophical configuration in which it appeared in France—tended, either, to foreclose any further inquiry (as did Rorty's memorable evaluation of "the textual inscription of the sexual" in French philosophy as merely provocative stylistic play, serving at best to exhibit the "sexual overtones of most metaphysical debate")[4] or ultimately to divert this avenue of interrogation by proffering, in fact, less a general formalization of "the feminine" within the French philosophical configuration as a whole (and even less again a formalization of the "invariants" shaping this discursive ensemble) than, on the contrary, relatively isolated incursions into the functioning of "the feminine" in the individual corpuses of the various authors involved. This "inaugural" failure to fundamentally address the question of the functioning of "the feminine" within some of the most important philosophical texts published in France from the sixties on is important to redress, it seems to me, not simply in order to further our comprehension of that body of texts commonly designated under the (both somewhat monolithic and increasingly temporally askew) rubric of "contemporary French philosophy"—whose signatories include Deleuze, Derrida, Irigaray, Kristeva, Kofman, Lyotard, and Serres: all of whom, moreover, mobilize the philosopheme of "the feminine" in very different ways—but also, *perhaps*, to permit a renewed perception of certain topoi of the discussion around sexual difference (especially as regards the essentialism versus constructivism controversy) in the light of the different inflexion accruing to these topoi within the philosophical texts in question.

The very fact that a historically delimited,[5] diverse array of French philosophical texts, written by a plurality of authors, had a common recourse to the category of "the feminine" (understood here in a sense large enough to encompass philosophemes such as "becoming-woman" or "the girl" in Deleuze and Guattari, the "hymen" in Derrida, the personages of "Penelope" and Ariadne" in Serres, or again, the "figures" of "woman" in Kofman, Lyotard, or Irigaray, amongst others: in short, what has been referred to as a "general tropology of the feminine"[6] in French theory) would indeed seem to indicate, both, that this category plays a specific *philosophical* role in the texts involved and that these works are themselves linked by a certain shared philosophical concern. This category's synchronized multifarious entrance on the scene of French philosophy would, then, have been called up by a process of conceptualization common to diverse authors, as though the movement of thought traversing this particular philosophical conjuncture discerned in the "feminine" the necessary "agent" for the drama it sought to unfold. In this sense, we might take a first step toward resituating "the feminine" in French philosophy by understanding it neither as a simple category floating in the air of the time (although the importance of psychoanalytic theory for French philosophy in the sixties and seventies, as well as the irruption of the women's movement at the same period were certainly determining factors), nor as a "figure" gleaned from literature, mythology, or history (even though all these sources undoubtedly constitute a repertory drawn upon by the philosophical texts in question), but, more rigorously, as a "conceptual persona" in the sense

Deleuze and Guattari give to this term in *What is Philosophy?* Defined as one of the three elements characterizing philosophy per se, the conceptual persona plays a crucial role in the creation of concepts and the "laying out" of what Deleuze and Guattari term the "prephilosophical plane of immanence"—consisting of an "image of thought," in the sense of the image thought gives itself of what it means to think, or an "intuitive understanding"—which ensures a coherency to the concepts so grouped and serves, as a result, as "the ground of philosophy."[7] The conceptual persona fills a role of intermediary between this prephilosophical plane and the features of the concepts that populate it, going from one to the other in such a way as to constitute the conditions under which this plane finds itself filled with concepts of the same group.[8] Plato's "Socrates," Kierkegaard's "Knight of the faith." Nietzsche's "Zarathoustra," "the Antichrist," and "Dionysos" are all examples of conceptual personae—but so too are "the Friend," "the Claimant," "the Rival," and "the Boy" in Greek philosophy, Pascal's "Gambler," Kant's "Judge," or again, significantly, Le Doeuff's "woman-philosopher":[9] all constitute points of view according to which planes of immanence are laid out and distinguished from another or brought together, at the same time as they condition the creation of concepts that correspond to the "topology" of the plane. While Deleuze and Guattari suggest that each great philosopher institutes his or her own plane of immanence, they also raise the question of whether one and the same plane might not be shared by several philosophers, such that we could speak of a pre-Socratic plane, or a plane of so-called classical thought. However complex this question is—for every plane is interleaved, with its layers entering into different relationships, and susceptible to cut across others—it would seem possible to postulate a common plane, or at least a family of planes, populated (be this only partially, on certain layers) by the concepts invented by the different French contemporary philosophers, and this all the more so precisely insofar as these concepts are accompanied by a shared conceptual persona.

Now, clearly, the fact that "the feminine" constitutes a conceptual persona common to a multiplicity of different authors is related to the historical conjuncture, which is the context in which the issue of its relationship to "women," understood as a "psychosocial" category or "type," arises. Of course, all the French theorists deploying this persona have explicitly disclaimed, at a moment or other, that "the feminine" has for referent "women," with this constituting one of their major criticisms of feminist thought, denounced as perpetrating, in this respect, a hypostasis or "ontologization" of "the feminine." Yet, this obviously doesn't mean that there is no relation whatsoever between "the feminine" as employed by the French philosophers and "the existence of those in history named women."[10] Paraphrasing Deleuze and Guattari's distinction of conceptual personae and psychosocial types, we might indeed say that "the feminine" has a relationship with the epoch or historical milieu in which it appears that only the psychosocial category of "woman" or "women" enables us to evaluate. On the other hand, however, the attributes associated with women as a psychosocial type—their physical and mental movements, their pathological symptoms, relational attitudes, existential modes, and legal status—must be understood as undergoing a "determination purely of thinking and of thought" that wrests them from both the historical state of affairs of a society and the lived experience of individuals, in order to turn them into features of the conceptual persona of "the feminine"—that is to say, into *thought*-events on the plane laid out by thought or under the concepts it creates. In this way, though there is a system of referrals between the conceptual persona of "the feminine" and the psychosocial type "woman," the two can never be reduced to one another, or merged.[11]

That admitted, it is now possible to formulate more precisely the function performed by "the feminine" in the philosophical texts that have recourse to this conceptual persona. For "the determination purely of thinking and thought" that transforms psychosocial attributes of "women" into thought-events operates above all, I would argue, by the "extraction" of spatio-temporal relations that are inherent to the attributes in question. Such spatio-temporal relations are, in this sense, to be understood as so many coordinates implied in the "images of women" that French philosophy borrows from literature (for example, the "girls" of Proust, Carroll, or Kleist), mythology (Ariadne and Penelope, but also Persephone, Medea, and Hestia, amongst others), history (for instance, the place of women in the Greek city) or psychoanalysis ("the feminine" as that which exceeds the binary opposition of sexual difference), as well as from politics and the history of philosophy itself. Conversely, this means that we can only understand the philosophical function performed by "the feminine" in contemporary French texts by grasping that this persona presents, or one might say "personifies," complexes of space and time that correspond to the concepts operative within these texts. In short—to put this more technically—the philosophical operation of "the feminine" can be qualified as that of a *schema* in the sense Kant gives to this term in the *Critique of Pure Reason* as a (pure) spatio-temporal determination that corresponds to a concept.[12]

It is imperative to grasp that this operation of "the feminine" as a schema is all the more accentuated insofar as the concepts that find thereby a transposition or "intuitive presentation" themselves partake of what can be broadly characterized as a new conceptualization of "time"—or, more precisely, "a proto-temporality"—within the framework of French philosophy's elaboration of a radically revamped "transcendental aesthetic." In the terms of this "collective" elaboration—whatever may be the diverse inflexions proper to each author—the Kantian formulation of space and time as pure, a priori, forms of human sensibility is replaced by the formalization of a pure and "an-egological" differential transcendental field characterized by the movement of a "(spatio-)temporalization"[13] constitutive of the conditions of both meaning and the real. Further, this movement or process of (spatio-)temporalization—which is, in fact, what is to be understood by the notion of "difference" (or *"différance"*) emblematic of the contemporary philosophical project—is itself a reworking or "repetition" of Kant's doctrine of transcendental schematism. Without going into great detail, it is nonetheless important to underline in this context that Kant's qualification of the pure schemata as transcendental determinations of time rendering possible an a priori relation between the concepts of the understanding and pure intuition (that is, between thought and being) constitutes for the contemporary French philosophers nothing less than the "discovery of Difference."[14] Hailing the Kantian doctrine, in these terms, for "introducing time into thought itself", the protagonists of the contemporary repetition of transcendental schematism nevertheless denounce Kant for confining his discovery within a metaphysics of representation. Along these lines, Kant is notably criticized for placing the schematism under the jurisdiction of the understanding and the apperception (the "I think"), such that a transcendental subject and its cortege of categories dictate the conditions of possibility that the schema, understood as a merely *external* intermediary between the concept and intuition, is called upon to realize, as it were. Sundering any such allegiance to a limited number of a priori categories imposed as functions of a subject erected in the form of unity and identity, the French philosophers, for their part, situate their revised schematism within what Lyotard describes as a transcendental "horizon of multiplicity and diversity"[15] and claim for it the status of a veritable "genetic principle" implicated in the production as much of concepts as of space and time qua phenomenological constructs, or, again, of actualized entities, such as individualized subjects and objects. Interestingly, Deleuze gives to his particular—multi-layered and extremely dynamic—variant of this revamped transcendental schematism the name of "dramatization", on the basis that the correspondence of a system of spatio-temporal determinations to a concept consists in "replacing a logos by a 'drama.'"[16] It is then as the "agent", or more strictly the "patient" of such a drama, that "the feminine" can equally be qualified as either a *conceptual persona* or a *schema*: both designations mark that the operation it performs is that of presenting, or of rending perceptible (or intuitable), the new conceptualization of (space-) time that is, in fact, what is equally to be understood by the concept of "difference."[17]

In the light of the above precisions, we can now advance that the reason why "the feminine" was elected to fill this role of presenting the proto-temporalizing process elaborated within French philosophy in an "intuitive" form (in the sense that intuition is the sphere of spatio-temporal determinations) is that the French philosophers were to deem it possible to extract from the attributes associated with "women" as a psychosocial type a determination of time or temporality radically at odds with the conception of time shared by both common sense and metaphysics. In other words, the conceptual persona of "the feminine" was called up, as it were, by the project of contemporary philosophy insofar as it was judged capable of questioning the notion of time as a linear and homogeneous succession of present moments—which is, of course, the notion that Heidegger analyzes in *Being and Time* as determining not only the Kantian conception (even if, for Heidegger, Kant—precisely with his doctrine of transcendental schematism—nevertheless touched upon a completely original figure of temporality) but the entire history of metaphysics, from Aristotle to Bergson.[18] The resources upon which this critical functioning of "the feminine" draws (in the sense of extracting therefrom the temporal determinations that

thought transforms into "thought-events," qua features of a conceptual persona)
are perhaps nowhere more succinctly set forth than in the description given by
Julia Kristeva of "female subjectivity" as incompatible with the "conception of
linear time that, easily qualifiable as masculine, can be characterized both as
inherent to [our] civilization and as obsessional."[19] Referring to the "images"
that the western tradition bequeaths us of this "female (or 'feminine')
subjectivity," Kristeva specifies that, contrary to the linear time "inherent to the
logical and ontological values of a given civilization," the temporal modalities
associated with women might not only be qualified as "cyclical" and
"monumental," but indeed, ultimately "have so little to do with linear time that
passes that the very name of temporality is unsuitable." Insofar then as we can
speak of another conception of "time" associated with "the feminine," Kristeva
argues that we should rather refer to recent scientific notions of a time
inseparable from space, such as modern physics' conception of a space-time in
infinite expansion.

A particularly clear example of "the feminine's" transposition of the
proto-temporizing process elaborated in French philosophical texts is given with
the conceptual persona of "the girl" mobilized by Deleuze and Guattari in *A
Thousand Plateaus*. Inseparable from the notion of "becoming-woman"—"it is
not the girl who becomes a woman; it is becoming-woman that produces the
universal girl"[20]—this conceptual persona offers a spatio-temporal
determination corresponding to the authors' concept of a pure empty form of
time, "Aeon" or "the time of the event." The very term "becoming-woman"
marks this correspondence with a concept that sets up against the traditional
linear notion of time, as the pure homogeneous succession of points of presence,
a nonchronological "time-line" composed of an unlimited and content-free past
and future that infinitely subdivide each present. "Becoming," state Deleuze and
Guattari, is always an affair of the relations and determinations characterized or
given by "the time of the event," namely "the floating line that knows only
speeds and continually divides that which transpires into an already-there that is
at the same time not-yet-here, a simultaneous too-late and too-early, a
something that is both going to happen and has just happened."[21] Accordingly,
the girl is defined by Deleuze and Guattari as "pure relations of speeds and
slownesses, and nothing else." There is no psychology involved here, no "lived
experience"; we are not in the order of attributes or forms (such as that of a
"subject") but of spatio-temporal features: "A girl is late on account of her
speed: she did too many things, crossed too many spaces in relation to the
relative time of the person waiting for her."[22] It is precisely as such a "block of
space-time" that this persona can then serve to transpose intuitively the
movement of the pure empty form of time that is inseparable from Deleuze and
Guattari's conception of a differential transcendental field whose principle of
regulation is given not in the form of a Subject or the One but in an immanent
ordering of its components by just such a proto-temporalizing process. In short,
it is in the strictest conformity with their definition of the conceptual persona in
What is Philosophy? that Deleuze and Guattari's own conceptual persona of the
girl not only "assembles" a number of fundamental concepts elaborated in *A*

Thousand Plateaus—sc.: becoming, the time of Aeon, the pre-individual, pre-egological plane of immanence, and the auto-organization of this transcendental field into a continuum—but also enacts the very movement by which this plane or field is assured of a consistency.

Other instances of "the feminine's" calling into question the linear conception of time which we might cite in this context are: Derrida's early use of the term "hymen" as a "figure," or, more strictly on our understanding, a "schema," marking—through its play on an undecidability of temporal modality, since the term refers as much to marriage and the (past) consummation of desire as to virginity and desire's anticipation—the spacing or interval of an impossible present (presence) between the already perpetrated and yet-to-come;[23] Lyotard's association of the "space-time of the event," defined as strictly incompatible with the linear and prospective unfolding of mutually exclusive instants, with what he designates, via a reference to the myth of the "Primordial Mother," as a "feminine" or "maternal" medium or plasma;[24] or, again, Irigaray's morphological "motifs" and models of female *jouissance*, which function as so many schemata serving to delineate the spatio-temporal determinations of a "sensible transcendental" unthinkable within a metaphysics based on a "phallogocentric" conception of time and transcendence.[25] And yet, despite these explicit schematizations of temporal processes, what emerges from an attentive examination of the "feminine's" functioning as a schema of a proto-temporalization within contemporary French philosophy is that such an operation does indeed—as Kristeva suggested in her article, "Women's Time," referred to above—seem to favor a determination less of time "as such" than of space. In fact, it may well be insofar as "one thinks of space when evoking the name and destiny of women, more so than time,"[26] that "the feminine" lends itself so well to functioning as a schema of the notion of "difference" (or its equivalents) by which the French philosophers oppose to the metaphysical conception of time what we might, to a certain degree at least, describe as "the repetition of space in a time that is itself in ruins."[27] We could even say that it is precisely to the extent that the "images" conveyed by the tradition show a singular association of women with space (or, conversely, of space with a "feminine principle") that these images constitute such a propitious source for the philosophers seeking to formulate another "articulation" of what is named "time." It would then be the fact that "women" have traditionally been linked to space—i.e., to an order "outside of time" and, hence, "outside of the sign"—that explains why "the feminine," as a conceptual persona translating this socio-historical link into a thought-event, is able to schematize a "process" that seeks to circumvent the categories of metaphysical discourse establishing presence as the value determining the complicity of time and the sign. Whence certain declarations in Irigaray's *Ethics of Sexual Difference* take on a quasi-programmatic status for the contemporary French philosophical project as a whole: "[P]erhaps we are again passing through an epoch in which *time should redeploy space.* . . . A recasting of immanence and transcendence, notably by that *threshold* never interrogated as such: the female sex." "Some 'thing' would have always/already served being that has never been thought by philosophy? . . . A spatial necessity that has been forgotten within the economy of time?"[28]

Certainly, once the operation of "the feminine" as a schema of a proto-temporalizing process is grasped as entailing a "redeployment of space by time," one can better understand the constant association of this persona with the references frequently found in contemporary French philosophy to non-Euclidean spaces. It is, of course, in keeping with their elaboration of a new transcendental aesthetic, characterized by a proto-temporizing movement in virtue of which the transcendental field is assured of a continuity (or what Deleuze and Guattari refer to as a "consistency"), that the French philosophers turn to spatio-temporal models other than those—utilized by Kant—of Euclidean geometry and Newtonian physics. The work of Michel Serres is in this instance exemplary since he explicitly situates topology as the first *objective* elaboration of a transcendental field ("field of invariants"). Given the importance that thus accrues to topology, it is extremely significant that, through his references not only to Penelope and her weft or to Ariadne and her thread but also, via a play on the homophony of *"mère"* ("mother") and *"mer"* ("sea"), to the amorphousness of "the mother" or primal matrix, Serres associates "the feminine" with preconceptual elaborations of spaces endowed with topological structure.[29] Similarly for Lyotard in *Discours figure* designates the "topological" space that conditions the event as he understands it (and which he additionally relates to the Freudian unconscious) as maternal, as the "matrix" of difference.[30] Again, the schema of the "hymen," like that of "double invagination," used by Derrida, equally involves a "transformation or deformation of space" that is topologically connoted,[31] while Deleuze and Guattari's concept of "becoming-woman" is, in its turn, put in correlation with the "smooth" nonhomogeneous spaces that these authors qualify by reference to Riemannian (differential) manifolds.[32]

Yet, of the multiple examples we could proffer of such a correlation in French philosophy, the most pertinent for us to elaborate here (since, in this way, we shall discover that the "the feminine's" schematization of space [-time] betrays a peculiar twist) is undoubtedly the contemporary philosophers' reinvestment of the Platonic notion of an infinitely diversified, irrational—and, in a certain sense, *feminine*—"space," known under the name, amongst others, of the *chora*. Introduced in the *Timaeus*, this notion is presented by Plato as the necessary complement to the cosmogonic system he had hitherto set up in terms of the relation between the ontological sphere of Forms or Ideas, intelligible and perpetually selfsame, and the phenomenal copies that, subject to generation and ever-changing, only participate in "being" insofar as they imitate the noetic sphere. It was the inability of this dualistic framework to explain the genesis of the sensible world as such that prompted Plato to add a "third kind" (trítou géuoV) to the two pre-established kinds of "nature" (júsiV)—with this *triton genos* first being qualified as "the receptacle and, as it were, the nurse of all generation" (49a). While English language commentaries on the *Timaeus* have retained, above all, the term "receptacle" (upodocń) as the way to refer to this "third nature," French commentaries have traditionally preferred the term "*chora*" (cώra): variously translated as "space," "place," or "room" in the sense of "volume"), which, in fact, only appears in the Platonic text after a series of other names or "figures"—ranging from "receptacle" and "nurse" to "mother," "imprint-bearer," "place," and "amorphous plastic material or medium"—have been advanced as ways of designating the requisite "nature," qualified from the outset as seeming to defy rational apprehension. For this reason, some commentators have argued *"chora"* to yield the meaning of the chain of preceding names—qualified as "metaphoric," or "non-technical"—such that Plato's use of the term in the *Timaeus* would constitute "the first occurrence in Greek literature of the word cώra in the sense of space in general, as distinct from the space occupied by any particular thing."[33] Even Heidegger subscribes, in a certain sense, to such an interpretation—despite his being one of the rare commentators *not* to speak of "metaphors" in this context[34]—when he situates "*chora*" as preparing the way for the later metaphysical conception of space as defined by extension.[35] However controversial such a position may be— especially if the notion of "space in general" is, indeed, understood in the Euclidean or Cartesian sense of a pure *extensio*—the fact remains that, by attributing to this "third kind" the role of "that in which" all becoming and change occurs, Plato would, in effect, seem to be trying to conceptualize "something" that one can difficultly avoid qualifying, despite all the reservations such designations inspire, as being of the order of an *originary* or *primordial "space," "spatiality"* or, again, *"spatial medium."*

Indeed, Plato's very association of the *chora* with a "feminine principle"—as in the passage where he compares the third kind to a "mother," while describing the Ideas and copies as, respectively, "father" and "child" (50d3-5)—must be understood as contributing to the elaboration of just such a "primordial spatiality." By characterizing the *chora* as a "mother," "nurse of all generation", and "receptacle of all bodies," Plato is, in fact, drawing on prior formulations of what must be at the "origin" of the sensible world, relying, in particular, on the Orphic cosmogonies according to which all that exists proceeds from a "place" or "element" pre-existing the formation of the cosmos and connoted as "feminine." Such an association of a "feminine principle" and a "space-like" element was equally conveyed by the image, common within the Greek thought of Plato's time, of woman or, more specifically, the womb, as a receptacle which harbors and nourishes, like the earth, the seed planted therein. As such, Plato's reference to a "feminine principle" is a way of demarcating, as it were, the general "space-like" traits that can be understood to characterize the "third kind" of "nature" required by his cosmology, even while insisting on the fact that this "difficult and obscure nature" eludes reason's grasp. Indeed, any rational definition of the *chora* seems impossible given that, on the one hand, qua "place" or "medium" existing prior to the formation of the cosmos, it is characterized by constant movement and division, while, on the other, qua "that in which all things come into existence," it must be devoid of any essence or identity of its own and, as such, without any corresponding Form or Idea. Thereby thwarting any attribution of identity, the *chora* can only be apprehended, states Plato, by a sort of bastard reasoning: "this, indeed, is that which we look upon as in a dream and say that anything that is must needs be in some place and occupy some room (χώραν)."[36] It is in the context, then, of this extreme difficulty to grasp what has no status in the world of Forms that Plato first turns to prior attempts to formulate what such an originary element must be before he himself quite literally *enacts* in the pages of the *Timaeus* the subordination of this primordial and preconceptual "space" to the realm of measure and reason. Drawing in this perspective upon the mathematics of his time, Plato will indeed bring to bear upon the *chora*, through the intervention of the Demiurge, a veritable arsenal of operations of commensuration, stereometrization and geometrization in the aim of rendering this primitive "*spatium*," without "order or measure," amenable to the generic unity of the Ideas.

The fact that the *chora* remains, however—on Plato's own admission—refractory to order, reason and measure even after the intervention by the Demiurge, thus thwarting the tentative to subordinate it to the categories structuring Platonic metaphysics, explains why the French philosophers almost unanimously hail it as a precursor of their own notion of "difference." Deleuze, for example, speaks of the *chora*, in this context, as an "intensive spatium," "matrix of the unequal and different";[37] Serres describes it as a "manifold swarming with diverse primordial spaces";[38] while Lyotard, for his part, claims for it the status of an "invisible matrix" harboring "the initial alterity of the sensible event."[39] Of course, insofar as all these characterizations equally show that the French philosophers understand the "space in general" that Plato would be attempting to delineate under the name of "*chora*" as decidedly topological in nature (Serres' "manifold" refers directly to the Riemannian notion, while both Lyotard and Deleuze qualify their respective notions of the "matrix of the event" and the "intensive *spatium*" as topological), they can at the same time be seen to link the *chora* with "the feminine" since the latter is deployed by the same philosophers as a schema of just such a space. That said, however, the most explicit explorations of the correlation between the *chora* and "the feminine"—albeit from very different perspectives—are to be found in the work of Kristeva, Irigaray, and Derrida.

Succinctly put Kristeva's contemporary reformulation of Plato's association of a preconceptual "space" and a "feminine principle" takes the form of the mobile and provisional configuration of the drives preceding and underlying language's logical and syntactic (symbolic) function that she precisely names the *semiotic chora*. This configuration is related not only to "the feminine," understood as a modality or process that precisely exceeds the ordering of subjectivity and meaning correlative to the instauration of the symbolic function, but also—on a genetic level—to the maternal body, which, in its function as a "regulatory principle," acts to canalize the movements of division and rejection characterizing the drives and thus gives rise to the "rhythmic space"—as Kristeva refers to the *semiotic chora*—where the first conditions of signifiance and a becoming-subject are assembled.[40] Derrida, for his part, equally claims the *chora* as a "concept" congenial to his own undertaking, and indeed—in a gesture not unlike Kristeva's appropriation of the

Platonic term to name the pivotal notion of a "heterogeneity" exceeding all closure within metaphysical categories—situates the *chora* as a precursor of his own notion of *différance* by qualifying it (in his later texts, at least) as "an irreducible spacing," "site of writing, of inscription, of the trace or type," that exceeds all the major determinations of Platonism and metaphysics.[41] At the same time, however, he maintains that, while the *chora* escapes in this way an ontological appropriation, certain aspects of its description by Plato remain irreducibly enmeshed in metaphysics: most notably, the entire sequence of "tropes" (with the exception of "receptacle") in the *Timaeus* that refer either to the figure of the "mother" or to "space" as such. In this respect, Derrida acknowledges, as it were, that the figure of the mother in Plato's text is itself a figure of a primordial spatiality, but he must, for this very reason, disqualify the description of the *chora* in terms of space and the feminine since any such notion of a primordial spatiality is antithetical to his own understanding of the *chora* as a site of differential inscription. Finally, Irigaray also denounces the association of the *chora* and "the feminine" as metaphysical but does so on the grounds that Plato, by describing the *chora* as a mother and nurse, refers sexual difference to the binary oppositions of intelligible/sensible and form/matter, such that "the feminine," in the same way as the *chora*, is identified as a purely passive matter-support—without any identity, essence, or productivity of its own—awaiting the virile impression of the forms. On Irigaray's own understanding, however, not only does "the feminine" exceed any such representation or sexual modelization in terms of activity and passivity, matter and form, but it must be understood to exceed and condition every representation and figuration, functioning in this sense—again like the *chora* itself, strangely enough—as the nonrepresentable site of inscription of all that finds expression in an economy based on the rule of the father/forms.[42]

That said, I should at once state that, as regards my argument that "the feminine" functions within French contemporary philosophy as a schema of a certain "spatialization" (ultimately referred to a "proto-temporalization"), it is of little importance that of these three theorists, only Kristeva, in fact, "endorses", as it were, the association of the *chora* and "the feminine," while both Derrida and Irigaray criticize Plato's conflation of the two notions. What does matter, on the other hand, is the fact that all three theorists in their reading of the *chora* want to distance themselves from a certain notion of spatiality (be this identified with "the feminine" as Derrida—and, in a certain sense, Irigaray—would have it,[43] or, in a significant twist, identified rather with a *hypostasis* of "the feminine," as Kristeva—or, again in a certain way, Irigaray[44]—contends) in order to, thereby, either reclaim the *chora* from Platonic ontology (as is the case for Kristeva and Derrida) or, on the other hand, dismiss it as irreducibly metaphysical. For all three theorists, the problem lies predominantly with Plato's description of the *chora* as "amorphous and undifferentiated,"[45] since such a characterization—as Irigaray's critique of the *chora*'s "sexual modelization" has just shown—is understood to be the hallmark of a metaphysical conception of a "negative, homogeneous and virgin space . . . without marks, opposition or determination, ready . . . to receive and reflect the types [i.e., *tupoi*] inscribed therein."[46] Derrida, of course, consistently contests throughout his corpus the notion of a pure, homogeneous space, which he situates as belonging to the metaphysical myth of an uninhabited, unmarked origin: myth of the pure presence of the pure present, while Kristeva—taking up, in fact, an elliptic early remark by Derrida himself, criticizing Plato for "ontologizing" Democritus' notion of *"rhuthmos"*[47]—argues in *Revolution in Poetic Language* that Plato's description of the *chora* as amorphous erases the rhythmicity suggested by the changing movement of its "elements" and thus acts to immobilize the infinitely repeatable divisibility and ever-changing configuration said to characterize the *chora* as it exists primordially, before the "cosmos comes into being." In this way, Plato is claimed to have turned a moving differential multiplicity into a container or "receptacle," with the *chora* thus indeed being situated, on Kristeva's reading, as an "ontologization" or hypostasis of rhythm.[48] This is, moreover, the context conditioning Kristeva's claim that "what we take for a mother . . . is nothing but the place where rhythm stops and identity is constituted":[49] far from reducing "the feminine" to the maternal and thereby essentializing the former—as Judith Butler and other critics of her association of the semiotic *chora* with "the feminine" have argued[50]—Kristeva understands, on the contrary, our representation, and, indeed, our very naming, of the maternal body as being, in themselves, a hypostasis and ontologization of the semiotic rhythm that she associates with "the feminine."[51]

Both Derrida and Kristeva argue that, in order to wrest the *chora* from the metaphysical determinations relative to its characterization as an amorphous space or receptacle, it is necessary to restore to, or re-inscribe within, it, the rhythm and differentiation that Plato would have attempted to efface. This is the reason why Kristeva so stresses that the *semiotic chora* must be thought of as a "rhythmic totality"; whenever this rhythmicity is stymied or blocked, the *chora*, strictly speaking, becomes "a-semiotic" as it were,[52] such that Kristeva speaks in this context of an "indifferentiation" of the drive facilitations and of the *chora*'s "immobilization."[53] Likewise, in a similar perspective of reclaiming the language in the *Timaeus* that supposedly eludes Plato's attempts to efface the "rhythmicity" said to mark Democritus' conception of a differential multiplicity, Derrida distinguishes between the tropes in Plato's text that testify to an ontological appropriation of Democritus' notion of *"rhuthmos"* (which Derrida glosses as "rhythm" and "writing," relating it in this way to his own notion of "différance") and those that, on the contrary, resist any such appropriation. Crucially, as we seen, Derrida disqualifies as metaphysical all the sexual-spatial tropes in Plato's text (such as "mother," "nurse," "space," and "place"), while hailing, on the other hand, the series of "typomorphical" tropes (related to the thematic of inscribing or impressing forms in a soft, malleable material) which he situates as referring to a differential multiplicity composed of the movement of "traces" or "marks" alone and, thereby, strictly irreducible to any notion of a "pre-existing" space as such.

That admitted, it should be evident that the "re-inscription" of differentiation and rhythm promoted by Kristeva and Derrida is, in fact, tantamount to introducing within Plato's spatial medium a vector, or movement, of temporalization—for what, after all, is rhythm but the introduction of a temporal movement within space, such as is given with a "linked sequence" (as Kristeva herself defines rhythm),[54] or Derrida's "play of differences," "writing," and so on, where the differences or diacritical marks constantly refer "back" and "forward" to one another? It is, moreover, precisely this introjection of a temporalizing movement within what Plato conceived, for his part, as an archaic spatial matrix existing before "time and the cosmos" that constitutes the very crux of the contemporary French "reinvestment" of the *chora*: for, clearly, it is indeed only as such a differentiated and rhythmic totality that the *chora* can be claimed as a model of the French theorists' own conception of a proto-temporalizing movement "producing differentiation in general," whether this be formulated in terms of an "originary" pre-ontological "difference" or as a heterogeneous semiotic process in which the constitution of the subject and signification find their condition.

And yet, for this very reason, one might well be advised to examine more attentively the contemporary French theorists' disqualification of the terms and tropes in Plato's text that testify to the conception of an amorphous and non-differentiated "originary spatiality" ("without marks, opposition, or determination"), functioning as the site in which differentiation in general is produced. After all, the archaic spatial matrix that Plato describes in the *Timeaus* as a moving "irrational" configuration, without "measure or order," refractory to the dominion of the transcendental forms and ever-rebel to an imposition of geometric objectivity, is surely somewhat difficult to identify with the "homogeneous space" of metaphysical "pure presence"—or, for that matter, with an inert, passive support docilely awaiting the impression of virile forms. Even the specific attribution of "amorphousness" that Plato uses to underline the formal indetermination of a "space" ever eluding a stable nomination while simultaneously displaying a constant motility and imbalance of "forces," clearly cannot be equated with the homogeneity, isotropy, or "passivity" proper to a space *partes extra partes*, but would seem, quite to the contrary, to open up a conception of "space" resolutely "marked" by an ontological undecidability. This being the case, it would indeed seem that the French theorists' decision to disqualify as metaphysical all Plato's references to a pre-existing space—even while they variously acknowledge the "topological" pertinence of Plato's description in other respects—is principally motivated by the aim of securing their own understanding of the "site in which differentiation in general is produced" in terms, shall we say, not of an "originary space" but of an "originary time" (on condition that the term "originary" here be distinguished from any and all notions of a punctiform pure origin). Which brings us back, logically enough, to the functioning of "the feminine."

The feminine, we have stated, operates as a schema by which to give an intuitive transposition of the notion of a "differential transcendental field" characterized preeminently by a proto-temporalization ("originary time") that may be understood to carry, in a certain manner, space within itself—much as rhythm can be defined as the articulation of space and time. Yet, as we intimated above, there is indeed a peculiar twist to this schematizing operation of "the feminine", for, while the association of "the feminine" and space is central to this operation—being, in fact, what primarily explains why the conceptual persona of "the feminine" is so suitable for schematizing a process seeking to circumvent the categories of metaphysical discourse instituting the complicity of the value of presence and a linear conception of time—it is, nevertheless, equally capable of calling into question the very proto-temporalizing process it is supposed to schematize. Indeed, the very project of elaborating an "originary temporality" under the name of "difference" would seem undermined by certain variants of this association of space and "the feminine" insofar as these cast doubt on the degree to which such a temporality can, in fact, qualify—if we may put it this way—as *"originary."* Which is to say that they pose the problem of whether such a temporal process is not always/already subsidiary, or secondary, to a "space" that, as on Plato's own comprehension of the *chora*, would manifest neither a principle of "synthesis" (as underlies, for example, a "linked sequence"), nor any differentiation—other, at least, than the "diversity" that is inherent to this notion of "space" itself: a space that, described by Plato as mobile and energetic, is indeed revealed to give, "in itself" (without the intervention of a "time-like" element), multiple and changing "form" to its "elements." In this respect, Derrida's disqualification of all the sexual-spatial tropes in the *Timaeus* that testify to a problematic of an originary spatiality exemplarily underlines that the problem posed is well and truly that of whether the proto-temporalizing movement elaborated by the contemporary French philosophers under the name of difference (or *différance*, or heterogeneity, and so on) can legitimately qualify as "the primordial milieu in which differentiation in general is produced."[55] In fact, as we have seen, the only way Derrida can secure his interpretation of "the site of inscription of all that is" in terms of a proto-temporalizing "rhythmotypical structuration," is if he first disqualifies as metaphysical—however tenuous such a gesture seems to be—all the figures in Plato's text (including those connoted as "feminine") that refer to an archaic spatial matrix, ultimately as irreducible to any form of temporalizing process as it is to the metaphysical notion of linear time. In this sense, then, the very recourse to "the feminine" as a schema of a different ordering of time and space was to confront the contemporary French philosophers with the question of whether the proto-temporalizing process they thereby sought to transpose in intuitive terms was not itself dependent upon a more primordial "spatium" or "groundlessness" (as Deleuze designates the *chora*). Suffice it to say, in this context, that such a question is not without very precise precedents in the philosophical genealogy informing the elaboration within the contemporary texts of the concept of "difference." It is, for example, extremely significant that Kant, whose doctrine of transcendental schematism is, as we have seen, the source of the contemporary concept of "difference," consistently argued that the temporal schemata constitutive of experience were themselves premised upon the structural (ontological) opening of human sensibility to an exteriority independent of itself: an "opening" that Kant identified (with ever-greater emphasis, as is shown both by the modifications he introduced in the second edition of the *Critique* and by his posthumous notes) as given with the pure (nonsynthetic) intuition of *space*.[56]

That "the feminine" can function as a schema of such a space should not be construed as implying an "essentialist" conception of "the feminine," such that this would consist in establishing an a-historical and ontological relation between "the feminine" (understood in this instance as rigorously referring to "women") and an originary "space." Not only is "the feminine" as a schema or conceptual persona quite simply impossible to identify with "women" as a socio-historical type, but even the fact that the association of "a feminine principle" and a "space" before, or outside of, time and the sign has existed throughout the Western tradition—notably since the Orphic cosmogonies, under the influence of which, as we know, Plato conceived his *chora*—in no way acts to secure any sort of "ontological" or "a-historical" relationship between two terms supposedly endowed with a stable signification. Certainly, the French contemporary philosophers draw upon this association in their invention of the conceptual persona of "the feminine"—as they do upon other "images" of women given either by the tradition or contestations of the same (such as the women's movement)—yet they never simply reproduce it, as indeed, the very utilization of "the feminine" to schematize a different ordering of time goes to show, and this even (or indeed, perhaps, all the more so) if such an enterprise proves to be put into question by the question of space itself. Moreover, the very characterization that one finds in the *Timaeus* of a spatiality, connoted as "feminine" and ever-eluding a transcendental determination by the forms, radically complicates traditional (sexual) modelizations distinguishing between "female" and "male" in terms of the preeminently metaphysical opposition of "passivity and "activity," no less than it does metaphysical determinations of "space" in terms of an homogeneous, isotropic, and, all in all, "passive" or "inert" extension. Far from ratifying such hylomorphic models of a space, or site, of inscription, connoted as feminine, which would passively await the virile incision of the forms for the donation of a structure or movement, Plato's association of an originary spatiality and a "feminine principle" seems to me to summon us to rethink anew the question (posed not only in contemporary philosophical thought but also in recent feminist debates articulated around the essentialism versus constructivism controversy) of whether one can conceive of a "site—or space—of inscriptions" as constituted by differential (and fundamentally "equi-valent") "inscriptions" or "traits" alone, or whether a distinct, if ontologically undetermined, "milieu" of some sort must be postulated to serve as the principle of differentiation orientating the multiple and changing "form" assumed by the various marks that "inscribe themselves" or, perhaps more strictly, "emerge," therein.

In this respect, re-situating "the feminine" in contemporary French philosophy not only serves to show how central this "conceptual persona" was to the philosophical project uniting a plurality of texts and authors at a certain epoch but also indicates that the role it played in these texts both ultimately exceeded authorial control and would, indeed, prove to be as yet unexhausted.

Notes

1. See, for example, Elizabeth Grosz, *Sexual Subversions* (Boston: Allen and Unwin, 1989), 95

2. See, for example, Alice Jardine, *Gynesis· Configurations of Woman and Modernity* (Ithaca and London: Cornell University Press, 1985). Of course, Irigaray was to make such a criticism very early on in respect of Deleuze and Guattari's concept of "becoming woman." In a 1981 text, she denounces the fact that: "as soon as women are valorized in some way, men want to become women . . . i.e., not to lose the position of a subject who is in control of the situation and in control of discourse." See: *Le Corps-à-corps avec la mère* (Montreal: Editions de la pleine lune, 1981), 64. Similar remarks are made in: *Ce Sexe qui n'en est pas un* (Paris: Minuit, 1977), 138, sq. Eng. trans. Catherine Porter with Carolyn Burke, *This Sex which is not One* (Ithaca: Cornell University Press, 1985).

3. Diane Jonte-Pace was to declare in the early nineties: "If the unanswerable question for an earlier decade was Freud's 'What do women want?', the comparable question in today's conversation is surely 'What does "woman" mean?' See: "Situating Kristeva differently: Psychoanalytic Readings of Women and Religion," in *Body/Text* in *Julia Kristeva· Religion, Women and Psychoanalysis,* ed. David Crownfield (Albany: State University of New York Press, 1992), 1–22.

4. Richard Rorty, "Philosophy as a Kind of Writing," *Consequences of Pragmatism* (Brighton: The Harvester Press, 1982), 90–109. Admittedly, Rorty's remarks apply to Derrida's work alone and not to contemporary French philosophy as a whole. It seems clear, however, from his characterization of Derrida's references to sexual difference as "funny" and "shocking" that Rorty esteems "the feminine" *as such* to be devoid not only of any *philosophical* function in general, but of any serious function whatsoever.

5. This is not to imply that French theorists no longer work with the category of "the feminine." Irigaray and Kristeva both still refer, in different ways and with different intentions, to "the feminine"—indeed, Kristeva's relatively recent trilogy on "female genius" shows an extremely interesting inflexion in her thought on the subject—while Derrida frequently invoked such a category (or at least, shall we say, its semantic field) in his work up to the moment of his (recent) death. That said, however, the functioning of "the feminine" as a "schema" of philosophical concepts that overlapped or interconnected an array of texts by a variety of authors in France started to wane from the beginning of the eighties. Indeed, whereas "the feminine" had previously served to schematize that which—as Sarah Kofman put it—preceded and exceeded "all oppositions, such as the man/woman one, . . . [at least if] by the feminine one understands an undecidable oscillation," this category was increasingly relegated, in the eighties, to precisely just such an opposition, being re-inscribed as the simple counterpart to "masculine," qua "parts of a pseudo-whole" (cf.: Kofman, "Ça cloche," in *Les Fins de l'homme,* ed. Philippe Lacoue-Labarthe and Jean-Luc Nancy, Paris: Galilée, 1980; republished in *Lectures de Derrida,* Paris: Galilée, 1984, 150). As early as 1983, Derrida was to object: "Why do you still want to call 'feminine' that which escapes this contract (of phallocentric terror)" (in "voice II," text-dialogue with Verena Andermatt-Conley, *Boundary* 2, no. 2, Winter 1984, 86), while in 1987 Lyotard was to speak of "the feminine" as revealing itself as finally too dependent "on the intrigues stemming from the difference of the sexes" *(Que Peindre? Adami, Arakawa, Buren,* Paris: La Difference, 1987, 61) Another reason for discerning a historical delimitation to the functioning of "the feminine" in French contemporary philosophy is an empirical one. The deaths of Deleuze, Kofman, and Lyotard in the nineties effectively signed the end of

a *certain* configuration of French contemporary philosophy, which would seem duly countersigned and dated with Derrida's death in 2004.

6. The term is coined by Alice Jardine, *Gynesis.*

7. The first three chapters of *What Is Philosophy?* (trans. Hugh Tomlinson and Graham Burchell, New York: Columbia University Press, 1994; originally published as *Qu'est-ce que la philosophie?,* Paris: Minuit, 1991) are devoted to this triad of elements—the plane of immanence, the concept, and the *conceptual persona*—by which Deleuze and Guattari define philosophy. While the conceptual persona plays a role of intermediary between concepts and the prephilosophical plane, it also intervenes between this plane and the chaotic state from which thought must draw its determinations: the conceptual persona is precisely what extracts these determinations and constitutes a point of view by which they are given a consistency and transformed into coordinates of the plane of immanence. Not only does this conception of philosophy seem indebted to Kant (in a certain sense, the *schema* that Kant described as a "third thing," mediating between the intuition and the concept, finds a singular incarnation in Deleuze and Guattari's conceptual persona), but it is also a conception that conforms to Deleuze's portrayal, in *Difference and Repetition,* of a philosophy that, starting with Nietzsche and Kierkegaard, would be an equivalent of theatre: the conceptual persona is, on this understanding, the hero, or heroine, of such a theatre, agent of a "movement that would directly touch the soul." Concerning this last point, see the introduction to *Difference and Repetition* (trans Paul Patton, New York: Columbia University Press, 1968), especially 5–11.

8. *Ibid,* 1994, p. 75.

9. Deleuze and Guattari refer, in these terms, to Michele Le Doeuff's *Hipparchia's Choice.* See: *What Is Philosophy?,* 71, note 7.

10. I borrow this expression from: Catherine Chalier, *Figures du féminin Lecture d'Emmanuel Levinas* (Paris: La Nuit surveillée, 1982), 75-76.

11. *What Is Philosophy?,* 70.

12. "The Schematism of the Pure Concepts of the Understanding" forms the first chapter of the section of the *Critique* dealing with the Analytic of Principles (i.e., Book II of the *Transcendental Analytic).* Although this chapter comprises but seven pages, it has been argued to be the very "kernel" of Kant's work: a view with which Kant himself would seem to have concurred, given both the importance he attributed to this chapter in his correspondence and the fact that it is the only part of the *Analytic* to have been retaken in its original form in the (extensively modified) second edition of the *Critique.* One should, however, note that this appreciation has, from Kant's time on, been rudely contested: many commentators (amongst whom figure Schopenhauer and Kemp Smith) have indeed argued this section to be not only obscure and redundant, but to have no other ostensible motivation than considerations of architectonic symmetry. Contemporary French philosophers' reading of this doctrine is very heavily influenced by Heidegger's interpretation in *Kant and the Problem of Metaphysics* (trans. Richard Taft, Bloomington and Indianapolis: Indiana University Press, 1997) and, indeed, a knowledge of this latter text is indispensable for anyone who desires to understand the conceptualization of "difference" developed in France

13. There are several reasons why, in this paper, I sometimes speak of a "proto-temporality" or "temporalization," sometimes of a "(spatio-)temporalization" and, at other times again, of a "space-time" or "spatio-temporalization," without any bracketing of the "spatial component." I hope that these reasons, which vary according to whether what is discussed is Kant's own understanding of schematism or the French philosophers' "repetition" of the Kantian doctrine, will become clear as the paper progresses. That said, I would note here two points. First, in respect of Kantian schematism, while Kant defined the schemata as transcendental determinations of *time,* these determinations so depend on the contribution of pure spatial intuition that several commentators have suggested that

one should more strictly speak of the schemata as *spatio-temporal* determinations. Second, although the French philosophers clearly give a transcendental privilege to "time" or "temporality"—insofar as their shared philosophical project centers precisely on a differential and an-egological "proto-temporalization"—they equally claim that such a "temporality" is inseparable from a "spatiality" that it, in a sense, bears within itself.

14. See: Deleuze, *Difference and Repetition*. 86 Similarly, when Derrida writes, in *Of Grammatology,* that "imagination . is the other name of *différance* as auto-affection," while attributing "the entire chain that makes possible the communication of the movement of temporalization and the schematism of imagination, pure sensibility and the auto-affection of the present by itself" to "all that Heidegger's reading has strongly repeated in *Kant and the Problem of Metaphysics:*" he is explicitly indicating that *"différance"* must be understood as another name for the process of proto-temporalization that he elaborates in the wake of Heidegger's "more originary," "ecstatic-horizonal" interpretation of Kant's doctrine of transcendental schematism. See: Jacques Derrida, *Of Grammatology* (trans. Gayatri Chakravorty Spivak, Baltimore: Johns Hopkins University Press, 1976), 186–187 and 342—343, note 21. I have already indicated, in a previous note, how important Heidegger's interpretation of the Kantian doctrine is for the contemporary French philosophers.

15. Jean-François Lyotard and Jean-Loup Thebaud, *Au Juste* (Paris: Bourgeois, 1979), 167.

16. Gilles Deleuze, "La méthode de dramatisation," *Bulletin de la Société française de Philosophie,* 62 (1967): 107—108.

17. See in this respect the note 7, supra.

18. Martin Heidegger, *Being and Time* (trans. John Macquarrie and Edward Robinson, Great Britain: Basil Blackwell, 1980), Introduction, paragraph 8 and Division II, chap. 6, with the very important note 30 to this chapter.

19. Our translation from: "Le Temps des femmes, " 34/44: *Cahiers de recherche de sciences des textes et documents,* no. 5 (1979): 7–8. An English version of this text, "Women's Time," trans. Alice Jardine and H Blake, can be consulted in *Signs,* 7:1, Autumn, 1981.

20. Gilles Deleuze and Felix Guattari, *A Thousand Plateaus* (trans. Brian Massumi, Minneapolis: Minnesota University Press, 1987), 277. Originally published as: *Mille Plateaux* (Paris: Minuit, 1980).

21. Deleuze and Guattari, *A Thousand Plateaus,* 262.

22. Deleuze and Guattari, *A Thousand Plateaus,* 271

23.See: Jacques Derrida, "La double séance, " *La Dissémination* (Paris: Seuil, 1972), 260, sq. English trans. Barbara Johnson, *Dissemination* (Chicago: University of Chicago Press, 1981).

24. Jean-François Lyotard, "Argumentation et présentation: la crise des fondements," in *L'Univers philosophique,* vol. 1, ed André Jacob (Paris: P.U.F.), 746.

25. While Irigaray uses the term "sensible transcendental" specifically in *Ethique de la différence sexuelle* (Paris: Minuit, 1984, eng. trans. Carolyn Burke, *The Ethics of Sexual Difference,* Ithaca: Cornell University Press, 1993), she employs morphological motifs and models of female *jouissance* in the perspective of a "new transcendental" throughout her early work. Amongst other places, see: *Speculum of the Other Woman,* trans. Gillian C. Gill (Ithaca: Cornell University Press, 1985), originally published as: *Spéculum De l'autre femme* (Paris: Minuit, 1974); *This Sex which is not One"* (1977); and *Passions élémentaires* (Paris: Minuit, 1982).

26. " Le temps des femmes, " 6. My translation.

27. I borrow this expression from G. Préli, *La Force du dehors Extériorité, limite et non-pouvoir à partir de Maurice Blanchot* (Paris: Recherches, 1977)

28. *Ethique de la différence sexuelle,* 24, and *L'Oubli de l'air* (Paris: Minuit,

1983), 136. My translation. It might be noted in passing that, although Irigaray does indeed—contrary to the other French philosophers under consideration here—link "the feminine" to women as a referent, the terms in which she couches such an association clearly show that the conditions required for "the female sex" to accede to representation entail the opening up of a "real transcendental field" or what she equally names a "sensible transcendental."

29. Specific reference is made here to: *Hermes IV La Distribution* (Paris: Minuit, 1977), 145–170, 197–210, and *Les Origines de la géométrie* (Paris: Flammarion, 1993), 21, 30, 233 sq. Nevertheless, the importance of topology for the elaboration of an "objective transcendental" is stressed throughout Serres' work.

30. Jean-François Lyotard, *Discours, Figure* (Paris: Klincksieck, 1978), 275 sq. and 327 sq.

31. Jacques Derrida and Christie V. McDonald, "Choreographies" (interview), *Diacritics,* vol. 12 (1982): 74.

32. Deleuze and Guattari, *A Thousand Plateaus,* chaps. 10 and 11.

33. David Ross, *Plato's Theory of Ideas* (Oxford: Clarendon Press, 1951) 125. See equally: D. Keyt, "Aristotle on Plato's Receptacle," *American Journal of Philology,* no. 82 (1961): 291–300.

34. As Derrida points out in a long note to his essay, "Chora," in *Poikilia Etudes offertes à Jean-Pierre Vernant* (Paris: EHESS, 1987). This essay was subsequently republished in a slightly modified form as: *Khôra* (Paris: Galilée, 1993). English trans. Ian McLeod, "Khôra," in *On the Name* (Stanford: Stanford University Press, 1995).

35. Martin Heidegger, *An Introduction to Metaphysics* (trans. Ralph Mannheim, New Haven: Yale University Press, 1959)

36. Plato, *Timaeus,* 52b. I've referred here to the English translation by Francis M. Cornford, *Plato's Cosmology. The* Timaeus *of Plato Translated with a Running Commentary* (London: Kegan Paul, 1937).

37. *Difference and Repetition,* 233.

38. *Hermes IV: La Distribution,* 210.

39. *Discours, Figure,* 21 and 339.

40. Concerning Kristeva's theorization of the semiotic modality, the principal reference is: *Revolution in Poetic Language* (trans. Margaret Waller, New York: Columbia University Press, 1984; this is an abridged version of *La Revolution du langage poétique,* Paris: Seuil, 1974), 25 sq. A more succinct presentation of the semiotic modality can be found, among other places, in "From One Identity to an Other," *Desire in Language A Semiotic Approach to Literature and Art* (trans. Thomas Gora, Alice Jardine and Leon S. Roudiez, New York: Columbia University Press, 1980).

41. Jacques Derrida, "Comment ne pas parler, " *Psyché Inventions de l'autre* (Paris: Galilée, 1987). It should be noted, as regards the qualification of the *chora* as an "irreducible spacing," that Derrida's "spacing" is a notion that strictly relates to his elaboration of *différance* as proto-temporalization, and not, in fact, a conceptualization as such of "space". See, in this respect, my article: "In-between 'Spacing' and the *Chora* in Derrida: A Pre-originary Medium?," in *Intermediality as Inter-esse Philosophy, Arts, Politics,* ed. Henk Oosterling, Ewa Plonowska-Ziarek, and Hugh Silverman (London: Continuum Press, forthcoming).

42. Irigaray, *Spéculum De l'autre femme,* 382–384. It should be noted that these are the only pages in Irigaray's text where she refers directly to Plato's own passages on the *chora* Elsewhere in *Spéculum,* she devotes a chapter—comprised almost uniquely of quotations—to Plotinus' commentary on the *chora,* which leads her to adopt Plotinus' identification of Plato's notion with Aristotle's "matter" (ϋλη) despite the fact that Plato himself never uses the word ϋλη in relation to the *chora* and that his (rare) use of it

elsewhere in his work is always in the sense of a building material such as wood Judith Butler perpetuates Irigaray's "misreading" in her *Bodies That Matter* (New York and London. Routledge, 1993) not only insofar as she accepts Irigaray's interpretation of the *chora* through Plotinus but also by endorsing Aristotles' assimilation of the *chora* to his own notion of *hyle* (42) and, more generally, by consistently situating the *chora* as a notion of "materiality" that thereby belongs to the "history of matter." One can certainly interpret the *chora* as a notion of a "spatial materiality"—or as a "spatial medium," as I myself have upheld—but, despite her references to the *chora* as a "space of inscription," Butler never really problematizes the identification of *chora* and materiality, and often slips into a simple identification of *chora* and "matter."

43. Admittedly, given her assimilation of the *chora* to Aristotle's notion of *hyle,* Irigaray talks in terms of matter or materiality more so than in those of "space" when dealing directly with Plato's concept. She does, nevertheless, make many indirect references to the *chora* in contexts where its spatial "nature" (as a "place", "site," or "space") is brought to the fore and, at these moments, her criticisms of the *chora* remain couched in much the same terms as when she refers to it as "matter": namely, she denounces it as a notion of a "passive, formless, sensible support," serving the intelligible as the receptacle of its (re)productions of the same. Irigaray, of course, criticizes what she views as Plato's identification of "the feminine" with such a "passive support," while Derrida in a sense accepts this identification and, as a result, disqualifies both "the feminine" and "space" as irreducibly metaphysical.

44 On Irigaray's reading, Plato's identification of "the feminine" with a "passive spatio-material support" must be situated as a *representation* of "the feminine" which inevitably fails to capture that which remains unfigurable in a phallogocentric economy pretending to a systematic closure.

45. Plato, *Timaeus,* 50d7 to 50e4. The Greek term ἄμορφον that is rendered as "amorphous"—or more precisely, as "amorphe"—in French translations of the *Timaeus* (for example, that by Joseph Moreau and Leon Robin, in: Plato, *Oeuvres Completes,* t. II, Paris: Gallimard, Bibliothèque de la Pléiade, 1942) is often not translated as such in English translations, which content themselves with rendering the adjectival expression Plato uses to qualify this term, namely "free from all characters" (Francis M. Cornford, *Plato's Cosmology,* 1937) or "devoid of all character" (Desmond Lee, trans. *Timaeus and Critias,* London: Penguin Classics, 1977).

46. Jacques Derrida, "Tympan," *Marges—de la philosophie* (Paris: Minuit, 1972), xxiv. My translation.

47. Jacques Derrida, "Positions," interview with Jean-Louis Houdebine and Guy Scarpetta, in *Positions* (trans. Alain Bass, London: The Athlone Press, 1981), 75, 106, note 39.   """

48. Kristeva, *Revolution in Poetic Language,* 26, 239, note 13.

49. Kristeva, "The Novel as Polylogue," *Desire in Language,* 191

50. See, for example: Butler, *Bodies That Matter,* 41, and "The Body Politics of Julia Kristeva," in *Gender Trouble· Feminism and the Subversion of Identity* (NewYork: Routledge, 1990).

51. See on this point: Kristeva, "Motherhood according to Bellini" and "Place Names." in *Desire in Language,* especially, 238 and 291

52. It should be remembered that Kristeva employs the term "semiotic" in virtue of its preponderant etymological sense of "distinctiveness." See: *Revolution in Poetic Language,* 25.

53 Kristeva, "Le sujet en procès, " *Polylogue* (Paris: Seuil, 1977), 76–79.

54. *Desire in Language,* 286.

55. Derrida, *La Dissemination,* 144.

56. I examine the philosophical genealogy informing the elaboration of the

concept of difference *(différance)*—specifically as regards Heidegger's "temporalist" interpretation of Kantian schematism—in my article "In-between 'Spacing' and the *Chora* in Derrida: A Pre-originary Medium?," cited above.

Bibliography

Burchill, Louise. "In-between 'Spacing' and the *Chora* in Derrida: A Preoriginary Medium?" In *Intermediality as Inter-esse. Philosophy, Arts, Politics,* edited by Henk Oosterling, Ewa Plonowska-Ziarek and Hugh Silverman London: Continuum Press, forthcoming.

Butler, Judith *Gender Trouble: Feminism and the Subversion of Identity.* New York: Routledge, 1990.

———. *Bodies That Matter.* New York and London: Routledge, 1993.

Chalier, Catherine. *Figures du féminin. Lecture d'Emmanuel Lévinas* Paris: La Nuit surveillée, 1982.

Cornford, Francis M. *Plato's Cosmology The Timaeus of Plato Translated with a Running Commentary* London: Kegan Paul, 1937.

Deleuze, Gilles "La méthode de dramatisation. " *Bulletin de la Société française de Philosophie,* 62 (1967): 90–118.

———. *Difference and Repetition* [1968]. Translated by Paul Patton. New York: Columbia University Press, 1994.

Deleuze, Gilles, and Felix Guattari *A Thousand Plateaus* [1980]. Trans. Brian Massumi. Minneapolis: Minnesota University Press, 1987.

———. *What Is Philosophy?* [1991]. Translated by Hugh Tomlinson and Graham Burchell. New York: Columbia University Press, 1994.

Derrida, Jacques. *Of Grammatology* [1967]. Translated by Gayatri Chakravorty Spivak Baltimore: Johns Hopkins University Press, 1976.

———. *La Dissémination.* Paris: Seuil, 1972.

———. *Marges—de la philosophie.* Paris: Minuit, 1972.

———. *Positions.* Translated by Alain Bass. London: The Athlone Press, 1981

——— *"Chora "* Pp. 265–296 in *Poikilia. Etudes offertes à Jean-Pierre Vernant* Paris: EHESS, 1987.

———. *Psyché Inventions de l 'autre.* Paris: Galilée, 1987.

———. "Khora." In *On the Name.* Translated by Ian McLeod. Stanford: Stanford University Press, 1995.

Derrida, Jacques, and Christie V. McDonald.""Choreographies" (interview). *Diacritics,* vol. 12 (1982): 66–76.

Derrida, Jacques, and Verena Andermatt-Conley. "voice II." *Boundary* 2, no. 2 (Winter 1984): 68–93

Grosz. Elizabeth *Sexual Subversions.* Boston: Allen and Unwin, 1989.

Heidegger, Martin. *Being and Time* Translated by John Macquarrie and Edward Robinson. Great Britain: Basil Blackwell, 1980.

———. *Kant and the Problem of Metaphysics* [1929]. Translated by Richard Taft. Bloomington and Indianapolis: Indiana University Press, 1997.

———. *An Introduction to Metaphysics.* Translated by Ralph Mannheim. New Haven: Yale University Press, 1959.

Irigaray, Luce. *Spéculum De l'autre femme* Paris: Minuit, 1974.

———. *Ce Sexe qui n'en est pas un* Paris: Minuit, 1977

————. *Le Corps-a-corps avec la mère* Montreal: Editions de la pleine lune, 1981.

————. *Passions élémentaires* Paris: Minuit, 1982.

———— *Ethique de la différence sexuelle* Paris: Minuit, 1984.

Jardine, Alice. *Gynesis Configurations of Woman and Modernity.* Ithaca and London: Cornell University Press, 1985

Jonte-Pace, Diane. "Situating Kristeva differently: Psychoanalytic Readings of Women and Religion," in *BodylText in Julia Kristeva: Religion, Women and Psychoanalysis,* edited by David Crownfield. Albany: State University of New York Press, 1992.

Kant, Immanuel, *Critique of Pure Reason* [1781]. Translated by Norman Kemp Smith. London: MacMillan, 1985.

Kofman, Sarah. *Lectures de Derrida* Paris: Galilée, 1984.

Kristeva, Julia. *Revolution in Poetic Language* [1974]. Translated by Margaret Waller. New York: Columbia University Press, 1984.

————. *Polylogue.* Paris: Seuil, 1977.

————. *Desire in Language A Semiotic Approach to Literature and Art.* Translated by Thomas Gora, Alice Jardine and Leon. S. Roudiez. New York: Columbia University Press, 1980.

————. "Le temps des femmes. " 34/44: *Cahiers de recherche de sciences des textes et documents,* no. 5 (1979): 5–19.

Keyt, David. "Aristotle on Plato's Receptacle." *American Journal of Philology,* no. 82 (1961): 291–300.

Lyotard, Jean-François. *Discours, Figure.* Paris: Klincksieck, 1978.

————. *Que Peindre? Adami, Arakawa, Buren* Paris: La Difference, 1987.

————. "Argumentation et presentation: la crise des fondements. " In *L 'Univers philosophique,* vol. I, edited by Andre Jacob. Paris: Presses Universitaires de France.

Lyotard, Jean-François and Jean-Loup Thebaud. *Au Juste.* Paris: Bourgeois, 1979.

Plato, *Timaeus* Translated by Desmond Lee. London: Penguin Classics, 1977.

————. *Le Timée.* Translated by Joseph Moreau and Leon Robin. In *Œuvres Complètes,* t. II. Paris: Gallimard, Bibliothèque de la Pléiade, 1942.

Préli, Georges. *La Force du dehors. Extériorité, limite et non-pouvoir à partir de Maurice Blanchot* Paris: Recherches, 1977.

Rorty, Richard. *Consequences of Pragmatism* Brighton: The Harvester Press, 1982.

Ross, David. *Plato's Theory of Ideas.* Oxford: Clarendon Press, 1951.

Serres, Michel *Hermes IV La Distribution* Paris: Minuit, 1977.

————. *Les Origines de la géométrie* Paris: Flammarion, 1993.

Chapter 7

Being and Time, Non-Being and Space . . . (Introductory notes toward an ontological study of "Woman" and *chora*)

Jana Evans Braziel

> Existence, reality, truth, meaning, values—all the standards and concepts that metaphysics celebrates are implicated in an illusion that metaphysics sustains without unraveling, that it knows the truth about time and Being.[1]

In the history of the western metaphysical tradition, questions of ontology—most frequently posited in the Platonic terms, "Being" and "Becoming"—have been central to the study of philosophy. The western conceptions of space and time—as well as materialism, ethics, and politics—have been grounded on this ontological and metaphysical plane; however, twentieth-century thinkers have interrogated this *a priori* grounding of space and time within ontological constructions, beginning with Heidegger's *Sein und Zeit* in the early twentith century, Sartre's *Être et néant* at the mid-century, and more recently, by Luce Irigaray in *Speculum* and other works.

In *Éthique de la différence sexuelle*, Irigaray asserts that "un changement d'époque exige une mutation dans la perception et la conception de *l'espace-temps*, l'*habitation des lieux* et des *enveloppes de l'identité*. Il suppose et entraîne une évolution ou transformation des formes, des rapports *matière-forme* et de l'intervalle *entre*: trilogie de la constitution du lieu" ["the transition to a new age in turn necessitates a new perception and a new conception of *time* and *space*, our *occupation of place*, and the different *envelopes known as identity*. It assumes and entails an evolution or transformation of forms, or the relationship of *matter* to *form* and of the interval *between* the two: the trilogy of the constitution of the place''] (15). Historically, Irigaray theorizes *le féminin* has been constructed as *espace*, *le masculin* as *temps*. Irigaray's archaeology of the *féminin* challenges these constructions as metaphysically predicated on "woman's" absence.

This paper is part of a larger study (tentatively entitled *Choric Becomings*) that analyzes the philosophical configurations of *le féminin*, spatiality, temporality, *sophia* (or wisdom), and even nihilism in western metaphysical thought. This work attempts to both construct and simultaneously deconstruct the histories of the terms space and time, while exploring metaphysical (and postmetaphysical) representations of embodiment. Primarily, it addresses the feminist and queer deconstructions of space and time as gendered philosophical categories, utilizing ideas from cultural studies, philosophy, poststructuralism and literature. Beginning with a rereading of Plato's *Timaeus*, especially the passages on the *chora*, the study diachronically examines spatiality as a gendered (yet obscured) philosophical construct, from its Platonic *arche*, or even pre-Socratic beginnings, through late antique theological sources and into the modern and postmodern works of Bergson, Heidegger, Levinas, Derrida, Deleuze and Irigaray.[2]

The affiliation of the "feminine" with the spatial and the material demands revaluations, not only of time, but also of generation, motion, and temporality, as central to language and to constructions of knowledge. The larger ontological study on "woman" and *chora* proposes just such a transvaluative reading of western metaphysics, and specifically, conceptions of space and time in relation to gender. In this study, I explore both the material and the spatial as constructions of *le féminin* (the "feminine"), although the two often seem to be either scientifically collapsed, or conversely, regarded as contradictory and mutually exclusive manifestations. In analyzing the philosophical ramifications of this *en-gendered* "space", I draw on the feminist and queer theories of Luce Irigaray, Judith Butler, Elizabeth Grosz, and Jacqueline Zita.

To rewrite space and time is to revise the very parameters of one's own existence. To interrogate these terms as *a priori* given categories for the construction of knowledge and subjectivity in western metaphysics, and even, in modern rationalist thought, is an *archic* and *archaic* turn: not a return to 'origin', as deconstructionist strategies would confound the very notion of origin or *arche*, but a turn to the space that has been posited as the foundation of knowledge itself in the west—an inscrutable and discursive becoming, a genesis, like all others, but neither primordial nor quintessential. Yet, this turn is an *archaic* one in the sense of *a* beginning, however distorted it may be within the trajectories of western thought as prime beginning. It involves a turn to earlier cosmogonies and mythologies, philosophies and ideologies, some forgetful of their own beginnings and becomings, their own roots, and most of all, forgetful of the systems that they displaced and supplanted. As such, this work "represents a fable or mythic unfolding of a fantasied—an impossible—origin . . . rather than as a historical archaeology."[3]

I offer here, then, a theorization of certain ideas or concepts, constructed through a process of *bricolage* with *le féminin*, within the "western" tradition. I do not theorize these concepts as ahistorical universals of *le féminin*. Nor do I see the historicity of these ideational constructs as fixed, but rather in constant flux and exchange.

In doing so, however, I do not wish to reiterate and reify the *diachronic* as a historical teleology, with a finite and isolable "origin" and established "end". Nor do I intend to essentialize a meaning of history. As such, this study attempts to treat history *not* "as a hermeneutic whole," but rather as "a heterogeneous set of meanings."[4] I concur with Catherine Zucker's sentiments, expressed in her discussion of Derrida's deconstruction of Plato in *Postmodern Platos*: "In *Khora*, [Derrida] argues, there has been a certain instability or 'doubling' of meaning within the history of philosophy from the very 'beginning' in Plato. Heidegger was mistaken, therefore, to think that 'history' had an identifiable beginning or end. What we have in the history of philosophy is, rather, a series of different accounts that have some common elements, but that also leave something out."[5] Similarly, like Judith Butler and Luce Irigaray, I write with a certain apprehension, if not trepidation, about the ostensible "origins" of "western" thought.

Confounding *arche* and *telos*, the *archic* and the *anarchic*, the *diachronic* and the *synchronic*—and theorizing a revaluation of these terms which both revisit their etymological roots, while severing them from their banal connotations and further theorizing their circulation in contemporary discourse—I hope ultimately to discombobulate the organizing chronology of history and of ideas, and the contemporary preference (*dominance?*) for *synchrony* over *diachrony*.

The Diachrony of the Other

Structuralist and poststructuralist theorists alike, especially Claude Lévi-Strauss and Michel Foucault after him, following their modernist precursors (Saussure in Linguistics and Heidegger in Philosophy) valorize the *synchronic* as a paradigmatic reservoir of knowledge over the *diachronic* as a historical (i.e., *artificial?*) attenuation of ideas, if not an amnesiac enervation of thought itself. I argue for a rethinking of *synchrony-diachrony* here. I am indebted to the subtle, and suggestive, ideas of Emmanuelle Levinas, who intimates that the totalizing gesture of the *synchronic* attempts to reduce all to a paradigmatic sameness, a reduction only exceeded through the ideational and temporal transcendence of the *diachronic*.[6] Like Levinas, I reject a reading of the *diachronic* as a monolithic and homogeneous stretch of knowledge across time, across history; like Levinas, I see in the *diachronic* only a reaching toward the irreducibility of the other, different at different times, yet still a grasping which is always exceeded and surpassed by that other.

Hierarchical constructions of gender, race, class, sexuality, citizenship/belonging, and foreigner/outsider (as well as revolutions, sometimes egalitarian, that disrupt such hierarchical positioning) clearly operate synchronically—deployed and meaningful relative to cultural, historical, geopolitical, and linguistic location. Synchronic constructions, however, also persist diachronically, latently or even manifestly signifying residual significance. However differently deployed synchronically (*a synthesis within chronos?*), the constructs (or signifiers) also attain and accrue meaning historically, primarily through textual (and canonical) systems of thought— philosophy and literary canons, for example—which are constituted, however elusive such a constitution might actually be, as historically coherent systems, capable even of storing contradiction and heterogeneity. As such, these constructs are overdetermined signifiers, excrescences of social and political meaning. Each, then, is a significatory and historical reservoir of meaning—a receptacle (*hypodoche*). As constructs, though, each has a constitutive outside— synchronically constructed and diachronically residual. This constitutive outside is also an excessive reservoir of meaning not yet constructed, not yet deployed, not yet embodied.

The diachronicity of other . . . In Levinas' words, *diachrony and the other.*

Engaging Irigarayan *Espace*

"*Chaque époque—selon Heidegger—,*" Luce Irigaray writes, "*a une chose à penser. Une seulement*" ("According to Heidegger, each age has one issue to think through, and only one").[7] The issue for our age, Irigaray pronounces, is the thinking of "sexual difference" (*la différence sexuelle*).[8] In alluding to Heidegger, she places *her* question on par with *his* own, the question of the meaning of being; without thinking "sexual difference"(*la différence sexuelle*), Irigaray believes that we have not yet begun to think about being (*être ou étant*). Irigaray and feminists *engaging* her theory—notably Tina Chanter and Rosi Braidotti, who both make passionate arguments for the necessity of thinking "sexual difference"—insist that "*la différence sexuelle est probablement celle de notre temps. La chose de notre temps qui, pensée, nous apporterait le «salut»?*" ("sexual difference is probably the issue in our time which could be our 'salvation' if we thought it through").[9]

In the essay, "*Éthique de la différence sexuelle,*" Irigaray reiterates that one idea belongs to an age, reflecting on Descarte's *l'admiration* ("*wonder*"), Spinoza's *la joie* ("*joy*"), and Hegel's "blood" ethic (« *du sang* »), an analysis of "*le monde éthique et l'interprétation de la différence sexuelle à partir de ce couple frère-soeur repris à la tragédie antique*" ("the ethical world and the interpretation of sexual difference he founds on the brother-sister couple he borrrows from ancient tragedy"),[10] a sexual difference Hegel bases on his reading of Sophocle's *Antigone*. She writes that "*l'exigence éthique demanderait de revoir théoriquement et pratiquement ce rôle historique imparti à la femme*" ("an ethical imperative would seem to require a practical and theoretical revision of the role historically allotted to woman").[11] As such, it would require a revision of tragic, Hegelian "sexual difference": "*Autrement dit, dans cette scission des deux versants de la différence sexuelle, une partie du monde demanderait comment pouvoir trouver et dire son sens, son versant de la signification, tandis que l'autre s'interrogerait sur le sens que peut encore avoir le langage, toutes valeurs, et la vie*" ["In other words, this division between the two sides of sexual difference, one part of the world would be searching for a way to find and speak its meaning, its side of signification, while the other would be questioning whether meaning is still to be found in language, values and life"].[12] Such is the impasse of the question of "sexual difference" in the postmodern era, Irigaray suggests. The possibility for a new "ethics", the possibility for thinking "sexual difference", the possibility for breaking the *same*-old logic defining the past two millenia—these are the ideas which imbue the lines composing Irigaray's book *L'Éthique de la différence sexuelle*, as well as her later works such as *Sexes et Parentes, Le temps de la différence, Je, Tu, Nous*, and *J'aimé à toi*.

Irigaray echoes Heidegger's evocation of Hölderlin's poetic words, « *Seulement un dieu peut encore nous sauver* » ("Only a god can save us now").[13] For Irigaray, an "ethics of sexual difference" would necessitate that the *"le dieu reviendrait d'avant la constitution de notre espace-temps en monde clos par une économie des éléments naturels pliés aux affects et vouloirs de l'homme"* ("god would refer back to a time before our space-time was formed into a closed world by an economy of natural elements forced to bow to man's affect and will").[14] Irigaray's "return" to a pre-Socratic, specifically Empedoclean, model is a beginning in her interrogation of space and time.

Space, or the feminist reconstructions of space, to be certain, is integral to Irigaray's philosophical project, the deconstruction of phallocentric discourse and its *monosexual economy* which entangles *le féminin* within its constructions. Carolyn Burke reads Irigaray's reinscriptions of space as a return to the elementalism of the pre-Socratics, an elementalism also evident in *Marine Lover of Friedrich Nietzsche* (*Amante marine: de Friedrich Nietzsche*), *Elemental Passions* (*Passions élémentaires*) and *L'oubli de l'air: chez Martin Heidegger*. Burke refers to Irigaray's methodology as a "return to a prerational, elemental, and transmutational model" in which gender difference can be rethought.[15] Burke also offers an insightful synopsis of this elemental methodology: "In her most recent texts, Irigaray evokes a conceptual space that has, in her view, been repressed by philosophy since the pre-Socratics: the 'elemental' worldview preceding our own 'reasoned' science in which the earth, air, fire and water combine and interact to generate forms of life still in a state of becoming, within the human microcosm as well as in the larger macrocosm" (230); "In a similar spirit, Irigaray's recent work emphasizes this space between 'l'intervalle,' a mediate position between two polarized terms which requires us to abandon 'either/or' thinking in favor of the 'both/and' model. For she abandons the definitions and distinctions of conventional discourse to explore those intermediary rhythms and spaces in the human passions" (236). All of Irigaray's work has engaged notions of *espace, temps, le sujet*, and *corps*, from her earliest works which are deeply informed by Freudian and Lacanian psychoanalysis, such as *Speculum. De l'autre femme* and *Ce Sexe qui n'en est pas un*, to her "middle" elemental, philosophical works examining and deconstructing a male philospher's oeuvre for the element he ignores or subsumes within his thought— water in *Amante Marine. De Friedrich Nietzsche*; air in *L'Oubli de l'air chez*

Martin Heidegger; earth in a polyvocal, lyrical text called *Passions elementaires*; the last elemental book, on fire, has yet to be written.

However, her most explicit engagement with the en*gendering* of *espace* and *temps* clearly begins in *L'Éthique de la différence sexuelle*, where she insists, following Heidegger, that *the* question defining our era is the question of "sexual difference," a question which if thought would require rethinking even the most basic of parameters—those of *espace* and *temps*. A manifest critique of Heidegger's own neglect of 'spatiality', and thus the body, pervades the poetic-philosophical *L'Oubli de l'air* as well. In *"Différence sexuelle,"* the opening essay of *L'Éthique de la différence sexuelle* [*An Ethics of Sexual Difference*], Irigaray writes that *"pour que cette différence ait lieu d'être pensée et vécue, il faut reconsidérer toute la problématique de l'espace et du temps"* ("In order to make it possible to think through, and live, this difference, we must reconsider the whole problematic of *space* and *time*").[16] Historically, Irigaray posits that *"le féminin est vécu comme espace mais souvent avec les connotations de gouffre et de nuit"* (*"the feminine is experienced as space, but often with connotations of the abyss and night"*), whereas *"le masculin [est vécu] comme temps"* ("the masculine is experienced as time").[17] These en*gendered* and *sexuated* spatio-temporal constructions, Irigaray argues, have privileged time (interior, subjective) over space (exterior, objective). "Le temps" ("Time"), Irigaray writes, *"deviendra l'intériorité du sujet lui-même, l'espace, son extériorité"* ("becomes the *interiority* of subject itself, and space, its *exteriority*").[18] She commiserates that *"Le sujet, maître du temps, devient l'axe de la gestion du monde, avec son au-delà d'instant et d'eternité: Dieu. Il opère la passage entre le temps et l'espace"* ("The subject, master of time, becomes the axis of the world's ordering, with its something beyond the moment and eternity: God. He effects the passage between time and space").[19]

A priori? Feminist and Queer Interrogations of Space, Time and Bodies

For postmodern feminist theorists, the constructions of space and time are immediately and intimately connected with issues of embodiment. This section explores the metaphysical representations of the body as constructed and the metaphysical conceptions of the space or *chora*? in which it is *en-gendered* and generated. I am most interested in the theoretical, conceptual, and even lived possibilities suggested by feminist and queer theorizations of corporeity, sexuality, and subjectivity as culturally constructed; these theorists, largely influenced by the works of Luce Irigaray, think beyond her theorization of "sexual difference" as *two*. They theorize subjects, bodies, and desires as constructs but refuse the construction of *a* female identity, and thus *a* feminist politics around this category. Such universalizing (and therefore reductionist) constructions, as offered in part by Braidotti and Alcoff, however they allow latitude for other difference(s), imply gender commonality and sexual similitude, if not as innate then as historically produced, socially understood, and relationally positioned.

These feminist and queer theorizations of corporeity have extensive and provocative ramifications for feminist thought. The reconfiguration of bodies allows feminist scholars to address material, even corporeal issues, without essentializing bodily sites. It also allows feminists to reconsider bodies as epistemological sites for the manifold constructions of meaning and to recover bodies as loci for locating politics, without predicating this theorization of corporeity on an essentialist, irreducible, and monolithic conception of the body. Conversely, it allows for the production of meaning through the multifarious, heterogeneous construction of bodies.

Feminist critics whose works have been influenced by Luce Irigaray—Naomi Schor, Carolyn Burke, Margaret Whitford, Elizabeth Weed, Sue Best, Tina Chanter, Judith Butler, and Elizabeth Grosz—all offer intriguing, yet different alternatives for conceptualizing the constructions of the body. More importantly, these critics all read the work of Irigaray in alternative, philosophical ways that diverge from the "standard" interpretations of her work by Anglo-American literary critics: traditional interpretations that posit her ideas as essentialist and universalizing. These critics (Butler, Best, Burke, Chanter, Grosz, Vasselau, Schor, and Whitford) all offer readings of Irigarayan theory as informed by the field of philosophy, rather than literary studies, and thus, offer a more nuanced understanding of Irigaray's engagement with the history of philosophy: Irigaray's groundbreaking *Speculum. De l'autre* femme deconstructively reads the metaphysical tradition (and engages with a diverse array of thinkers, such as Plato, Aristotle, Plotinus, Descartes, Hegel, Kant, and Freud) for its constructions of *la femme*; however, her later work also continues her project of metaphysical deconstruction—of Nietzsche's thought in *Amante Marine*; Heidegger's ideas in *L'Oubli de l'air*; and more contemporary thinkers such as Levinas, Lacan, and Merleau-Ponty in other works. Following Irigaray who interrogates the constructions of *la femme* as *matière* or *corps*, the feminist and queer theorists formulate new ways for thinking about bodies, gendered bodies, and the locations of women.

Several books from the 1990s reveal a *tour de force* deployment of "body theory" or feminist-queer theorizations of corporeity. I outline three separate trajectories that mark receptions and postmodern deviations from Irigarayan morphology, outlining Judith Butler's, Elizabeth Grosz's, and Jacqueline Zita's rethinking of bodies as constructed and offering lines of thought for en*gendering* and *queering* bodies.

In contrast to what Butler perceives as the naïveté of feminist theories of "embodied materialism," such as proposed by Braidotti, Judith Butler warns against a feminism that would "simply retrieve the body from what is often characterized as the linguistic idealism of poststructuralism."[20] Butler explains that many feminists have maintained that "in order for feminism to proceed as a critical practice, it must ground itself in the sexed specificity of the female body."[21] Butler disagrees with this premise of "sexual difference" grounded in materiality, asking "why *materiality* has become a sign of irreducibility, that is, how is it that the materiality of sex is understood as that which only bears cultural constructions and, therefore, cannot be a construction?"[22]

In *Bodies that Matter: On the Discursive Limits of "Sex"* Butler interrogates the historical and philosophical speciousness of a feminism rooted in the "female body" yet the conceptual seeds of this position were already sewn, however cursorily, in the third chapter of *Gender Trouble*, "Subversive Bodily Acts." In this final chapter, Butler asks, "Is 'the body' or 'the sexed body' the firm foundation on which gender and systems of compulsory sexuality operate? Or is 'the body' itself shaped by political forces with strategic interests in keeping that body bounded and constituted by the markers of sex? (128–29). Butler contends that "embodied materialism," such as Braidotti proposes, presumes the body as a prediscursive given and gender and/or sexuality as the discursive inscriptions of culture. Butler suggests that "this 'body' often appears to be a passive medium that is signified by an inscription from a cultural source figured as 'external' to that body"; thus, Butler further asserts that "any theory of the culturally constructed body . . . ought to question 'the body' as a construct of suspect generality when it is figured as passive and prior to discourse" (129). This reconfiguration of the body, and the cultural constructions of corporeality, form the basis of Elizabeth Grosz's important work, *Volatile Bodies: Toward a Corporeal Feminism*.

Counter to postmodern, poststructuralist theorists (including most feminist and queer theorists) who regard "gender" as a social, cultural construction but regard biological "sex" as natural" or given, Grosz seeks to problematize this bifurcated division between "gender"/"sex" (so instrumental and fundamental to feminist thought). She does not exclusively theorize and interrogate "gender" as constructed, but the body as constructed also. She refuses to accept the "naturalness" of the body, arguing instead for a revaluation of corporeity as a "socio-cultural artifact."[23] Grosz writes in "Bodies-Cities" of *Space, Time and Perversion* of her own desire to "rethink" corporeity and subjectivity:

> I have been interested in trying to refine and transform traditional notions of corporeality so that the oppositions by which the body has usually been understood (mind and body, inside and outside, experience and social context, subject and object, self and other—and underlying them, the opposition between male and female) can be problematized. Corporeality can be seen as the material condition of subjectivity, and the subordinated term in the opposition, can move to its rightful place in the very heart of the dominant term, mind. Among other things, my recent work has involved a kind of turning inside out and outside in of the body. I have been exploring how the subject's exterior is psychically constructed; and conversely, how the processes of social inscription of the body's surface construct a psychical interior: [. . in order] to reexamine the distinction between biology and culture and explore the way in which culture constructs the biological order in its own image. Thus, what needs to be shown is how the body is psychically, socially, sexually, and representationally produced.[24]

The *corporeal feminism* that Grosz suggests is not based on an essentialist notion of materiality, but rather on the culturally constructed heterogeneities of multifarious bodies: Grosz contends that bodies "cannot be adequately understood as ahistorical, precultural, or natural objects," insisting that bodies are "not only inscribed, marked, engraved by social pressures external to them but are the products, the direct effects, of the very social construction of nature itself" and further concluding that these representations and cultural inscriptions quite literally constitute bodies and help to produce them as such."[25] Thus, Grosz agrees with Butler in acknowledging that materiality itself is *always already* a construct, but she does not agree that materiality thus loses its viability within feminist, queer thought; rather, Grosz maintains, "these kinds of inscription are capable of reinscription, or transformation."[26]

Against Butler's skepticism about a material feminism, Grosz insists that, if we accept Irigaray's premise—that the "male" is normative and valorized, but the entire binaristic paradigm male/fe/male is a "self-amplifying" phallogocentric construct that erases women—we must also begin to interrogate all "masculinist" constructs and knowledges—including the most basic, those of *space* and *time*. Irigaray herself urges this revaluation of the most rudimentary of philosophical precepts. Against feminist *"discursivization"* of materiality, what Grosz posits as a "process of sanitization or neutralization—that is, a strange de-corporealization" among feminist cultural theorists (Butler's work seems implied, given the subtitle of her latest book *Bodies that Matter: On the Discursive Limits of "Sex"*)—whereby "analyses of the *representation* of bodies abound, but bodies in their material variety still wait to be thought,"[27] Grosz advocates a direct engagement with the constructions of materiality itself.

The bodies examined in Jacqueline N. Zita's *Body Talk. Philosophical Reflections on Sex and Gender*, for example, are located "in the tensions between modernism and postmodernism, feminist theory and queer theory, and philosophical and more experimental ways of writing about the body" (4). Readers of *Body Talk* follow a trajectory of creative vacillation between the modernist body and postmodern conceptions of the body—between the fixed constructions of sexuality informed by the former and the alternate conceptions of sexuality (as fluid, intertextual, and protean) theorized by the latter. Zita refers to this labyrinthine trajectory as a "circle of bodies, theories, and revolt.[28]

Drawing on feminist and queer theorizations of the body—such as those offered by Butler in *Bodies That Matter* and Grosz in *Volatile Bodies*, which Zita reviewed for *Signs*—*Body Talk* examines the corporeal spaces, contested sites, and often contradictory meanings of embodied subjectivity. Postmodernist theories and practices, Zita suggests, rightly expose the contingencies of epistemological categories—sexual identities, biologistic conceptions of gender, and essentialized notions of race. "Postmodernism," Zita writes, "supplies a set of ontological commitments needed for a world in which the body appears to be malleable, protean and constructed through and within discourse" (105). For Zita, the body is a *"materialization"*, "a sturdy but fragile thing, an historical matter of political struggle" (4).

A historicity of the body is precisely what *Body Talk* brings to the philosophical discussions of bodily constructs. Corporeal constructions, Zita maintains, are neither "lightweight" nor "detachable" (107); the body, even as culturally constructed, "carries its own historical gravity," an historical weight which "bears down on the 'sexedness' of the body and the possibilities of experience" (107). Refusing pure abstraction and overly abstruse theorizations, Zita examines corporeality in its most concrete, tangible, and political locations. Take, for example, the multiple and varied bodies which proliferate in Zita's analysis: she speaks of *border bodies*, situated between both national, geopolitical, and linguistic borders, and even the more microphysical barriers of bodily contact, such as latex gloves; she conceptualizes *antibodies*, paradoxically and punningly, both the queer bodies which attract-repel and the homophobes who are *anti-body* in their cultural production of "straight repulsion" (37); she critiques *prozac-feminist bodies*, or *pharmorgs* (Zita's neologistic spin on Donna Harraway's *cyborg*), who are part pharmaceutical, part organism. Other examples include the infected, rhetorically disinfected, and excessively heterosexualized reconstructions of Magic Johnson's multiply-imaged bodies and the postmodernist, transgendering bodies of the *male lesbian* and the *lesbian male* "trapped in a genetic female body" (101). More intimately, Zita rhapsodically sings of her passion for the seductive *femfire bodies* of "theory in drag". Zita's work also analyzes *nomadic bodies*, which mark the bisexual and transsexual "softening of the edges of the hetero/homo divide" (132). Through the multifarious movements of these postmodern bodies, Zita theorizes new ways of thinking about the intersections and imbrications of corporeality and subjectivity.

An-arche? A Footnote[29] for *Queer Eschatology and Space for Resisting Closure* . . .

> In eschatology the beginning overtakes the end and puts an end to the end; in teleology, the end fulfills the beginning and puts an end to the beginning. In eschatology the beginning outstrips the end so that the end is driven beyond itself. The most extreme end is consequently the point of transition to a new beginning. . . The beginning is eschatology, the gathering together [of beginnings and ends], thus supplies a logic of reversal, a movement in which the beginning spins itself out into oblivion, and then turns itself around into a new beginning.[30]

The feminist and queer theorizations of corporeity run counter to the synchronizing stream of the western metaphysical tradition and the history of onto-theology in which affiliations between materiality and nihilism underlie and subtend metaphysical constructions of space; although time (and the flux that accompanies it or coincides with it) has also been regarded as inferior to the stasis, presence, and immutability of eternity, time still remained the realm through which man conceptualized mind/*nous* and thought/*noesis*, the realm in which he apprehended the shadow of the presence of forms and the eternality of being, however fragmented or perverted by flux and becoming. Whereas time was conceptualized in relation to being, if only as a fallen state of being, space was erased or subsumed within these ontological speculations, and thus, radically *de*-ontologized. The affiliations between materiality and nihilism also underlie and subtend metaphysical constructions of gender. Where as the *masculine* has been ontologically defined, the *féminin* remains *in*essential, negated, and thus radically *de*-ontologized.

Having faced the end of one millennium and the beginning of a new era, are we moving toward the *anarchic*, a space-time severed from the historical foundations of western thought? Surely, the end of colonialism, the rise of postcolonial nations, and the infiltration of nonwestern ideas and ideologies into Europe and North America have fertilely expanded our knowledges in the late twentieth century; however, even in these geopolitical shifts, the *anarchic unraveling of time* and western history remain the ineluctable and residual traces of their own *archic* (if also violent) beginnings. To think the *anarchic* still remains invested—even in acts of subversions and divestments—with the notion of *arche*, of origin. The *anarchic* annihilates the *archic*, overturning "origin" merely (*thus absolutely?*) through its alpha-negation; yet the *anarchic* presupposes the *archic*, even as it poses it as the site of radical (*thus absolute?*) dismemberment.

In a deconstructive reading of Heidegger's *Destruktion*, Christopher Norris writes that the "'destruction' of metaphysics is intended not, like Derrida's, to release [*gelassen?*] a multiplicity of meaning but to call meaning back to its proper self-identical source."[31] Similarly, Butler resists a utopian vision which would mimetically embrace "repressed feminine sensibilities" (such as Irigaray's?) but holds that a proliferation of sexed, gendered identities might, as Patricia Huntington phrases it, "create a future identity in which all current language and sexual and gender identity would no longer be applicable or necessary."[32] Some questions persist· What is the "place" of "origin" in utopia? What is the "place" of Heidegger's own shift from "origin" to "topology" in his philosophy of Being (*Sein, Dasein*)? "Being-there" . . . *aber wo?* but where? The "place" of utopia?

Carol Bigwood, in *Earth Muse: Feminism, Nature and Art*, explains Heideggerian "origin", not as a "virginal a priori," or first cause but rather an event, a genesis where things emerge into unconcealment but without ground or reason."[33] Butler has also footnoted a response to an Irigarayan conception of "origin". Responding to Donna Haraway's critique that Irigaray reinforces "Plato as the origin of Western representation," obscuring the work of Martin Bernal (in *Black Athena*) and others who argue that "the 'West' and its 'origins' are constructed through a suppression of African cultural exchange and influence," Butler argues that "Haraway may be right, but Irigaray's point is to expose the violent production of the European 'origins' in Greece and so is not incompatible with the view that Haraway outlines."[34] For Butler, the violence of "origin(s)" remains at the "site of representational inscription"—in Plato and in Irigaray (*and also in Butler?*)—as the remainder of "founding exclusions."[35] The important question for Butler then is, "What becomes stored in that receptacle?"[36] This question seems to reiterate Heidegger's question about the excess of meaning stored within the meaning of Being (*Sein*).

In *Ecstatic Subjects, Utopia and Recognition*, Patricia J. Huntington writes that the "identitarian dream of symmetrical recognition sets history on an assimilative course which can only be described as nihilistic and dystopian from the standpoint of those who represent difference."[37] However, a utopian vision and methodology which attempts a "critical mimetic recovery of origins"[38] also entails risk, and even danger. Huntington interrogates this quest for "origin(s)", asking,

> Does not every methodology of mimetically recovering origins itself prove an obstacle to overcoming the Hegelian dream of symmetrical recognition? Would not every conception of origin lead back to a fixed telos or final vision of utopia? . . . Do not, then, Irigaray and late Heidegger simply foster yet additional phantasmatic utopian projections of a perfect, ideal, harmonious community in which we get our Eden back? Would not their archaeological projects enact new fetishes of the lost (m)other of our current humanity?[39]

Irigaray's own work is utopic, although she herself is critical of "masculinist utopias" that constitute "static rationalizations of some objectified lost origin that, projected as the future," symbolizing "the possibility of man's self-transcendence." Margaret Whitford suggests that it is strategically (or deliberately) so, resistant to the Freudian dystopic death drive and the Nietzschean (poststructuralist?) nihilism.[40] Huntington, following the work of Drucilla Cornell and her reading of the "unerasable trace of utopianism" in Irigarayan thought,[41] believes that Irigaray is indeed utopic, "but without lapsing into an uncritical reification of origins and ends."[42]

Huntington poses Irigarayan "origin" not as a fundamental *a priori*, but rather as "whatever constitutes the suppressed economy of desire supporting a symbolic system."[43] Drucilla Cornell explains that, for Irigaray, "the origin that is lost is resurrected as fantasy, not as an actual account or origin. When we remember the origin, we remember the future of a feminine irreducible to the castrated other of the masculine imagery."[44] Huntington suggests that Irigaray's project is the construction of a new sexuated imaginary, precisely through a critical mythologizing, in the Heideggerian sense of creating a new *poiesis*.

In a footnote to "Critically Queer" in *Bodies that Matter*, Butler interprets Cornell's reading of the "feminine" as an impossibility (282–283, fn 11). Although not explicitly acknowledged as such, I see Butler's reading of "critically *queer*" as indebted to Irigaray's own thought which could be defined as "critically *féminin*." Indeed, Butler seems to be influenced throughout *Bodies that Matter* by Irigaray's thinking of "sexual difference" in *L'Éthique de la différence sexuelle*, which is cited several times in the footnotes of the text, as are other works by Irigaray and secondary readings of her work. I mention this fact, because in general critical *parlance*, I have heard (and I have read) statements positing Butler's theorizations of gender performativity as diameterical (or at least radically divergent) from Irigaray's theorizations of sexual difference. While I admit that the critical ends and discursive aims of the two are—perhaps radically—divergent, Butler remains indebted to Irigaray in numerous ways: clearly, her theorization of performativity, which displaces the notion of an heterosexual "original" through its mimetic proliferation of deviant nonheteronormative sexual copies, owes something to Irigaray's notion of *mimetisme* (or "mimicry") as a deconstructive strategy which dislocates *différence* from its relegation to *l'autre de la même* (the "other of the same").

Both, however, are also clearly indebted to Deleuze's reading of *simulacre* as the "bastard" or anomalous in *Logique du Sens* (Paris: Minuit, 1969). In this early book, Deleuze sees *simulacre* as that which displaces the hegemony of resemblance underlying, Deleuze argues, Platonic dualism (specifically, Plato's definitions of form and copy, the latter of which, however inferiorly, must mimetically resemble the former). Irigaray asks, however, "what about the screen?" What about the site of representation (*its true "origin"* . . . *?*), whether copies (mimetic and resembling) or simulacra (deviant and dissembling)? In this sense, she—*originally?*—dis/places Deleuze back into the cave; or at least this interpretation constitutes my own (bastard?) reading of "L'æstera de Platon" (from *Speculum. De l'autre femme*). And yet, Deleuze, Irigaray, Butler—all three suggest a dis/placement of, if not a Heideggerian re/turn (*Kehre, Umkehr*) to, "origin". As such, all three (like Heidegger before them) constitute a reiterative (if also deviant) gesture toward "origin". And toward the "place" of utopia . . .? How can one situate oneself outside this closed circle of "origin" (*arche*) and "end" (*telos*), this *eternal return*? How can one find the "place" (*topos*) of utopia?

Butler herself resists a "radical constructivism," which regards all as textual, as discursive, and thus, easily (even volitionally) re-in-scrib(b)able . . . or conversely, regards all as constructed (*by entry into the symbolic?*)—for once and for all. Butler argues that the very iterative construction constitutes the ground of inscription, which cannot be thought of as prediscursive or as given. Such "radical constructivism" either submits to a linguistic idealism which disavows (even eradicates) all human agency; or, conversely, it (*unconsciously?*) reiterates a humanistic sense of agency and subjectivity, because it posits inscriptions as mutable, transient, malleable, and thus capable of re-inscription, reconstruction. "The paradox of subjectivation (*assujetissement*)," Butler writes, "is precisely that the subject who would resist such norms is itself enabled, if not produced, by such norms"; "the citation of the law," she argues, "is the very mechanism of its production and articulation"; "What is 'forced' by the symbolic, then," Butler writes, "is a citation of its law that reiterates and consolidates the ruse of its own force."[45] Such "radical constructivism," Butler herself recognizes, leaves one mired in the circular ruse (the *eternal return?*) of thought itself. The logical end of Butler's queries (anti-essentialist and antifoundational) leads back again to a determinist and essentializing system of subjectification (*assujetissement*). Foucaultian discourse (especially as conceived through Althusserian interpellation?) persists as the unacknowledged, though still presumed ground (*origin?*) of Butler's performative, manifesting another form of determinism (*ineluctably?*). Do we find ourselves, yet again, in an insidious "logic of the same"? Do we even dare to suggest an "original" or primary "logic of the same"?),—that of *logos* itself?

And the "place" of utopia? After all, despite charges of false etymologies (could one really be charged with such an egregious Socratic crime, since all etymologies are merely creative concretizations of usage and desire and not absolute, prediscursive truths, the thing inherent in the word itself, as Cratylus himself *always already* proposes?—unless, of course, we believe in the absolutism of language, despite the death of all other gods . . . ? And the lectures of Saussure? forgotten? . . . *a-letheia*?) . . . "*utopia*" is "no place at all" (*ou-topos*), regardless of the ambiguity it poses as not only a genuine place, but indeed the best (*the most "original"?*) of all places (*eu-topos*)?, the place of the *Go(o)d* itself?

In this conclusion, I have attempted to frame the archaeological (from *arche*) through a theorization of the *anarchic*. At end (*telos?*), I question whether or not *anarchic* thought is possible, being linked etymologically (*do we perceive Kore here? or at least the voice of Persephone, in the words of Diotima spoken to Socrates . . . to Cratylus . . . to the Symposium?*) and ideationally (*and thus absolutely?*) with the *archic* foundation it attempts to interrogate—in this study the *archaic roots* of the philosophical concepts of space and time, although these *archaic roots* are often, in Deleuzian terms, less "arboreal" more "rhizomatic." Certainly they do not grow in one direction, unilaterally, rigidly, and continuously; such a misnomer presupposes *diachronic continuity*, a persistent and residual "sameness" across time. Neither do they rhizomatically spread along a *synchronic path*, completely cut off from the continguousness (or contiguity[46]) of the *dia-chrony*: such a path presupposes a *synchrony* (a synchronization?) which collapses into paradigmatic "sameness". Rather, these *archaic roots*—both their "arboreal" sedimentations, as well as their "rhizomatic" proliferations—are *diachronic*, in Levinas's sense of the term, in their radical alterity, transcendent [?] only in their irreducibility to a synchronizing (or even diachronizing) "logic of the same." In proposing such a rethinking of terms (ineluctably a Heideggerian "turn"? *Kehre?*), I hope to offer a (*millennial? "original"?*) "space" (*chora*) for resisting closure, although I realize that many of the terms I have proposed—*arche* and *anarche*; *synchrony* and *diachrony*—even in their traversal of the liminal and the ambiguous "interval,"[47] may be inextricably linked, and thus, unthinkable one without the other *Et l'une ne bouge pas sans l'autre*. "And the one doesn't move without the other."

In the tension between metaphysical constructions, 'radical constructivism', and their *anarchic* unravelings, however, perhaps *chora* (or the *choric*) may persist as a liminal and indeterminate category (*archic? anarchic? an-anarchic?*): thus, perhaps, a space (*still the* place—no-*place?—of utopia?*) for other multifarious and *choric* becomings . . . and not the foreclosure (*teleological? eschatological? logical? or merely a-logical?*) of becoming itself. And in the dialectic tension between these discursive and structural poles, however, perhaps new *choric (queer) becomings* can be mobilized and alternative *sophic spaces* can be created, embodied, and inhabited in the post-western twenty-first Century.

Notes

1. Tina Chanter, *The Ethics of Eros. Irigaray's Rewriting of the Philosophers* (London and New York: Routledge, 1995), 153.

2. I do not seek a prepatriarchal, or prediscursive, space or time; I do not seek a spatio-temporal "before" as another ontological ground; I merely seek to reveal these beginnings as one of many *choric becomings*; one of many *sophic spaces*; and in this sense only, do I seek to *unravel time,* a time constructed as interior, immutable, transcendent, and as the prime movements of an unmoved mover, to use Aristotelian terms. Time is so posited by Aristotle in the *Physics*, Plato in the *Timaeus*, Plotinus in *Enneads III 6–7*, Augustine in *Confessiones*, Kant in the *Critique of Pure Reason*, Bergson in *Essai sur les données immédiates de la conscience*, and Heidegger in *Sein und Zeit*. All of these theorists construct time as the interior movements of the soul; time as subjectivity itself.

3. Elizabeth Grosz, "Irigaray and the Divine," in *Transfigurations Theology and the French Feminists*, edited by C. W. Maggie Kim, Susan M. St Ville, and Susan M. Simonaitis (Minneapolis: Augsburg Fortress Publishers, Augsburg, 1993), 206.

4. Patricia J. Huntington, *Ecstatic Subjects, Utopia and Recognition* (Albany, N. Y.: State University of New York, 1998), 220; hereafter cited as Huntington, *Ecstatic Subjects*.

5. Catherine Zucker, *Postmodern Platos* (Chicago: University of Chicago Press, 1996).

6. Emmanuelle Levinas, *Temps et L'Autre* (Montpellier: Fata Morgana, 1947, 1979).

7. Luce Irigaray, *L'Éthique de la différence sexuelle* (Paris: Minuit, 1987), 13; *An Ethics of Sexual Difference*, translated by Carolyn Burke and Gillian C Gill (Ithaca, N. Y.: Cornell University Press, 1993), 5 Henceforth cited as Irigaray, *L'Éthique* and *Ethics* respectively.

8. Irigaray, *L'Éthique* 13; *Ethics* 5. The necessity of thinking "sexual difference" does not establish this category as primary; it merely establishes it as one identitary element constituting one's position and positionality. The category of "sexual difference" is singular only as an intellectual or epistemological category constituting positionality; however, it is not actually singular, but manifold. As the *sex which is not one*, we must also refuse the idea that we are also only *two*. Sexual difference(s) are multiple, historically and culturally located, plural in their multifarious variations. This "intellectual singularity" and "multifarious variation" are not meant to suggest a commonality of sexual difference, or even a common ground of "sexual difference," but only to indicate (and *name*) an intellectual rubric or category for thinking difference in relation to en-*gendering* and sexuation: as such it both constitutes a category of interrogation (philosophically, politically, socially, materially, etc) and an element of identitary construction. I contrast *identitary* from *identity* as an individual model versus a collective one, the former (hopefully) evading the universalism of the latter, although I realize that subjective models can also be reified and abstracted as universal; in other words, the *identitary* would be an individualistic model—specific rather than generic, micropolitical (indeed individual) rather than macropolitical. While few would deny the parameters of racial difference(s), national difference(s), class difference(s), linguistic difference(s), or religious difference(s)—however interpellated, internalized, socially

constructed, or deconstructed—there is a chilling and dead silence (or antithetically, an acrimonious and cacophonous rumble in the feminist rabble) surrounding the category of sexual difference(s), a refusal to occupy a position of gendered and sexuated difference(s) in a maneuver that both obscures and paradoxically reifies the binarism same/different (de Lauretis, cite). While I would resist the excesses and critical violations of making sexual difference(s) primary, as does Rosi Braidotti (*Nomadic Subjects*, 1994), I would equally resist the hegemonic, critical excess which negates and denies difference(s) of sexuation and gender.

9. Irigaray, *L'Éthique* 13; *Ethics* 5.

10 Irigaray, "Éthique de la différence sexuelle," from *L'Éthique*, 113–114; *Ethics*, 116–117.

11 Irigaray, *L'Éthique*, 114; *Ethics*, 117.

12. Irigaray, *L'Éthique*, 122; *Ethics*, 126.

13 Irigaray, *L'Éthique*, 123; *Ethics*, 128.

14 Irigaray, *L'Éthique*, 123; *Ethics*, 128.

15 Carolyn Burke, "Romancing the Philosophers: Luce Irigaray," in *Seduction and Theory*, edited by Dianne Hunter (Urbana and Chicago: University of Illinois Press, 1989).

16 Irigaray, *L'Éthique* 15; *Ethics* 7.

17. Irigaray, *L'Éthique* 15; *Ethics* 7.

18. Irigaray, *L'Éthique* 15; *Ethics*, 7.

19. Irigaray, *L'Éthique* 15; *Ethics* 7.

20. Judith Butler, "Bodies that Matter," in *Engaging with Irigaray Feminist Philosophy and Modern European Thought*, edited by Carolyn Burke, Naomi Schor, and Margaret Whitford (New York: Columbia University Press, 1994), 141—74; hereafter cited as Butler, "Bodies."

21. Butler, "Bodies," 150.

22 Butler, "Bodies," 142.

23 Elizabeth Grosz, *Space, Time and Perversion* (London and New York: Routledge, 1995), 103; henceforth cited as Grosz, *Space*.

24. Grosz, *Space*, 103–104.

25. Grosz, *Volatile*, xii

26 Grosz, *Volatile*, xiii

27 Grosz, *Space*, 31.

28 *Body Talk* is comprised of three major sections: "Articulations," "Disarticulations," and "Rearticulations" and interrogates traditional assumptions about gender, race, sexuality, and the foundational, corporeal matrix of these constructions, the body. The first section, "Articulations," explores the construction of normative bodies and the "deployments of power across sexuality, gender, race, disability and class" (4). Specifically, it challenges biologistic discourses, which establish heteronormative and racially-positioned cultural-corporeal sites. Zita challenges these discourses in the essays, "The Magic of the Pan(eroto)con," "Heterosexual Anti-Biotics," and "Prozac Feminism " The essays in "Disarticulations" examine postmodernist erosions of ontological categories and "engage a process of 'disarticulation' in which the articulated bodies of modernism's normativity" are "disassembled and refigured" (80). This section includes Zita's provocative "The Male Lesbian and the Postmodern Body," a creative theoretical piece called "FemFire: A Theory in Drag," and "Fiddling with Preference," which challenges the sexual demarcation between hetero- and homo-.

The third (and longest) section of the book, "Rearticulations," discusses contemporary theorizations of corporeality—specifically, the feminist, lesbian, and textual theorizations by Monique Wittig and Gloria Anzaldùa. In "Rearticulations," Zita offers these two models of corporeality—the Wittigian body and the Anzaldùan body—

which mediate between the fixity of modernist bodies and the alter-fluidity of postmodernist bodies, yet still understand bodies as both socially constructed *and* materially meaningful In "Hard Traits/Fluid Measures," Zita splices sections of Simon LeVay's *The Sexual Brain* with Wittig's *The Lesbian Body*, moving between the former's categorical science of sexual identity and the latter's textuality of desire. "Anzaldùan Body" offers a critical analysis of the material textualities and the textual materialities of Gloria Anzaldùa's *Borderland/La Frontera*. In "Venus: The Looks of Body Theory," Zita offers rejoinders to bell hooks' and Judith Butler's readings of *Paris is Burning*. The last essay, "A Suite for the Body (in Four Parts)," creatively circles back to issues raised in the Introduction, those of theory-making and body-writing, material articulations, and corporeal transcendences.

29. *"Mais, en ce qui concerne le seul corpus écrit, les notes en bas de pages sont parfois le lieu le moins accessible"* ("However, taking the written corpus alone, the footnotes are often the least accessible place") [Luce, Irigaray, *"Écrire en tant que femme,"* de *Je, Tu, Nous. Pour une culture de la différence* (Paris: Éditions Grasset & Fasquelle, 1990) 62, "Writing As a Woman," from *Je, Tu, Nous. Toward a Culture of Difference*, translated by Alison Martin (New York and London: Routledge, 1993), 54. This interview with Luce Irigaray by Alice Jardine was also published in part in "Exploding the Issue· 'French' 'women' 'writers' and 'the canon,'" *Yale French Studies* 75: 229–258 and in full in *Shifting Scenes: Interviews on Women, Writing and Politics in Post '68 France*, edited by Jardine and Anne Menke (New York and London: Routledge, 1991).

30. John Caputo, "Incarnation and Essentialization: A Reading of Heidegger," *Philosophy Today* 35, no 1 (Spring 1991): 31–42; quoted in Huntington, *Ecstatic Subjects*, 217

31. Christopher Norris, *Deconstruction* (New York and London: Methuen, 1990).

32. Huntington, *Ecstatic Subjects*, 123.

33. Carol Bigwood, *Earth Muse. Feminism, Nature and Art* (Philadelphia: Temple University Press, 1993); quoted in Huntington, *Ecstatic Subjects*, 320, fn4.

34. Judith Butler, *Bodies that Matter· On the Discursive Limits of "Sex"* (New York and London: Routledge, 1993) 257, fn 44.

35. Butler, *Bodies*, 257, fn 44.

36. Butler, *Bodies*, 257, fn 44.

37 Huntington, *Ecstatic Subjects*, 120.

38. I have borrowed this phrase from Huntington's title for Chapter Four in her book, "A Critical Mimetic Recovery of Origins: Reading Heidegger with Irigaray and Cornell" (119–158).

39. Huntington, *Ecstatic Subjects*, 121.

40. Margaret Whitford, "Irigaray, Utopia, and the Death Drive," in *Engaging with Irigaray Feminist Philosophy and Modern European Thought* (New York: Columbia University Press, 1994), 379–400.

41. Drucilla Cornell, *Beyond Accommodation. Ethical Feminism, Deconstruction and the Law* (New York and London: Routledge, 1991). Huntington offers a lucid and insightful reading of Cornell's reading of Irigarayan ethics and utopia in Chapter Four of her work, offering a critical rejoinder to Cornell's reading of Irigaray's notion of "Woman" (nonexistent as an *a priori* concept, constructed only in its *a posteriori* incarnations in individual women) as still predicated around the primacy of the binarism *masculin/féminin* in Chapter Seven.

42. Huntington, *Ecstatic Subjects*, 122.

43. Huntington, *Ecstatic Subjects*, 122.

44. Cornell, 78; as quoted in Huntington, *Ecstatic Subjects*, 130.

45. Butler, *Bodies*, 15

46. "Contiguous relations disrupt the possibility of the enumeration of the sexes, i.e., the first and second sex. Figuring the feminine as/through the contiguous thus implicitly contests the hierarchical binarism of masculine/feminine. This opposition to the quantification of the feminine is an implicit argument with Lacan's *Encore: Le séminaire Livre XX* (Paris: Éditions du Seuil, 1975). It constitutes one sense in which the feminine 'is not one.' See *Amante marine*, pp. 92–93" (Butler, *Bodies*, 256, fn 40).

47. *Citational mimesis, re-production*: "For a discussion of a notion of an 'interval' which is neither exclusively space nor time, see Irigaray's reading of Aristotle's *Physics*, 'Le Lieu, l'intervalle,' *Éthique de la Différence*, 41—62" (Butler, *Bodies*, 252, fn 16).

Bibliography

Aristotle. *Physics* 4 (10–14), translated as *Physics* (2 volumes) by P. H. Wicksteed and Francis M. Cornford. London: Heinemann, 1968—1970.

———. *De Generatione animalium The Generation of Animals*. Greek text and English translation by A. L. Peck. *The Loeb Classical Library*. Cambridge: Harvard University Press, 1942, 1953, 1963.

Augustine. *Confessiones X-XIII* from *Augustine Confessions*, edited by James J. O'Donnell Oxford. Clarendon Press, 1992.

———. *De Trinitate*, from *Corpus Christianum. Series Latina*, edited by W. J. Mountain. Turnholti: Brepols, 1978.

———. *De Genesi ad literam. The Literal Interpretation of Genesis Volume II Books 7–12. Ancient Christian Writers. Volume 42*, Latin text and English translation by John Hammond Taylor, S. J. New York: Newman Press, 1982.

Bergson, Henri. *Essai sur les données immédiates de la conscience*. Paris: Presses Universitaires de France, 1889.

———. *Matière et mémoire* Paris: Presses Universitaires de France, 1896.

———. *Durée et simultanéité*. Paris: Presses Universitaires de France, 1922.

Bernasconi, Robert. "Levinas on Time and the Instant." Pp. 17–44 in *Time and Metaphysics*, edited by Robert Bernasconi and David Wood. Coventry: Parousia Press, 1985.

———. "The Trace of Levinas in Derrida." Pp. 17—44 in *Derrida and Différance*, edited by Robert Bernasconi and David Wood. Coventry: Parousia Press, 1985.

———. "Levinas and Derrida: The Question of the Closure of Metaphysics." Pp. 23—34 in *Face to Face with Levinas*, edited by Richard Cohen. Albany: University of New York Press, 1989.

Bernasconi, Robert and David Wood, eds *Time and Metaphysics*. Coventry: Parousia Press, 1985.

———. *Derrida and Différance* Coventry: Parousia Press, 1985.

———. *The Provocation of Levinas*. London: Routledge, 1988.

Bernasconi, Robert and Simon Critchley, eds. *Re-reading Levinas*, Bloomington: Indiana University Press, 1991.

Berry, Phillipa. "Woman and Space According to Kristeva and Irigaray." Pp. 250–264 in *Shadow of Spirit· Postmodernism and Religion*, edited by Berry and Wernick. London: Routledge, 1992.

Best, Sue. "Sexualizing Space." Pp. 181–194 in *Sexy Bodies· the Strange Carnalities of Feminism*, edited by Elizabeth Grosz and Elspeth Probyn New York and London: Routledge, 1996.

Bigwood, Carol. *Earth Muse Feminism, Nature and Art*. Philadelphia: Temple University Press, 1993.

Braidotti, Rosi. *Nomadic Subjects Embodiment and Sexual Difference in Contemporary Feminist Theory*. New York: Columbia University Press, 1994.

Burke, Carolyn. "Romancing the Philosophers: Luce Irigaray." Pp. 226–240 in *Seduction and Theory: Readings of Gender, Representation, and Rhetoric*, edited by Dianne Hunter. Urbana and Chicago: University of Illinois Press, 1989.

———. "Irigaray through the Looking Glass." Pp. 37–56 in *Engaging with Irigaray*, edited by Carolyn Burke, Naomi Schor, and Margaret Whitford. New York: Columbia University Press, 1994.

Butler, Judith. "Bodies that Matter." Pp. 141–274 in *Engaging with Irigaray. Feminist Philosophy and Modern European Thought*, edited by Carolyn Burke, Naomi Schor, and Margaret Whitford. New York: Columbia University Press, 1994.

———. "Bodies that Matter." Pp 1–26 in *Bodies that Matter: On the Discursive Limits of "Sex"*. New York: Routledge, 1993

———. *Antigone's Claim: Kinship between Life and Death*. New York: Columbia University Press, 2000.

Caputo, John. "Incarnation and Essentialization. A Reading of Heidegger." *Philosophy Today* 35, no. 1 Spring (1991): 31—42.

Carson, Ann. "Putting Her in Her Place: Woman, Dirt, and Desire." Pp. 135—69 in *Before Sexuality. The Construction of Erotic Experience in the Ancient Greek World*, edited by David M. Halperin, John J. Winkler, and Froma I. Zeitlin. Princeton: Princeton University Press, 1990.

Chanter, Tina. "Feminism and the Other." Pp. 32–56 in *The Provocation of Levinas*, edited by Robert Bernasconi and David Wood London: Routledge, 1988.

———. "The Alterity and the Immodesty of Time: Death as Future and Eros as Feminine in Levinas." Pp. 137–154 in *Writing the Future*, edited by A. Benjamin and David Wood. London: Warwick Studies in Philosophy and Literature, Routledge, 1990.

———. "Antigone's Dilemma." Pp. 13–46 in *Re-Reading Levinas*, edited by Simon Critchlcy and Robert Bernasconi. Bloomington: Indiana University Press, 1991.

———. *The Ethics of Eros: Irigaray's Rewriting of the Philosophers*. London: Routledge, 1995

———, ed. *Feminist interpretations of Emmanuel Levinas*. University Park: Pennsylvania State University Press, 2001.

Cohen, Richard, ed. *Face to Face with Levinas*. Albany: State University of New York Press, 1986.

———. Introduction to *Time and the Other*, translated by Cohen. Pittsburgh: Duquesne University Press, 1986.

Cornell, Drucilla. *Beyond Accommodation Ethical Feminism, Deconstruction and the Law*. New York and London: Routledge, 1991.

Critchley, Simon. *The Ethics of Deconstruction Derrida and Levinas*. Blackwell: Oxford, 1992.

Critchley, Simon and R. Bernasconi, eds. *Re-reading Levinas*. Bloomington: Indiana University Press, 1991.

Critchley, Simon, Adriann T. Peperzak, and Robert Bernasconi, eds. *Emmanuel Levinas. Basic Philosophical Writings*. Bloomington and Indianapolis: Indiana University Press, 1996.

Deleuze, Gilles. *"La conception de la différence chez Bergson."* Les Études Bergsoniennes 4 (1956): 77–112.

———. *Le Bergsonisme* Paris: PUF, 1966

———. *Logique du Sens*. Paris: Minuit, 1969.

——— *Différence et répétition*. Paris: 1968

Derrida, Jacques. *"Violence et métaphysique Essai sur la pensée d'Emmanuel Levinas."* Pp. 117–128 in *L'Écriture et la différence.* Points; Paris: Seuil, 1967.

———. *"En ce moment même dans cet ouvrage me voici "* Pp. 21–60 in *Textes pour Emmanuel Levinas,* edited by François Laruelle Paris. Jean-Michel Place, 1980.

———. *"En ce moment même dans cet ouvrage me voici "* Pp 159–202 in *Psyché: Inventions de l'autre.* Paris: Galilée, 1987.

———. "Plato's Pharmacy." Pp 61—71 in *Dissemination,* translated by Barbara Johnson. Chicago: The University of Chicago Press, 1981

———. *Khôra.* Paris: Galilée, 1993.

———. *Apories.* Paris: Galilée, 1994.

———. "Adieu." *L'Arche* 459 (February 1996): 84–91.

duBois, Page. "The Platonic Appropriation of Reproduction." Pp. 169—83 in *Sowing the Body: Psychoanalysis and Ancient Representations of Women.* Chicago and London: The University of Chicago Press, 1988.

Fraser, Nancy, and Sandra Lee Bartky, eds. *Revaluing French Feminism· Critical Essays on Difference, Agency, and Culture.* Bloomington: Indiana University Press, 1992.

Gill, Mary. "Matter and Flux in Plato's *Timaeus "* *Phronesis* 32 (1987): 34–53.

Grosz, Elizabeth. "Irigaray and the Divine." Pp. 199-214 in *Transfigurations· Theology and the French Feminists,* edited by C.W Maggie Kim, Susan M. St. Ville, and Susan M. Simonaitis. Minneapolis: Augsburg Fortress Publishers, Augsburg, 1993.

———. *Volatile Bodies: Toward a Corporeal Feminism.* Bloomington: Indiana University Press, 1994.

——— . "Women, *Chora,* Dwelling." Pp. 47–58 in *Postmodern Cities and Spaces,* edited by Sophie Watson and Katherine Gibson Malden, Mass., and Oxford, UK: Blackwell, 1995.

———. *Space, Time and Perversion. Essays on the Politics of Bodies* London and New York: Routledge, 1995.

Halperin, David M. "Why is Diotima a Woman? Platonic Eros and the Figuration of Gender." Pp. 257—308 in *Before Sexuality. The Construction of Erotic Experience in the Ancient Greek World,* edited by David Halperin, John J. Winkler, and Froma I. Zeitlin. Princeton: Princeton University Press, 1990.

Heidegger, Martin. *Sein und Zeit.* Tübingen: Max Niemeyer, 1986.

———. *Einführung in die Metaphysik.* Tübingen: MaxNiemeyer, 1966

———. *Was heisst Denken?* Tübingen: Max Niemeyer, 1954. 174–175

Hodge, Joanna. "Irigaray Reading Heidegger." Pp. 191–210 in *Engaging with Irigaray,* edited by Carolyn Burke, Naomi Schor, and Margaret Whitford. New York: Columbia University Press, 1994.

Huffer, Lynne, ed. *Another Look, Another Woman· Retranslations of French Feminism.* New Haven, Conn.: Yale University Press, 1995.

Huntington, Patricia J. *Ecstatic Subjects, Utopia and Recognition.* Albany, N. Y.: State University of New York, 1998.

Irigaray, Luce. S*peculum. De l'autre femme.* Paris: Minuit, 1974.

———. *Ce sexe qui n'en est pas un.* Paris: Éditions de Minuit, 1977.

———. *Amante marine. De Friedrich Nietzsche.* Paris: Éditions de Minuit, 1980.

———. *Passions élémentaires.* Paris: Minuit, 1982.

———. *L'Oubli de l'air chez Martin Heidegger.* Paris: Minuit, 1983.

———. *L'Éthique de la Différence Sexuelle.* Paris: Minuit, 1984.

———. *Speculum of the Other Woman,* translated by Gillian C. Gill. Ithaca, N. Y.: Cornell University Press, 1985.

———. *Parler n'est jamais neutre.* Paris: Éditions de Minuit, 1985.

——— *This Sex which is Not One,* translated by Catherine Porter with Carolyn Burke. Ithaca, N. Y: Cornell University Press, 1985

————. *Sexes et parentés*. Paris: Éditions de Minuit, 1987.

————. *Je, Tu, Nous Pour une culture de la différence* Paris: Éditions Grasset & Fasquelle, 1990.

————. "Questions à Levinas," *Critique* 522 (Novembre 1990): 911—20

————. *Marine Lover of Friedrich Nietzsche*, translated by Gillian C. Gill New York: Columbia University Press, 1991.

————. *Elemental passions*, translated from the French by Joanne Collie and Judith Still. London: Athlone Press, 1992; New York: Routledge, 1992

————. *J'aime à toi. Esquisse d'une félicité dans l'histoire*. Paris: B. Grasset, 1992.

————. *Sexes and genealogies*, translated by Gillian C. Gill. New York: Columbia University Press, 1993.

————. *An Ethics of Sexual Difference*, translated by Carolyn Burke and Gillian C. Gill. Ithaca, N. Y.: Cornell University Press, 1993.

————. *I, you, we. Toward a Culture of Difference*, translated by Alison Martin. New York, N. Y.: Routledge, 1993.

————. *Je, tu, nous: Toward a Culture of Difference*, translated by Alison Martin. New York: Routledge, 1993.

————. *Thinking the difference: For a Peaceful Revolution*, translated by Karin Montin. New York: Routledge, 1994.

————. *I love to you: Sketch for a Felicity within History*, translated by Alison Martin. New York: Routledge, 1996.

———— *Etre deux*. Paris: B. Grasset, 1997.

————. *The Forgetting of Air in Martin Heidegger*, translated by Mary Beth Mader. Austin: University of Texas Press, 1999.

————. *To Speak Is Never Neutral*, translated by Gail Schwab. New York: Routledge, 2000

————. *To Be Two*, translated by Monique M. Rhodes and Marco F. Cocito-Monoc. New York: Routledge, 2001.

————. "Writing as a Woman." Pp. 44–46 in *Feminism-Art-Theory. An Anthology, 1968 2000*, edited by Hilary Robinson. Oxford; Malden, Mass.: Blackwell Publishers, 2001.

————. *Between East and West: From Singularity to Community*, translated by Stephen Pluhácek. New York: Columbia University Press, 2002.

————. *The Way of Love*, translated by Ilcidi Bostic and Stephen Pluhácek. London: Continuum, 2002.

Irigaray, Luce, and Sylvère Lotringer, eds. *Why Different?. A Culture of Two Subjects. Interviews with Luce Irigaray*. New York: Semiotext(e), 2000.

Kant, Immanuel. *Critique of Pure Reason [Kritik der rreinen Vernunft]*, translated and edited by Paul Guyer and Allen W. Wood. Cambridge and New York: Cambridge University Press, 1998.

Kristeva, Julia. "*La chora sémiotique· ordonnancement des pulsions,*" *de La Révolution du langage poétique*. Paris. Éditions du Seuil, 1974.

Lacan, Jacques. *Encore· Le séminaire Livre XX* Paris: Éditions du Seuil, 1975.

Levinas, Emmanuelle. *Temps et L'Autre* (1947). Montpellier: Fata Morgana, 1979.

————. *Totalité et infini Essai sur l'extériorité* La Haye, Nijhoff, 1961

————. *Autrement qu'être ou au-delà de l'essence*. La Haye, Nijhoff, 1974.

————. *Éthique et Infini* dialogues con Phillipe Nemo. Librairie Arthè Fayard Radio France, 1982.

Lingis, Alphonso. "Face to Face." Pp. 135–155 in *Deathbound Subjectivity*. Bloomington: Indiana University Press, 1989.

Llewelyn, John. "Levinas, Derrida and Others vis-à-vis." Pp. 185–198 in *Beyond Metaphysics? The Hermeneutic Circle in Contemporary Continental Philosophy*. Altlantic Highlands, N. J.: Humanities Press, 1985.

———. *The Middle Voice of Ecological Conscience: A Chiasmic Reading of Responsibility in the Neighbourhood of Levinas, Heidegger and Others*. London: Macmillan, 1991.

——— "En ce moment même . . . une répétition qui n'en est pas une." Pp. 245–248 in *Le passage des frontières: Autour du travailde Jacques Derrida* (proceedings of the colloqium held at Cerisy). Paris: Galilée, 1994.

———. *Emmanuel Levinas. The Genealogy of Ethics*. London: Routledge, 1995.

Lyotard, Jean-François. "Jewish Oedipus." Pp. 35–55 in *Driftworks*. New York: Semiotext(e), 1984.

Mortensen, Ellen. *The Feminine and Nihilism· Luce Irigaray with Nietzsche and Heidegger* Oslo: Scandinavian University Press, 1994.

——— "Woman's Untruth and *le féminin*: Reading Luce Irigaray with Nietzsche and Heidegger." Pp. 211–228 in *Engaging with Irigaray*, edited by Carolyn Burke, Naomi Schor, and Margaret Whitford. New York and London: Routledge,1994.

Norris, Christopher. *Deconstruction, Theory and Practice*. New York and London: Methuen, 1982.

Philo Judaeus of Alexandria, *De Opificio Mundi* in *Philo. In Ten Volumes,* edited and translated by F. H Colson and G. H. Whitaker. *The Loeb Classical Library* Harvard University Press; London: W. Heinemann, 1929—1962.

Plato, *Timaeus* [TIMAIOS]. Greek text and English translation by R. D Archer-Hind London and New York: Macmillan and Co., 1888.

Plotinus, *Ennead III.6· On the Impassivity of the Bodiless*. Greek text edited with an English translation by Barrie Fleet. Oxford: Clarendon Press; NewYork: Oxford University Press, 1995.

———. *Ennead III 7 On Eternity and Time*. Greek text edited with an English translation by A. H. Armstrong. The Loeb Classical Library. Cambridge, Mass.: Harvard University Press, 1967.

Sartre, Jean-Paul. *L'être et le néant, essai d'ontologie phénoménologique* Paris: Gallimard, 1943.

———. *Being and Nothingness. A Phenomenological Essay on Ontology* New York: Washington Square Press: Pocket Books, 1992, 1956.

Whitford, Margaret. *Philosophy in the Feminine*. New York and London: Routledge, 1992.

———. "Irigaray, Utopia, and the Death Drive." Pp. 379–400 in *Engaging with Irigaray Feminist Philosophy and Modern European Thought*. New York: Columbia University Press, 1994.

Wyschogrod, Edith. "Emmanuel Levinas and the Problem of Religious Language " *The Thomist* 26, 1 (1972): 1–38.

———. *Emmanuel Levinas The Problem of Ethical Metaphysics* The Hague: Martinus Nijhoff, 1974.

———. "God and 'Being's Move' in the Philosophy of Emmanuel Levinas." *The Journal of Religion* 62:2 (1982): 145–55.

———. *Spirit in Ashes Hegel, Heidegger, and Man-Made Mass Death*. New Haven, Conn.: Yale University Press, 1985.

Ziarek, Ewa. "Kristeva and Levinas· Mourning, Ethics and the Feminine." Pp. 62–78 in *Ethics, Politics, and Difference in Julia Kristeva's Writing*, edited by O Kelly. New York: Routledge, 1993.

Ziarek, Krzysztof. *Inflected Language Toward a Hermeneutics of Nearness Heidegger, Levinas, Stevens, Celan*. Albany: State University of New York Press, 1994.

Zita, Jacqueline N. *Body Talk· Philosophical Reflections on Sex and Gender*. New York: Columbia University Press, 1998.

Zucker, Catherine. *Postmodern Platos*. Chicago: University of Chicago Press, 1996.

Chapter 8

"To Take a Chance with Meaning under the Veil of Words": Transpositions, Mothers, and Learning in Julia Kristeva's Theory of Language

Bettina Schmitz

The only truth in life is the love of the mother, James Joyce has written in *Ulysses*—"*amor matris*," subjective and objective genitive (Joyce, 444). That means the love the mother shows towards the child, and the love the child shows toward his or her mother. Every other thing in life turns out to be either uncertain or improbable according to Joyce. Is this certitude of the mother valid or just an unavoidable necessity? Some reflection within the framework of Julia Kristeva's theory of language shall put into question this certitude.

Two notions of the title of this paper seem to be problematic and it is the more problematic to put them together. Today how can we use the word "mother" from a feminist and a critical perspective? Feminist research, as we all know, has done this several times. Thus it is absolutely indispensable to reflect upon this notion, the idea as well as the reality of the mother. My reflections are based on Julia Kristeva's theory of language, in particular on her concept of *transposition*. Transgression, transference, and displacement are the most important movements of a language being-in-process. This is where Kristeva's notion of transposition is situated, at a point of intersection of formal and emotional aspects of language, of content, and structure.

I will begin with some general remarks to sketch the problems that come to the fore when we are talking about mothers and learning. Secondly, I will outline Kristeva's understanding of transposition as it is found in her book *The Revolution of Poetic Language*. There I will also give a brief outline of her theory of language. My deliberations will be concluded by a short analysis of the "Stabat Mater" chapter from her book *Tales of Love*. There I aim to show how—based on Kristeva's theory of the signifying process—a critical reference to both notions—to "mother" and "learning"—is possible. This critical reference also can be developed as a transpositional relation. Kristeva's theoretical work on language can be most helpful for a feminist investigation of the mother. Her philosophy of language therefore is the basis, but we need to transgress it.

Some Trouble with Mothers and Learning

Does not the word "mother" seem to be in a strange way provoking or even improper? On the one hand, what could be more harmless, whom could one trust more than a mother? In Germany, several years ago, on the traffic sign for pedestrians showing an adult man and a child, the shape of the man was changed into a woman. This has been done for good reasons, because in general being with a woman is supposed to be not as dangerous for a child as being with a man. On the other hand we have mythological persons like Medea murdering her children. Whom can we trust then? While reflecting on "the mother" everybody is concerned as a former child and many women are concerned as mothers or eventual mothers-to-be; but it is most important that all human beings are dependent on learning from others, from adults, and especially from their mothers. Everybody needs somebody who teaches him or her how to be in the world. Perhaps another sign for children should be set up, a warning of adult people.

If we now try to change perspectives, should not every educator and teacher have in mind such a thing? They should always take into consideration what it means to lead others in this very world, to give them knowledge about it, to teach them the abilities that they need to live in this society. So as teachers we are all agents of this world as it is, even if we would prefer to stay in a critical distance from it.

The trouble I have with the word "mother" is caused by historical, social, and biographical reasons. For German speaking people Johann Wolfgang von Goethe's drama *Faust II* is a good example of where the protagonist has to go to "the mothers". For Faust this is not only troublesome but even horrible. But let's leave alone these mythic figures by now. We have to bear in mind that real women are quite different: they act practically, they have practical knowledge, they stay in the middle of their lives, and perhaps they are also more prosaic figures than are those in myths or poems. On the one hand they are neither suffering like Faust's Gretchen, nor are they mother Goddesses. But on the other hand they have difficulties in freeing themselves from all those attributes that were transported with the topic of the eternal female, which men have tried to define, that they have sung of, or abused. All these traditional characteristics of the female do not only deter women; they may also be tempted to identify with them. In any case these images are a part of our cultural heritage that we cannot so easily get rid of.

I now want to speak about some of the difficulties that accrue with the topic of the mother in Western cultures. These traditional ideas form a kind of texture or network, even a labyrinth, full of meaning, sometimes seeming to be absurd and even meaningless. Not to get lost in this labyrinth we need not only a theoretical framework and a critical consciousness, but we also have to go back to our own experiences. That is not considered to restraint the investigation but to surpass it and to open new spaces.

Feminist research has made many investigations into the ideas and the images of the mother. A turn toward the mother can be a serious counterpart to patriarchal society that is orientated around the father. But to do so raises the danger of repeating merely male dominated structures, now under a female signature. We can observe this with the feminist discussion of equality if, instead of being orientated around the mother, they turn out to be no different than the order of the father. Most studies of the mother aim to correct male orientated one-sidedness while they refer to the experiences women had under patriarchal circumstances. To be successful in changing the androcentric worldview it is useful to refer to the experiences that originate from traditional social conditions, but the woman should not feel obliged to this very tradition. This is also a question of language as Adrienne Rich has written in one of her poems: "This is the oppressor's language, yet I need it to talk to you" (cf. hooks, 167). Here Kristeva's transposition concept of language can be helpful. The knowledge of traditional structures of language and the subjects it has transported, especially those that are descriptions of women, should lead us to surpass these attributes and functions of traditional femininity. Taking a closer look at this tradition proves it to be more complex, various, and also interesting than it was thought to be. So the feminist task to change traditional subjects, tales, and myths is situated within this very tradition. Kristeva's theory of the signifying process can be employed as a foundation of this analysis, which deals with the origins of a certain meaning as well as with meaning in a more general way.

What one can learn from "the mothers" during this process is more important perhaps for men than for women. All human beings are dependent on women. More generally their well-being depends on the responsibility all adults feel and especially that a mother feels—in fact women as mothers often are simply urged to feel so—for a sphere that is indispensable for all members of a community. We are dependent on mothers taking this responsibility even if they do not get the recognition they deserve because most social and political theories and practices do not adequately take into consideration this sphere, that is often called private. It is also important that the borders of this private sphere are called into question. Women themselves have to pay attention not to be restricted to the private. The main question even for feminist mothers is the tension between the process of learning and the process of criticizing, which exists as a tension within society as well as within the individual. The changes caused by the fact that people do not restrict themselves to learning but also develop their abilities to criticize is exactly what Kristeva has called a "revolution of language." This revolution not only comprises individual and political aspects but also the material basis of a society as well as that of the individual.

This has been a brief outline of the problems that arise from the processes of learning and teaching. To give instructions to other people at school or at the university implies being certain about one's own knowledge. From another point of view all people are dependent on learning from those who know something better than they do, from those who have developed their knowledge further than they have done, from people who are older than they are and have more life experience. People also seek to identify with their instructors (at least partially). This identification, however, may have temptations. But the interests and needs of pupils, students, and other learners restrict their identification and lead them to become more independent. Those who are learning have to resist their teachers and not adapt too much to them; they have to resist the impulse to be only good pupils who behave perfectly. This is simply a description of the border between learning and criticizing and to learn to know this very border is only possible as a personal experience (process). There exists no general rule to find this border and it can't be found once and for all. It is also a question of the dividing line between me and the other(s) that is able to protect me as an individual and that at the same time does not hinder communication so that the individuals stay open to keep contact with the others.

The Semiotic and the Symbolic. The Signifying Process According to Julia Kristeva

Kristeva's theory of language is concerned with the mutual relation between body and mind and with the relation between the individual and the society. Further, it offers a perspective from which to raise the question of femininity. With these issues Kristeva supplements two weak aspects of structuralist theory, subjectivity and history. Subjectivity and meaning come into being during the signifying process, which never comes to an absolute end. Text and subjectivity complement each other. The subject arises from the mediation of drives and stays in touch with his or her needs and seekings. A subject is by no means merely a speaking subject, but it is always quite material at the same time. Within the signifying process Kristeva distinguishes two modalities: the *semiotic* and the *symbolic*. Transpositional movements separate them from each other and at the same time *transposition* guarantees the constant relation between them. The whole sphere of spoken and written language is called the symbolic. The work of the symbolic consists in establishing the order of language as well as that of society and so any signifying system. Meanwhile the semiotic and the *semiotic chora* are nonverbal semiotic movements that can only come into speech in an indirect manner through the transpositional mediation. The semiotic forces do not belong to the system of language as such, but through transgressing symbolic language and being coextensive with it, the semiotic connects formal language with its outside, that is the body and all experiences that accrue from the bodily being of the speaking subject. To a certain extent we may compare the semiotic to the unconscious. We only can know what probably has taken place within the semiotic modality afterwards, reconstructing and constructing it in a deferred action (*Nachträglichkeit*).

Kristeva has developed the notion of the semiotic *chora* in reference to the *chora* in Plato's *Timeus* that also has the function of a mediator. Unlike Plato's metaphysical construction Kristeva's *chora* is not related to an absolute origin; *chora* according to Kristeva is no mediator between eternal ideas and mortal beings. The semiotic precedes the symbolic within the signifying process in a logical and in a chronological manner. The separation between mind and body originates from the work of the semiotic, which also functions to transfer bodily experiences to language. These bodily experiences are marked by society from the beginning. So within the signifying process language can never be totally detached from the body. Instead language stays in a vital and creative association with the body for a lifetime.

In the psychic realm that the semiotic *chora* opens, first structures are achieved: "Discrete quantities of energy move through the body of the subject that is not yet constituted as such" (Reader, 93). Kristeva calls the first structures an ordering (*ordonnancement*), not a law; these structures emerge along the rhythms of experiences of need and satisfaction, the organization of the day in a certain family and in a certain society. The *chora* is neither a marked position nor does it produce a certain sign, but it is "however generated to attain a signifying position" (Reader, 94). On the level of the text the *genotext* corresponds to the semiotic. Genotext is "language's underlying foundation" (Reader, 121). The *chora* precedes and underlies every figuration and stays to be a kind of reservoir (*le résau sémiotique*) of discontinuities that are not yet signs but may be temporally articulated.[1]

Kristeva explains language in reference to the drives and to the unconscious. But language is neither determined by unconscious movements nor by the body, but by transpositions that refer to bodily experiences and that stay in contact with the unconscious. The most important transpositional achievement is to set up the thetic during a phase that marks the principal break in preparation of the articulation of the sign and establishing the barrier between the semiotic and the symbolic. In comparison with Freud's theory of dream-work the thetic barrier is similar to censorship. Once the thetic is accomplished the subject cannot totally go back even if the barrier is permeable—otherwise there would be no language at all—and it may be displaced according to cultural differences that decide what can be spoken out and what has to remain unspeakable. Kristeva develops the term transposition[2] from the consideration of representability. With regard to the dream-work the process of language not only consists in condensation and displacement, but the consideration of representability—also mentioned by Freud as a third mechanism of dreams—gets the most important significance. As far as language acquisition is concerned, as well as for any use of language, language is always situated in a certain social and cultural sphere. In this sense society precedes language and stimulates it to establish an ordering (*ordonnancement*) that is "dictated by natural or socio-historical constraints" (Reader, 94).

"The mother's body is therefore what mediates the symbolic law organizing social relations and becomes the ordering principle of the semiotic *chora*" (Reader, 95). The ordering of the semiotic is first based on the body of the mother or "orientated around the mother's body" (Reader, 95) and relates the body of the subject-to-be to the mother. We have to take into consideration that the first ordering of the subject is not based on itself but on another and that this other in most societies and for most people is the mother. Thinking carefully about these relations we recognize that there does not exist any unmediated body before experience or any direct body experience. Instead a process that Kristeva calls transposition always mediates the body experience. Nevertheless there does not exist any object that could be mediated before the semiotic *chora* has started its work. Before a subject of speech comes into being, an exchange, a mutual relation not between subjects but between bodies has started. This intercorporeal relation first keeps the social situation of body and meaning. Of course we can identify a certain beginning of this process, but there is no absolute origin to be found.

Beyond manifest general rules of language, the language of a certain person is related to his or her life experiences, even if only a part of them can come into speech. Even if they are neither spoken out nor even conscious, all of these experiences are present while we are speaking. To get closer to these unspoken parts of language leads to Kristeva's investigation of the body and the unconscious. Methodologically she goes beyond a more linguistic or philosophical orientated approach to also discuss politics, psychoanalysis, and art. The interrelation between language and body goes together with a presence of early childhood in our speaking as well as a permanent presence of the emotions. The semiotic is not only a realm where the sign is prepared, but it continues to underlie manifest language. The semiotic is a space where the body and socio-cultural structures meet, intersect, and unite to become something that determines the psyche as well as language.

Kristeva's theory reaches to connect a subjective and a more general approach. She combines scientific distance with a personal identification and relation to the subject of investigation. Among feminists she has been criticized for essentialist aspects of her theory. One of the most important subjects of this critique has been the passages in *The Revolution of Poetic Language*, where she describes the semiotic. There she compares the purposes of the semiotic with those of the mother and calls the semiotic "motherly'." This is problematic to some extent. But in my opinion the notion of the mother is more problematic than the role she plays within the signifying process. Kristeva does not aim to give a definition of what the mother has to be. To argue with the mother instead may bring subversive effects. We must remember that already Plato's *chora* has been called a female principle and even a nurse of becoming. According to Astrid Nettling, Plato already subverted the relation between the eternal idea and mortal being by way of the *chora*.

Kristeva's main focus is the relation between language and experience. We have to keep in mind that the mother mediates early experiences in Western societies and they are made close to her body, "*corps à corps*" with her. Some of these experiences are necessarily associated with the body of the mother; others may be also made in relation to the body of the father or another person to whom the baby has a close relation. There exist good reasons to compare the *chora* with the mother, but by doing so we also have to rethink all the problems that arise with this idea of the mother and the period of early childhood experiences.

Stabat Mater

Now I will come to a text of Kristeva where she explicitly refers to the mother, the *"Stabat Mater," Tales of Love*. There she is concerned with motherhood not only in its relation to language acquisition and the process of language, but as an idea of femininity and as a female role. "If, however, one looks at it more closely, this motherhood is the *fantasy*, that is nurtured by the adult, man or woman, of a lost territory" (Reader, 161). The mother is in two senses situated at the border of the unspeakable. First, within the patriarchal tradition femininity is read and constructed in a specific manner. I want to emphasize that even if women have not always enjoyed this role, they must have felt fulfillment and approval to a certain extent. Second, this investigation of motherhood evokes the earliest experiences and period when the child could not yet speak. Both aspects contribute to make it nearly impossible to speak about femininity beyond all the too-well-known myths. "The mother then is alone and speechless," the Austrian author Marlene Streeruwitz writes,

> because—and there lays the true problem—there exists no language that brings into speech the sphere of motherhood. Patriarchy needs and needed a mother, who is speechless, expelled in her destiny (fate?) and who reproduces obediently his commands (demands?) and prohibitions. . . . All this rests enclosed within emotions which no language will help to give expression. It has to stay indescribable (Streeruwitz, 27, tsl)

For a critical discussion of this matter leading ideas, and yet tricks, are asked for which do not merely repeat the myths of the mother. Many traps have been set out by tradition. Careful working with and through language is needed. Otherwise one would have to agree that the mother remains unspeakable under any circumstances, that she even is the unspeakable by definition. In her reflections on the the child's early experience of the mother Kristeva is aware of the risks one takes by moving to this sphere that had been made unspeakable by tradition and that evokes a period of personal history when the individual did not have the capacity to speak for himself or herself. Kristeva's book *Tales of Love* can be read as a fragment of a history of human love based on psychoanalytic knowledge.[3] The theory of language is present in the background of this book. The author of this text about love is not only the speaking subject of an academic analysis—in French *nous*—but also the subject of drives, desire, and satiation, she is the subject in process as Kristeva's theory of language describes it—in French *moi*.

One of these tales of love, "*Stabat Mater*," is not only an "essay on the cult of the Virgin Mary and its implications for the catholic understanding of motherhood and femininity" (Reader, 160) but in a more general way it is an essay on the love of the mother and the love for the mother. The study coincides with Kristeva's own experiences on maternity, asking what experiences of motherhood modern women have. A "post virginal" (Toril Moi) discourse on maternity is required. In Kristeva's own words the revealing of the unspeakable in this context is described as follows: "Flash on the unnamable, weavings of abstractions to be torn. Let a body venture at last out of its shelter, take a chance with meaning under the veil of words" (Reader, 162). To be able to say at least something about the mother, i.e., an approach to the mother in the medium of the word, demands reflection on primary narcissism and the idealization of the mother that goes together with the primary narcissism. So we have to deal with the idea of a perfect, omnipotent mother whom no individual woman is able to embody. Some of these images of the multiplicity of representations are: maternity as the feminine par excellence; maternity as the precondition of artistic activity; maternity as a satisfying role for a woman; maternity as a construction that has not much to do with the real life of a woman.

The particular problematic of the reflection on the mother leads to a special structure of the "*Stabat Mater.*" There exist at least two tales of maternity that are confronted within the text. Personal observations break the main body of the text and the general analysis. These personal memories and reflections lead to an approach to the "real" experiences behind the fantasy of maternity. In this aim it is always indispensable to go through, to work through the cultural construction of the mother. According to this observation most passages of the "*Stabat Mater*" are split in two columns, which are intended to be two voices of maternity. The language of the left column is poetic; it includes personal experiences in all the one-sidedness of this perspective. The right column consists in more general explanations and it offers the cultural and historical background of the more personal part. The arrangement of the two texts already draws the attention to the mutual relation between them, showing allusions and influences. Even if the personal experience is some kind of material that has to be formed by culture later, this seemingly direct experience itself is already influenced and formed by cultural constructions. The tales and myths on motherhood are reflected by the personal experience and they give the experience a structure, but the construction is also influenced by personal experience. Any speaking or writing turns out to be a cultural technique that never is unmediated.

To write the tale of the love of the mother two times in one single text gives a closer look at the interrelation between personal and general text. Changes within these conditions of being a mother and speaking about mothers are only achieved by working trough personal experiences and socio-cultural ideas of the mother. The "*Stabat Mater*" is one of various tales of love that show how in a certain culture love is constructed and given a structure. Kristeva opens up possibilities of freedom by showing its boundaries at the same time. The freedom is given and limited by one's own bodily being, by the relation to other people and by a certain culture that can never be totally left.

The mother herself experiences these boundaries by giving birth to pain. The motto of the text, "*Stabat Mater*" reveals the Virgin as Pietà, as the mourning mother. "One does not give birth in pain, one gives birth to pain: the child represents it and henceforth it settles in, it continues," Kristeva writes (Reader, 167). The pains the mother feels are those of human vulnerability and mortality. She also feels the pain of her own speechless being and that of being necessarily an agent of patriarchal society, leading her children in this society. The mother is a point of intersection of body and language both for a theory of language and within her own feeling.

Not only women are concerned by the subject "maternity"[4] even if the discussion of the mother, as well as a discussion of sexual difference in general, often starts as one about femininity. Instead it would be crucial not to restrict motherhood to women, Sabine Gürtler writes (1994). But of course the possible pregnancy of a female body also gains significance in this context. Most important is the social framework of a tradition of motherhood.

Kristeva's reference to the representation of the Virgin Mary of the Christian tradition does not aim to promote it or to convince one of it, but she tries to understand it. Even if she criticizes Christianity for identifying femininity with maternity, in a most refined construction she acknowledges that it at least maintained what otherwise would have remained outside of any discourse. For Kristeva the Virgin Mary represents a supplement to patriarchy and at the same time she stands for a subversion of patriarchal God and law.

Subsequently to this subversive effect Kristeva outlines female ethics as a heretical ethics, as a *herethics*. This *herethics* on the one hand contains aspects of care—being a refuge in times of illness, passion, death—and on the other hand it is an ethics that does not avoid "the embarrassing and inevitable problematic of the law by giving it flesh, language, *jouissance*" (Reader, 185). Kristeva outlines the vision of a supplement and of an underlying basis for patriarchal law that is able to change it essentially.

Similar to her concept of the relation between the semiotic and the symbolic she does not intend to bring into speech something that has not been spoken out yet, merely veiled by a false language; she does not want to approach some hidden meaning. Instead, to be unspeakable underlines the border of language that is set conventionally, but is no mere convention. It reminds the thetic within the signifying process. Nobody can ever say everything; and this is not only a question of choice or of being mortal. Only with the emergence of language is there also constructed an unspeakable realm which has not existed before. That there is no paradise on the other side of language which, for instance, the mother could represent as the interrelation between the personal and general shows that no pure subjectivity is accessible in language because language always is a cultural construction. As soon as we start speaking we find ourselves within the symbolic, obliged to a social contract we may form (influence) only in a second step.

Kristeva's supplementary ethics, which is as subversive as it is constructive, does not want to exile women in the underground of the symbolic, of morality, and law. Within the signifying process men and women have to deal with semiotic and symbolic modalities with an underworld and a world above. Particularly women have to find a way of communication within the symbolic. That would be the way from the body relationship with their mother (Reader, 180), which no longer needs to be rejected because of the face-to-face with the daughter (Reader, 184).

At this very moment Kristeva's appreciation of traditional images of the mother comes to an end and her critique begins. She aims to arrive at new relationships among women which neither lead to mere repetition of former structures nor to ignore the achievements of the past. However, for several reasons this attempt has more the character of a vision than of a program. The starting point and continuing point of reference is the body, *le corps-à-corps*; the early relationship to the mother's body shall be transported to later periods of the individual's life. The body relationship continues to be the basis of one's own identity as well as of any communication; but according to the order of language and the symbolic it does not lead to a binding relation that is powerful in public space. A particular agreement among women within this corporal sphere may be deep, but without being symbolized it stays ineffective or even dangerous.

> Women doubtless reproduce among themselves the strange gamut of forgotten body relationship with their mothers. Complicity in the unspoken, connivance of the inexpressible . . . an ocean of preciseness . . . no communications among individuals, but connections between atoms. . . . The community of women is a community of dolphins. . . . Within this strange feminine see-saw that makes "me" swing from the unnamable community of women over to the war of individual singularities, it is unsettling to say "I". (Reader, 180–181).

Kristeva compares this difficulty with that of avoiding the personal pronoun in matriarchal civilization. But men have to find their own way from the body relationship with the mother to a face-to-face as well. Still, the Other of the female sex men have to confront usually does not remind them of the mother and this very early period of their life as much. So we suppose that reaching public space for men is easier than for women, but probably their relations within the public are not so deep or so rich. At the same time they seem to be in less danger. Psychoanalytic research has documented the gender asymmetries in early childhood. Different relations of the male and female child to father and mother concerning identification and desire lead to differently gendered personalities (identities) and even to different forms of the so-called oedipal stage.

Following Kristeva the relation of one woman to another can only obtain public character by passing through confrontation. It has to become a face-to-face relation. This face-to-face relation does not exclude the recognition of the other sex; instead it is the unspeakable community of women that may lead to a "repudiation of the masculine" (Reader, 184). And, if we put it the other way around, the symbolic relations among men—secluded from their semiotic roots and the early relation to the mother—also leads, as we all know, to a repudiation of the feminine.[5]

Kristeva aims to avoid the repudiation of the masculine and of the feminine. She intends to supplement the symbolic order, so that it finally is able to represent men as well as women and allows both sexes to access it. The differences between the sexes as well as those within one gender need to be confirmed to reach a balance within the symbolic that is no "pre-established harmony of primal androgyny" (Reader, 184). Being face-to-face with the daughter demands mutual respect, it demands taking the other seriously, and it implies a distance that is the very condition of knowledge. The body relation with the mother remains a foundation that never should be forgotten. We also can describe this process as a female way from the semiotic to the symbolic. But that does not mean that the semiotic would be female in principal, even if it comes into being in relation with the body of the mother. Also, women can find their place in public space. Femininity as such is as symbolical as it is masculinity.

Kristeva's theory of language is concerned with the corporal roots of the symbolic. In "*Stabat Mater*" it is a matter of the content, the myths, the tales, while in *The Revolution of Poetic Language* it is a more theoretical question. Her reflections aim to contribute that both sexes may remember the body relation with the mother without restricting to this body relation, while the patriarchal tradition demands we forget it and to exclude it. But this exclusion actually does not work very well because the repressed comes back from outside, from the underground, from the unconscious.

The reflections on the mother may have effects in various spheres:

1. As far as a model of language is concerned the "identity catastrophe" (Reader, 162) of maternity and especially of pregnancy marks a point of intersection where the semiotic and the symbolic meet and the subject is dissolved. This "identity catastrophe" takes place time and again so that the process of language can continue. To lose one's identity is the motor of the signifying process, but at first there has to have been built up an identity even if identity is a temporary effect for the subject. The most important moment within this process and the achievement of a certain identity is the thetic phase. Looking at this process—afterwards—we cannot find an absolute origin at the very beginning, but what we can do is retroactively give an interpretation when some transpositions already have taken place. We can only reconstruct this process while we are at the same time constructing. I do not want to interpret language too close to human procreation, but the linguistic interest in the mother should not be split totally from corporal aspects of sexual difference and this procreative function.

2. To take the risk of this identity catastrophe is the very condition not only for the signifying process as far as language is concerned but also for any artistic creation. We have to bear in mind that according to Kristeva's theory there does not exist a general difference between every day language creation and creation in art.

3. This analysis questions the myths, the tales of the mother. The image of the mother is at stake. This is the main issue of Kristeva's "*Stabat Mater*" and it is precisely at this moment when the reference to real mothers gets important. It is a question of learning from a real mother and of learning about the reasons that led to the fantasy of the mother, this idealized and repelled mother.

Finally I want to compare Kristeva's transpositional interpretation of language and of tradition with that of another philosopher with whom at first Kristeva seems to have not so much in common, even if she has written a book on her. I suggest Hannah Arendt's assertion of the break with tradition that has taken place. Arendt describes the paradoxes of human relatedness to tradition as a double bind. On the one hand we cannot simply continue with tradition because we know too much about its seamy sides, on the other hand we do not have the choice not to continue; continuing with tradition is our main duty as human beings and we owe most of our abilities to this tradition.

According to Arendt our knowledge about tradition only consists in fragments. We should seize these fragments and try to put them together, even if we know that we never are going to reach a complete picture. We cannot afford to refuse the knowledge of our tradition that has formed our own intellectual abilities and identity. The walk on the edge Arendt describes is exactly what we are doing when we want to change the traditional interpretation and practice of sexual difference. We have to start with the traditional images of being a man or a woman. Analyzing them we discover that they are more various and inconsistent then they are supposed to be. To get at least partially free from the restrictions they impose demands a second step and goes together with a change of these images within a certain society.

The truth of James Joyce's love of the mother may be undisputed; still there is no certainty accessible at any time, especially not from the perspective of the mother herself. Joyce can presuppose this absolute love of the mother because he splits up sexual difference and devalues the father and paternity at the same time. Kristeva's theory of transpositions can be a starting point to solve these problems of sexual difference even if we have to go beyond some of her presuppositions. Kristeva is aware that we need the "veil of words" but intends to stop splitting it up into sexual differences. This may lead to the restoration of the full meaning of the word *mother tongue* and, making use of what we have *learned from our mothers,* neither obeying them blindly nor stubbornly rejecting them.[6]

Notes

1. It is some kind of pantry, to which we do not have a key, which is not directly accessible.

2. Here it has to be mentioned that the most well-known notion of her earlier work, which is "intertextuality" also precedes the development of transposition, so she writes in *The Revolution of Poetic Language*, "The term *intertextuality* denotes this transposition of one (or several) sign-system(s) into another; but since this term often has been

understood in the banal sense of 'study of sources,' we prefer the term *transposition* because it specifies that the passage from one signifying system to another demands a new articulation of the thetic" (Reader, 111)

3. Here Kristeva refers to Freud.

4. In French *maternité* means motherhood as well as pregnancy.

5. See Buchfeld (1996); Schmitz (1993). '

6. I want to thank María Isabel Peña Aguado for the encouragement to question the image of the mother along the term of transposition, and many thanks to Deborah Orr for her indispensable help and her patience with the English version of this article.

Bibliography

Arendt, Hannah. *Between Past and Future.* New York: Viking Press, 1968.

Buchfeld, Ingrid, and Bettina Schmitz. "'La femme n'existe pas.' Identität, Differenz und Trauer der Frauen. Plädoyer für eine weibliche Dissidenz." Pp. 9–34 in *Anpassung und Dissidenz. Materialienband 18*, edited by Frankfur Frauenschule. Königstein/Taunus: Ulrike Helmer, 1996.

Butler, Judith. "The Body Politics of Julia Kristeva." Pp. 164–178 in *Ethics, Politics and Difference*, edited by Kelly Oliver New York, London: Routledge, 1993

Chodorow, Nancy *The Reproduction of Mothering* Berkeley: University of California Press, 1978.

Gürtler, Sabine. "Der Begriff der Mutterschaft in Lévinas' Jenseits des Seins." *Deutsche Zeitschrift für Philosophie* 4 (1994): 653–670.

hooks, bell. *Teaching to Transgress, Education as the Practice of Freedom.* New York-London: Routledge, 1994.

Joyce, James, *Ulysses*. Volume 1, ed. Hans Walter Gabler, New York, London: Garland Publishing Inc., 1984.

Kristeva, Julia. *La révolution du langage poétique*. Paris: Éditions du Seuil, 1974.

———. *Histoires d'amour*. Paris: Editions Denoël, 1983.

La révolte intime Pouvoirs et limites de la psychanalyse II. Paris: Fayard, 199 *Le génie féminin I Hannah Arendt*. Paris: Fayard, 1999.

Nettling, Astrid *Sinn für Übergänge Zur Parergonalität des Weiblichen in der Philosophie. Versuch über die Geschlechterdifferenz.* Wien: Passagen, 1992.

Oliver, Kelly, ed. *Ethics, Politics and Difference in Julia Kristeva's Writing.* New York, London: Routledge, 1993.

———. *Reading Kristeva. Unraveling the Double-bind,* Bloomington, Indianapolis: Indiana University Press, 1993

Rose, Jacqueline. "Julia Kristeva—Take Two." Pp 41–61 in *Ethics, Politics and Difference*, edited by Kelly Oliver, New York, London: Routledge. 1993.

Schmitz, Bettina. *Arbeit an den Grenzen der Sprache. Julia Kristeva.* Königstein/Taunus: Ulrike Helmer Verlag, 1998.

———. *Die Unterwelt bewegen Politik Psychoanalyse und Kunst in der Philosophie Julia Kristevas.* Aachen: ein Fach Verlag, 2000.

———. *Psychische Bisexualität und Geschlechterdifferenz.* Wien: Passagen Verlag, 1996.

Smith, Anne-Marie, Julia Kristeva *Speaking the Unspeakable.* London-Sterling/Virgina: Pluto Press, 1998.

Streeruwitz, Marlene. *Sein Und Schein. Und Erscheinen Tübinger Poetik Vorlesungen.*
    Frankfurt/Main: Suhrkamp, 1997.

Chapter 9

In Search of the Body in the Cave:
Luce Iirigaray's Ethics of Embodiment

Tonja van den Ende

> "We need to discover a language that is not a substitute for the experience of corps—corps as the paternal language seeks to be, but which accompanies that bodily experience, clothing it in words that do not erase the body but speak the body."
>
> —Luce Irigaray, *Body Against Body*

Introduction

Starting from a variety of perspectives, feminist theorists have contributed in massive ways to theorizing differences, all more or less agreeing that there is no such person as "the human subject." On the contrary, feminist theories have extensively shown that there are only specific subjects, coming from different backgrounds and different cultures, with a particular history and upbringing and with different genders and sexual preferences.

In this paper I wish to argue for thinking through the embodiment of differences in general and for an ethics of embodied differences in particular. With "embodied differences," I refer to differences as being lived and experienced in and through the body, and as constituting an important part of one's identity.

Although thinking through differences has traditionally been a priority on the feminist agenda, feminists have often considered theoretical emphasis on the body and embodiment of differences to be necessarily leading to an essentialist perspective that explains gender differences from a causal relation between certain body types and gender. According to this view, starting from *the body* always leads to a devaluation of *specific bodies* (female, black, handicapped, or anything considered to be 'other'). Consequently, the body has been relegated to the domain of biology or anatomy and for many years was rarely the object of feminist philosophy. Only recently, in the nineties, has feminist philosophical work on the body been published, starting with for example Judith Butler's *Bodies that Matter* (1993), Elizabeth Grosz' *Volatile Bodies* (1994), and Moira Gatens' *Imaginary Bodies* (1996).

As early as in 1974, two decades before the appearance of these publications, Luce Irigaray made embodiment her central theme in her Ph.D. thesis *Speculum of the Other Woman* (1985/1974). In this book she connects the devaluation of femininity and female bodies in psychoanalysis and classical philosophical texts by, among others, Hegel and Descartes, with the western tradition of devaluation of embodiment and the human body in general. Of this tradition she considers Plato's metaphor of the cave to be prototypical. Instead of the glorious departure from the cave into the light and vision of the philosopher, she proposes to return and search for the bodies we have left behind. Her publication, together with the more recent ones such as those by Butler, Grosz and Gatens, make quite clear that whereas there is no such person as "the human subject," there is no such thing as "the human body" either.

This conclusion raises several questions. What precisely is the relation between bodies and identities? How can we avoid the infamous dualisms between nature and culture, mind and body in theorizing this relation? And how should we understand embodied differences?

I find Luce Irigaray's work very helpful and inspiring when dealing with these questions: she brings bodily sensations to the fore, not only thematically, but also in her style of writing. Contrary to many interpretations of her work, I do not think her emphasis on sexual difference *theoretically* excludes other differences as important aspects of embodied identities. To argue this point, I will first explain in detail her understanding of bodies as imaginary bodies. She considers the body image to be the basis of our social lives and consequently crucial to our ethical lives. Starting from imaginary bodies, in my view both sexual and other differences can be taken into account in an ethics of embodied differences.

Then I will argue that "feminist theories of differences" should not only concentrate on deconstructing symbolic or socially constructed differences, but should also make room for the articulation of individually lived and experienced differences which form a crucial part of one's identity and lifeplans. These embodied differences are central to Luce Irigaray's ethics on which I will focus in the last part of my paper.

Body Images

The first two questions that need to be answered are: In which way are identities constructed? And how can we understand them as being embodied? Luce Irigaray answers these questions from a psychoanalytical perspective. Because of the attention she pays to the embodiment of identities, she is often considered to be promoting an essentialist perspective. Consequently, a careful reading of her notion of identity is required. So allow me to elaborate on this notion of "embodied identity."

As Freud described in his work *Das Ich und das Es* (1923), in the first few months of a child's existence, it is subjected to a multiplicity of bodily sensations, originating either from inside or outside the body. At this stage the infant is not yet capable of distinguishing inside from outside, self from other, or its different body parts from one another. Out of this multiplicity of bodily sensations, the child develops a sense of unity, an ego, which starts with the experience that its needs are not always fulfilled immediately—the most obvious example being the absence of the mother when the child wants milk. This is the first experience a child has of a separation between the inside and outside world, between self and other.

Lacan later explains this process of developing a sense of self in terms of *the mirror stage* (Lacan 1966), which can be taken literally as the stage—somewhere between six and twenty-four months—in which the child is held in front of a mirror. At first it will not recognize any image. Then it will learn to recognize the image of, for example, the parent holding it in front of the mirror. Finally it will come to recognize its own image and identify with it. But this identification is illusionary or imaginary: the image in the mirror is a Gestalt, which is not the same as the child itself. This image gives the child an illusionary sense of unity and identity and of difference from the other. A sense of identity with and difference from are therefore constructed in one and the same process.

Of course, the image with which the child identifies does not have to be the image in the mirror. It can also be, for example, the image of one or both of the parents, of a sister, or the ideal-type that the parents impose on the child. In later life this image will become a multitude of images with which a person consciously and unconsciously identifies and by which he or she is identified by others. Consequently, the construction of an identity is a never-ending process.

In one of her earliest articles dating from 1966, Luce Irigaray claims that language creates an *imaginary* that is equivalent to the one created in the mirror stage. Even before the child is born, it is being spoken about. After its birth, it is not yet capable of speaking for itself (it is literally "*in-fans*," nonspeaking). After a while the child experiences that it is being spoken about. In this stage the child is a signifier in conversations between, for example, the parents, in linguistic terms between a speaking "I" and a listening "you," whereas the child itself is not yet capable of signifying. It is still in the position of "he"/"she"/"it," the object of a narrative. This experience evokes a feeling of estrangement and abandonment, of what Luce Irigaray calls the child's "first death." To speak for itself, to tell its own narrative, it has to learn to identify with the position of the speaking subject, which is in linguistic terms the position of the "I."

This process of learning to identify with the subject-position in language is equivalent to the process of learning to identify with the mirror image. Both processes are necessary conditions for a child to develop a sense of self and articulate this "self." For that reason identity in Luce Irigaray's works must be understood as referring to both speaking for oneself, telling one's own narrative, and to the body image, or imaginary morphology as she prefers to call it. An identity, in other words, is "I who am this body and tell this narrative." and here I would like to add that having to place oneself in the position of the "I"-speaking subject and having to identify with a body image in order to create a sense of *unity* is, of course, a characteristic which pertains only to certain specific languages and cultures.[1]

Let me stress that the body image in these theories is much more than, for example, the photo in your passport. The body image, as Freud describes it, is a psychological representation of affective relations both toward the own body and toward others. Consequently, it has a personal, emotional, and physical significance, which is consciously and unconsciously informed by cultural and social significations. This is why a body image is a sort of ever-changing map or cartography, which is the result of the ways in which I, as an individual, sense and experience myself and the others around me, and of the ways others react to or affectively invest in my body. It is not a point-to-point registration of the anatomical body. Therefore, certain body parts can be overrepresented in the body image, and other parts completely negated. And if something changes in the anatomical or biological body, it can take a while before this change is integrated into the body image.

Oliver Sacks has given a very illustrative example of this time-consuming process of adapting changes in your body image in his book *A Leg to Stand on* (1984), in which he describes himself lying in a hospital bed with a broken leg. When he wakes up in the middle of the night, he senses a leg lying in his bed and throws it out, after which he falls on the floor. It was of course his own leg, but he could not yet experience it as part of his body.[2] The sensations of phantom limbs, i.e., body parts which are amputated but still "sensed," are another case in point.

Also, a body image does not end at the borders or the skin of an anatomical body. The pen with which I write, the car that I drive can—and maybe even must in order to function properly—become parts of my body image. Moreover, characteristics of another body can become part of my imaginary body by identifying with it. I can, for example, consciously mime the style of writing or dancing of my idol, or unconsciously incorporate my lover's manner of speech or laughing into my own.

What is, in my view, crucial to interpreting Luce Irigaray" writings on the body is, firstly, that according to her without bodies there would be no identities and that without others there would be no "self." In other words: "My body is never simple facticity, it is always a relation" (Irigaray, 1997, 62) Secondly, bodies are always libidinally invested, by myself and by others. Therefore, they are never "neutral" bodies, but are always lived, experienced bodies with an affective significance, both on an individual, and on a social or symbolic level. So bodies, and consequently identities, are both personal and social, the result of a personal working through of bodily sensations and of cultural images, and are continuously rewritten in "auto"biographical narratives that are in fact co-authored by many. Thirdly, when Luce Irigaray refers to embodied identities it is always in connection with *becoming*, because every identity consists of a never-ending dynamic process in which each person on the one hand "negotiates" (of course often unconsciously) between sensations of and affective investments in her own body, other bodies and the ways in which other bodies affectively invest in this body, and on the other hand works through and rewrites her "auto"biographical narrative and the narratives that are told about her[3] (cf. Ann Phoenix, 1998). Both narrative and body image are continuously changing and reconstructed.

This means that an identity is never static but is a continuous process of conscious and unconscious construction. It is both intersubjective or social *and* very personal in the sense that each person has a privileged relation to his or her own body and to his or her own story. It is in this sense that every identity and every body image is unique: no two bodies, no two autobiographies, and no two identities are the same. On the other hand, the body image and the autobiographical narrative must never be reduced to an intrasubjective construction but are to be understood as networks of conscious and unconscious personal, social and cultural meanings which bodies and narratives have. As Luce Irigaray writes in *Etre deux*: "Human beings are constituted from an interior core which integrates on different layers the many dimensions of our existence: bodily, mentally, genealogically, sociologically. . . . Described from the outside, these integrations are reduced to nothing; they only make sense in the way they together form a unity, an identity." (1997, 135) That is to say, they only make sense from the individual perspective, from the perspective of the "auto"biographical narrative of the speaking "I," which articulates these different layers in the way they make sense (or non-sense) to and are lived by the person in question.

This open and dynamic concept of identity is expressed in the words of the woman speaking to her female lover in Luce Irigaray's poetic text "When our lips speak together," "Be what you become, without holding on to what you could have been" (1977, 213). This dynamic concept of identity, which is a crossing of the personal and the social, the biological and the cultural, the body and the mind and which is expressed in an ever-changing and open-ended narrative, in my view contradicts an essentialist interpretation that considers an identity as fixed, unchangeable, and biologically determined.

Now before I get into Luce Irigaray's view on ethics, which is based on this dynamic concept of identity, I would like to expound on the notion of "incorporation" or "embodiment" of differences, because the next question is, of course, how are differences related to embodied identities?

A Feminist "Materialism"

The Fathers of Psychoanalysis have traditionally theorized sexual difference in terms of "more or less," "absence or presence": whether it is Freud's description of the clitoris as a smaller penis and of the girl as a little boy, or Lacan's definition of the feminine and masculine position in the imaginary and symbolic orders as a matter of having or not having the phallus. They hereby repeat a very troubled and complicated history that western cultures have with "othering," a process which defines "the other" in one or both of two possible modes. In the first mode, a dichotomy is posed between "the one" and "the other," considering the other to be of lesser value and on to whom, in psychological terms, negative aspects of the self or of "the own group" are projected. This is what I would like to call "the splitting mode of othering." In the second mode of othering, "the other" is thought in terms of complementarity, i.e., as complementing the deficiencies of the "I," thus adding to the "I" what the "I" is missing. This I would like to call "the romanticizing mode."

Femininity or Woman has traditionally been referred to in these romanticizing and splitting modes, i.e., as either the complementary or opposite other, as either the missing part of masculinity or the negative of Man. However, and here I firmly agree with Luce Irigaray, the embodied identity of a woman can never be fully understood in these terms. Ethics and social recognition of differences, as Luce Irigaray writes in the introduction to her book *Sexes and Genealogies* (1993/1987), must therefore be negotiated on the basis of particular identities and the differences that are part of them. These differences are situational and personal. Consequently, Luce Irigaray states in *This Sex Which Is Not One* that the social recognition a woman strives for depends on her country, her profession, her social class, her sexual preference, and the form of repression which is for her the most immediate and most unbearable (1977, 161). These differences between women cannot be expressed in the splitting or romanticizing modes.

Gender theories that try to avoid these modes of othering by considering masculinity and femininity solely in terms of characteristics on a gliding scale that can be acted out by both men and women seem to me to put the emphasis too much on a *conscious* rewriting of culturally and symbolically available positions and significations. My biggest fear is that we, as feminists, limit ourselves to deconstructing these symbolically and socially imposed norms. While part of our stories and theories should be about the ways in which culturally and symbolically reproduced truths mold and shape our bodies in a Foucaultian sense—a process that Judith Butler, when referring to sexual difference, so adequately labels as "boying" and "girling"—this, in my view, is not all there is to say. Not only are bodies to be understood as imaginary and symbolic or social constructions, but also the imaginary and symbolic or social orders are to be understood as informed by and interwoven with bodily sensations, feeding the images we create and sustain or oppose.

If differences were only symbolically constructed, there would be no resistance and feminism would not exist. It is because certain symbolic divisions do not *feel* right, both in an emotional sense and in the sense that they do not articulate certain sensations and perceptions, and that narratives or discourses do not open up to include our personal narratives, that we are motivated to work against them. As Rosi Braidotti writes, "I think that the imaginary identifications that constitute the unconscious types of interpellations by which identity unfolds are not only deep and powerful but also unpredictable. They help in following the cultural codes, but they also fuel possible forms of resistance" (1997, 35). I think that in order to articulate this resistance, attention should be paid to lived and experienced differences that are part of an individual's ever changing sense of self.

So I agree with Moira Gatens that there is a qualitative difference between the sense of self of a man who acts in culturally labeled "feminine" ways, and of a woman who acts in these ways (1996, 9–10). Of course, this difference can be attributed to the ways in which different gendered behaviors are culturally and symbolically valued, i.e., as a consequence of social constructions. But a sense of self is not only enacted in specific behaviors, it is also, consciously and unconsciously, constructed from bodily sensations. At least part of my body image or sense of self comes from impulses and sensations which originate in my body and which make my working through, my incorporating of, and resistance to these culturally constructed differences an individually lived difference.

Allow me to elucidate my point with the example of someone who is blind. This example is, I think, a case in point, because Luce Irigaray's comments on Lacan's mirror stage mainly focus on his emphasis on the visible and vision as constituting identity. She comments that a body image or *sense* of self must be understood as including *all* the bodily sensations, which is one of the reasons why she wants to pay more attention to e.g., smelling, tasting, breathing, and touching as important aspects of our identities and our relations toward others.[4]

The identity of someone being blind should, in my view, not be understood as reducible to a difference between seeing and not-seeing persons. This difference only reflects the way in which seeing and vision are highly valued in our societies, so that on a symbolic level a blind person is considered to be not-seeing, and not the other way around; i.e., a seeing person is not considered to be someone who is not-blind. Of course, this cultural importance of seeing has its impact on the sense of self of someone being blind. But this is just a part of her story, the other part being the qualitative difference in sense of self from someone who can see: the body image of someone being blind from birth may be constructed through intensified sensations of, for example, smell or touch. The autobiographical narrative of this person may express sensitivities toward the world and the persons around her that do not appear in a narrative told by one who can see. This is what I mean by a qualitative difference as lived and experienced by an individual, without implying that every "blind identity" is the same. On the contrary, there are no two identities that are the same. But what blind people *do* share is an experience of being considered "disabled" in a culture which stresses vision, and a radical alterity from a seeing person in regard to the sensations from which a body image and consequently an identity is constructed.

I read Luce Irigaray's concept of sexual difference in a comparable way. What women share in most cultures and either identify with or resist is a devalued position in phallocentric symbolic orders and societies, what Luce Irigaray refers to as the shared experience of *dereliction*. Like being blind is considered to be "less than seeing," from a phallocentric perspective being a woman is considered to be "less than a man." This binary difference, which is a difference in symbolic or cultural valuation, still needs to be deconstructed—and Luce Irigaray has done so extensively in all of her works—but is not the whole story that can be told about gendered or sexual identities. Differences, in other words, are not only symbolically written on, but also lived through the body: the very dissimilar differences in e.g., biological sex, color of skin, age, sexual preference, health, and wealth are lived differences, which form part of and constitute identities and lifeplans.

Luce Irigaray" project, although concentrating on the differences between the sexes, can be read as including these differences within one sex or gender. Such is Rosi Braidotti's point of view when she writes: "Sexual difference is not a metaphysical claim to a unitary and sweeping vision of subjectivity, but rather a recognition of the mutually shaping, yet internally contradictory, coexistence of asymmetrical power relations that are predicated along the very axes that shape subjectivity: sexuality, ethnicity and "race," class, age, and others" (1997, 27–28). Because these axes not only operate on a social or symbolic level, but are also lived and incorporated into our identities, I argue for sophisticated theories of the embodiment of these differences. In my view Luce Irigaray's works can be very helpful here. But, contrary to Rosi Braidotti, I prefer to reserve the term "sexual differences" for referring to the many, real, imaginary, and symbolical differences between the sexes.

Toward an Ethics of Embodiment

Ethics, as Luce Irigaray states in an interview published in 1996, has traditionally been theorized by philosophers as the sociocultural organization of intersubjective relations. This we can call a "top-down" approach, which allows for conceptualizing subjectivity as abstract, disembodied, gender-neutral and unsituated. What she proposes is to start off from the base and not from the summit, i.e., to theorize ethics as the practice of constructing and cultivating values in the relationships between "I" and "you." As these relationships cannot be grasped and certainly not lived without the bodily sensations of, for example, feeling, touching, moving, smelling, tasting, and hearing, embodiment should be "incorporated" into this ethics.

Ethics is concerned with the quality of life and of our living together. As embodiment forms a crucial part of our lives and radically influences our ways of living together, I argue with Luce Irigaray for the necessity of an ethics of embodiment or embodied ethics. For example, the quality of the relationship between a nurse and the patient he is bathing cannot be regulated by the number of minutes he is allowed to perform this task, but is to a large extent experienced by him and his patient in the way they both feel—emotionally and physically—while touching and being touched, in feeling comfortable or not during the process. These bodily sensations form a crucial part of the quality of our relationships toward others and ourselves and should therefore be part of our ethics.

As embodiment always implies differences and differences are part of every relationship, *respect for alterity* is central to Luce Irigaray's ethics. Respect for alterity implies a radical unsubstitutability of the positions of "I" and "you." This means never to usurp the position of the other, to enter communications with as few a prioris as possible, and to allow self and other to appear and articulate themselves in each communication. According to Luce Irigaray, the first ethical question we put to the other is: "Who are you?," which can then be followed by "Can we find common ground? Talk? Love? Create something together? What is there around us and between us that allows this?" (1993, 178).

The radical unsubstitutability of "I" and "you" challenges us to have the audacity to allow the other and our self to appear in all their differences. Of course, this is not an easily met challenge. I think that the articulation of our differences *can* be a joyful, liberating, and happy experience, but will often also be a very painful, dirty, and scary process. So I want to emphasize that the articulation of differences is not the solution to our moral problems. On the contrary, it is where the trouble—and moral debate—begins.

Notes

1. See, e.g , Gloria Wekker, 1994.

2. This is not an experience which is limited to human beings. A dog, for example, whose paw was broken, keeps regarding it as disfunctioning even after it has healed and will walk only on his three remaining paws. Only after being pushed into the water, will he use the paw to swim and from then on will keep using it.

3. As already stated, you never write your story by yourself. On the contrary, your "auto"biography is extensively informed by other narratives and is the product of a "co-authorship." This is why I write "auto"biography in this fashion.

4 One of the other reasons is of course that psychoanalysis defines the female sex as the invisible sex, referred to by Luce Irigaray as "the blind spot of psychoanalysis." Starting from other senses than vision, much more can be told of the female sex

Bibliography

Braidotti, Rosi. "Comment on Felski's 'The Doxa of Difference': Working through Sexual Difference " *Signs* 23 (1997): 23–40.

Butler, Judith. *Bodies that Matter. On the Discursive Limits of Sex.* London and New York: Routledge, 1993

Ende, Tonja van den. *In levende lijven. Identiteit, lichamelijkheid en verschil in het werk Van Luce Irigaray (In the Flesh Identity, Embodiment and Difference in the Works of Luce Irigaray),* Leende: Damon, (dissertation), 1999.

Gatens, Moira. *Imaginary Bodies. Ethics, Power and Corporality.* London and New York: Routledge, 1996.

Grosz, Elizabeth. *Volatile Bodies Toward a Corporeal Feminism.* Bloomington, Ind.: Indiana University Press, 1994.

Irigaray, Luce. "Communications speculaire et linguistique," 1966. republished in 1985a

———. *Ce sexe qui n'en est pas un.* Paris: Minuit, 1977.

———. *Parler n'est jamais neutre* Paris: Minuit, 1985a.

———. *Speculum of the Other Woman.* Ithaca, New York: Cornell University Press, 1985. (Trans. of *Speculum de l'autre femme.* Paris: Minut, 1974).

———. *Sexes and Genealogies.* Ithaca, New York: Colombia University Press, 1993. (Trans. of *Sexes et parentés.* Paris: Minuit, 1987).

———. *Etre deux.* Paris: B. Grasset, 1997.

Lacan, Jacques *"Le stade du mirroir comme formateur de la fonction du Je."* In *Ecrits. Editions du Seuil,* 1966

Phoenix. Ann. "Telling it like it was: Narrative Constructions of Identity." Unpublished paper presented at the research group *Humanisering, Zorg en Postmoderniteit.* Utrecht: University for Humanist Studies, 1998.

Pluhacek, Steven and Heidi Bostic. "Thinking Life as Relation: an   Interview with Luce Irigaray." *Man and World.* Dordrecht: Kluwer 29 (1996): 343–360.

Sacks, Oliver. *A Lleg to Stand on* New York: Summit Books, 1984.

Wekker. Gloria. *Ik ben een gouden munt Constructies van subjectiviteit en seksualiteit van Creoolse vrouwen in Paramaribo.* Amsterdam: Vita, 1994.

Chapter 10

Reconsidering the Notion of the Body in Anti-essentialism, with the Help of Luce Irigaray and Judith Butler

Annemie Halsema

Summary

In this chapter I aim at reconsidering anti-essentialism by thinking through the notion of the body in two accounts of gender identity, namely Luce Irigaray's and Judith Butler's. My claim is that both sketch different ways out of the essentialism-constructivism dilemma. Whereas Butler supersedes the dualism of matter and construction by introducing the notion of materialization, she doesn't reflect in a satisfying way on the phenomenon of the body. Irigaray's phenomenological approach of embodied identity instead offers good opportunities for rethinking an anti-essentialist notion of the body.

Reconsidering Anti-Essentialism

There is a strong and persistent tendency toward anti-essentialism and anti-naturalism in feminist theory. This tendency is initiated by Simone de Beauvoir in *The Second Sex* and is reflected in her famous formulation: "One is not born, but rather becomes a woman." In Anglo-American feminism this formulation anticipates the distinction between sex and gender, i.e., of some natural, biological fact and of culturally constructed identity. Distinguishing the sexed body from culturally constructed gender enabled feminists to avoid confinement of women to the bodily domain and to pursue change of the cultural significations of femininity.

Yet, in distinguishing sex and gender the Cartesian dualism of body and mind, matter and construction, prevails. The distinction presumes a view of the body as existing prior to language and cultural life, and a view of cultural significations of femininity and masculinity as immaterial, or disembodied. Anti-essentialists repeat the Cartesian dualism again, when they consider the body as a material ground that is fixed, a-historical and a-cultural. In this paper I take the anti-essentialist arguments for rejecting a naturalistic account of the body very seriously, yet aim at sketching an alternative for the inherent view of the body.

The problem I describe could be overruled by claiming that in present-day feminist theory the distinction of sex and gender has already been undermined. Feminist theoreticians, such as Judith Butler (1990) and Nelly Oudshoorn (1991) among others, have demonstrated that sex is as culturally constructed as gender. When the sex of bodies is a cultural effect as well as gender, the distinction is no distinction at all. However, this doesn't solve the problem. For even when sex is constructed as well as gender, we are left with the problem of materiality, in other words with our notion of the body. Overcoming the sex-gender opposition by claiming that sex is constructed does not in itself avoid repeating the dualism of matter and construction. The danger I want to reflect upon is that there prevails some nondiscursive rest, a residue, something outside of culture, which is bodily.

Two positions should be avoided: holding that "everything is constructed," which leads to linguistic monism, and holding that there is a fixed and stable outside to what is constructed, something which escapes construction. The last position is what anti-essentialists oppose against. In their definition essentialism comes to signify: holding that there is some stable outside to discourse, an origin, or something that is not constructed. My claim is that anti-essentialism in this form cannot avoid falling into either of the two traps that I just sketched, if it doesn't reconsider the body. Anti-essentialism should develop a new notion of the body: not as something outside of discourse and construction, neither as fully constructed.

In this paper I will sketch the outlines of such a notion of the body. Therefore I will join two conceptions of gender identity, that both in a different way overcome the dualism of considering the body as a stable materiality or as culturally constructed. The first one is Luce Irigaray's conception "becoming one's gender," which she develops in her works of the nineties (especially in *I Love To You*, 1996). This conception refers to the dialectical process of developing an identity by relating to one's gender. The second one is Judith Butler's notion of materialization. Acquiring a gender identity for her is a performative process of repeating cultural gender norms, a process in which gender norms materialize. I will first demonstrate that both accounts of the body are not essentialist—which is obviously so in the case of Butler and is to be demonstrated in the case of Irigaray. Next, the different approaches of the body these thinkers introduce call for further evaluation.

Irigaray: Becoming One's Gender

Developing a notion of embodied identity is Irigaray's aim indeed, because in her view patriarchal culture is characterized by the gender polarity of masculine disembodiment and feminine association with the bodily sphere. In patriarchy man is the one and only subject, who develops an identity that transcends embodiment. Women are defined by a masculine perspective that seeks to safeguard its own disembodied status through identifying women with the bodily sphere. This implies that both sexes are dependent on each other for the development of their identity. Women cannot develop an embodied identity, because they are excluded from the masculine transcendence of the body, and men are excluded from the bodily sphere, by subscribing it to women.

In order to overcome this hierarchical opposition of man/woman as spirit/body, Irigaray in her later works inquires the conditions for the development of embodied identities for both men and women. She aims at enabling both sexes to transcend their body, but *as* bodily beings, that is to say as beings that develop identities in continuity with their bodies. In other words, she aspires to formulate an alternative for the patriarchal transcendence of the body (which implies disembodiment) by developing a notion of identity that is embodied. Here, embodiment does no longer mean adding the natural to the cultural, but going beyond the natural. I will clarify this point by elaborating the notion "becoming one's gender"; a notion developed by Irigaray in her works of the nineties, in which she mimetically rereads Hegelian dialectics.

"Becoming one's gender" alludes to the development in a dialectical process of the particular individual to the universal, i.e., its gender. For Irigaray the universal is not one, but two: belonging to a gender is the universality we have to relate to. I quote, "Each man and each woman is a particular individual, but universal through their gender . . ." (1996, 51).

Becoming one's gender means, in Irigaray's words, ". . . recognizing that I am a woman. This woman's singularity is in having a particular genealogy and history. But belonging to a gender represents a universal that exists prior to me. I have to accomplish it in relation to my particular destiny" (1996, 39). Irigaray stresses the importance of relating to one's own gender: becoming does not so much entail differentiating oneself from the other sex but requires a development in relation to "the same," i.e., one's own gender.

Becoming one's gender implies a process of: 1. relating to one's particular history, 2. relating to one's collective history, and 3. relating to cultural constructions of gender. Firstly, relating to one's particular history, or also genealogy, means for women to relate to their predecessors in the female line, their mother, their grandmothers. Secondly, relating to one's collective history implies connecting to others of the same gender. And thirdly becoming one's gender involves relating to the societal norms, images, and descriptions of one's gender. These cultural constructions are normative; they function as social constraints that prescribe proper womanhood and manhood.[1] Irigaray proposes not to simply subscribe to these normative constructions, let alone repeat them, but to mimetically reinterpret them. In this context mimesis implies repetition with a distance, and in the end subversion of stereotypical constructions. The mimetical strategy implicates that in order to be able to subvert cultural constructions of femininity and masculinity, we need to relate to them and transform them for our aims. Irigaray explicitly writes that a woman should not comply with a model of identity imposed on her by anyone, neither her parents, her lover, her children, the State, religion, nor culture in general (1996, 27). Each individually, we should develop an identity by relating mimetically to cultural constructions and to others of our gender.

Becoming one's gender implies an identity that is developed in relationship to others. As such it has strong ethical implications, namely awareness of the given that you are only part of half of mankind, hence, that you are not the whole. It limits narcissism, and this limitation creates a space for the other to become. Irigaray holds that only by recognizing my own boundaries, I can meet the other in respect for his or her otherness, and recognize him or her as other. In other words, recognizing that one belongs to a gender is the foundation for Irigaray's ethics of alterity. Developing a gender by relating to others of one's gender and by mimetically reinterpreting cultural constructions implies recognition of the other (of the other gender) as fundamentally different than oneself.

Returning to the problem I started this paper with, let us investigate the implications of this notion of becoming one's gender for Irigaray's conception of the body. In Irigaray's account of gender identity the conception of nature has an important role to play. Belonging to a gender entails passivity, fidelity to the being I am, she writes, ". . . being given to me by nature and which I must endorse, respect and cultivate . . ." (1996, 107). In the light of present-day feminist critiques of the nature-culture distinction,[2] these references to nature seem naive, since they do not take into account the confusion of boundaries between nature and culture: nature and culture can hardly be supposed to have clearly defined boundaries. Yet, also Irigaray's references to nature do not aim at returning to a stable nature, or to a body as a stable point of reference for identity. In that respect they do not simply repeat the traditional distinction of nature and culture. As said earlier, Irigaray diagnoses patriarchy as abolishing the natural in the cultural (or spiritual) and describes her aim as "cultivating the spiritual." Cultivating the spiritual does not mean leaving the natural behind, but going beyond it in a process in which the natural keeps existing, as something we relate to. This is the alternative for the patriarchal transcendence of the natural, which implies subscription to the feminine sphere.

For Irigaray's conception of gender identity, this means that our relation to the body takes part in the construction of identity. Yet identity is not given with the body. In *I Love To You* she writes, "No doubt female physiology is present but not identity, which remains to be constructed" (1996, 107). Gender identity entails a process of construction: you have to become your gender; you are not your gender from the start. The fact of having a sex, which Irigaray describes as "natural," is not the same as having a gender identity. Identity rather is a cultural, or better: symbolical, construction, which differs individually, historically, and culturally. For this reason I consider it questionable, to say the least, that Irigaray's conception of identity is essentialist. It would be if she considered nature as the stable ground for identity,[3] but Irigaray instead thinks that identity entails a process of becoming. Neither is this conception naturalistic, because Irigaray does not reduce identity to nature. Her references to nature do not suggest that gender identity is only "natural": gender rather is a symbolic category, which includes being a body and relating to the societal possibilities and normative restrictions attributed to one's gender.

The question remains *which* role the body plays in becoming your gender. Irigaray clarifies it in the following sentence; "Of course, there is no question of [identity] being constructed in repudiation of one's physiology. It is a matter of demanding a culture, of wanting and elaborating a spirituality, a subjectivity and an alterity appropriate to this gender: the female" (1996, 107). The development of an embodied identity entails elaborating who you already are; it is a process which involves not only activity of a choosing subject, but also passivity, or respect for the boundaries that being a body inspire. The gender to which one belongs is a necessary boundary for developing one's identity. This boundary is an affirmative one, which protects from chaos, disorder, and disorientation.

The conception of "the negative," that Irigaray derives from Hegel (1996, 12–14), is a name for this boundary. The negative stands for the limit imposed on us by our gender. It is an affirmative limit which is necessary for the growth of gendered identity—namely through acceptance of the boundary formed by one's gender—and that is also necessary for recognition of the irreducibility of the other, in other words for considering the other *as other*. Irigaray considers this negative, which can be described in more general terms as finiteness, to be inscribed in the body already. The task for human beings is to cultivate their finiteness. I will come back to this notion in the conclusion of this paper.

Butler: Sexed Bodies as Effects

Whereas for Irigaray belonging to a gender is a necessary condition for developing an identity, in the work of Judith Butler we find a radically different view of the body. I will first describe her view and then return to Irigaray and evaluate both perspectives on the body.

Butler's notions of performativity and materialization of sex aim at defining gender by avoiding essentialism, and by also escaping the opposite pole of constructivism. Already in "Variations on Sex and Gender" (1987) and also in *Gender Trouble* (1990), Butler undermines the distinction between sex and gender which for so long has been dominant in Anglo-American feminist theory. Stressing the radical discontinuity of sexed bodies and culturally constructed genders, she concludes that the binarity of sex does not necessarily lead to assuming the binarity of gender. When gender is theorized as radically independent of sex, it becomes a free-floating artifice instead. And what is more, sex probably is as culturally constructed as gender: the so-called natural facts of sex seem to be discursively produced by various scientific discourses.

Butler continues the passage in *Gender Trouble* that I am referring to, with the point that seems to trouble her all along, namely the production of "natural sex" as prediscursive. I quote; "Gender is not to culture as sex is to nature; gender is also the discursive/cultural means by which 'sexed nature' or 'a natural sex' is produced and established as 'prediscursive,' prior to culture, a politically neutral surface on which culture acts" (1990, 7). Butler is troubled with the anti-essentialist assumption implicated in the sex/gender distinction that I mentioned in the beginning of this paper, the assumption namely of a sexed body prior to cultural inscription. In *Gender Trouble* she pursues alternatives for this assumption, an endeavor that is continued in *Bodies That Matter* by developing the notion of materialization, to which I will return later. The main reason for her concern seems to be that assuming sex as prior to cultural inscription precludes an analysis of the political constitution of the gendered subject. That seems to be the aim of Butler's work in general: she proposes to analyze the construction of gender identity as effect of power and therefore considers the gendered subject as produced in a gendered heterosexual matrix of relations (1993, 7).

What are the consequences of this analysis for Butler's notion of the body? In *Gender Trouble* she opposes considering the body as the ground, surface, or site of cultural inscription that pre-exists the acquisition of its sexed significance. She claims that the body cannot be taken as a passive medium on which cultural meanings are inscribed or as the instrument through which an appropriative and interpretive will determines a cultural meaning for itself (1990, 129).[4] Butler wants to evade a notion of the body as prediscursive. In an attempt to conceive of a nonprediscursive notion of the body she describes how "words, acts, gestures, and desire produce the effect of an internal core or substance, but produce this *on the surface* of the body" (1990, 136). At this point she introduces the notion of performativity; "such acts, gestures, enactments . . . are *performative* in the sense that the essence or identity that they otherwise purport to express are *fabrications* manufactured and sustained through corporeal signs and other discursive means" (Ibid.).

In *Bodies That Matter* this view of the body is radicalized. Whereas in *Gender Trouble* Butler perceived the body as inscribed surface, in *Bodies that matter* she speaks of the materialization of sex, which comes into being in the performative process of "assuming a sex." She reinterprets matter as "a process of materialization that stabilizes over time to *produce* the effect of boundary, fixity, and surface we call matter" (1993, 9). Successfully avoiding essentialism, Butler claims that bodies do not have a sex before cultural inscription, but that sex is a cultural construction, which materializes. Materialization is a process of sedimentation. Sexed beings come into existence through citing regulatory gender norms; these citations come to signify our bodies and cause us to perceive our body as sexed.

Overcoming the Dilemma of Essentialism and Constructivism

In the first part of this paper I claimed that the perspectives of both Irigaray and Butler succeed in overcoming the problems of stable materiality outside of discourse versus culturally constructed materiality. Both views imply that the body cannot be taken as something outside language or culture, or as completely constructed material. Both do so in different ways. In the next part, I will show how they do so. Because both perspectives cannot be considered to be indifferent to each other, or additional, after that I will analyze and evaluate the differences.

Butler explicitly argues against a view of the body as pre-existing cultural inscriptions. Therefore there can be no doubt that she escapes essentialism. But how does she perceive the body? In the former part of my paper I sketched how she envisions the body as an effect of cultural significations, and gender identity as a process of repeating binary and heterosexual gender norms. Does she thereby fall into the trap of constructivism? She carefully tries to avoid it, by not denying the reality of bodies. What she denies are all references to a pure and prediscursive body, which is no further formation of that body. Butler investigates the formations of the body in normative practices and pays attention especially to the practices that produce the effect that some bodies matter, and others do not.

Butler's work aims at destabilizing normative constraints, which cause exclusion. Her work enables change to normative practices, to locate the boundaries between inside and outside. However, I consider her account of bodies as signified in normative practices unsatisfactory, because it ignores the role of the phenomenological body in the construction of identity. Butler does not conceptualize the meaning that the body gives as it were "out of itself": we not only give meaning by means of language, but also bodily. Our embodiment is part of our lived experience and codecides our perception of the world and others.[5] Furthermore, Butler presumes something outside of discourse, a sort of Kantian *Ding an sich*: either in the form of something that "demands for articulation," or in the form of "abjected" bodies. In that respect she doesn't really escape the dualism of matter and construction: there remains a rest.

In Irigaray's work I find a phenomenological account of the body that gives a good alternative. Yet, first we have to see in what sense Irigaray sketches a way out of the traps of essentialism and constructivism. In her account of the process of becoming one's gender, identity is not precultural but is developed in a cultural and social environment. She claims that there is no identity outside of language and that the body is not the secure site of identity (1985, 15). Acquiring an identity rather is a dialectical process of becoming who you are. In this process nature is not abolished, but we relate to our body in a passive manner. Irigaray urges us to realize that we are bodily beings, and that our body is part of who we are: we have to accept and affirm that reality. Developing an identity is not only an active process but involves affirming the reality of our embodiment.

Projecting ourselves into Butler's point of view, we could ask whether Irigaray's conception of nature is not a reification, installed afterward as precultural. Is the body in Irigaray's account not a passive medium, which is inscribed from a cultural source? My thesis is that it is not, because the body is embedded, lived, and experienced in its cultural environment. I must admit that Irigaray seems to hold on to a naive nature-culture distinction at some places,[6] which gives rise to the suspicion that she does consider nature as something precultural. The main reason for doing so is presumably that she argues against patriarchal disembodiment. Her conception of becoming one's gender and her conception of the body in general, however, give rise to an interpretation of the body not as a fixed and stable point of reference for identity, but as experienced through language and to be articulated in language.

Conclusion: A Non-Essentialist Yet Embodied Notion of Identity

In the beginning of this paper I formulated its aim, namely reconsidering the notion of the body in anti-essentialism. I said that reconsidering anti-essentialism calls for rethinking materiality, i.e., the body. In the former part of this paper we have seen that Judith Butler's conception of materialization aims at doing so, by considering the sex of the body as the materialized effect of gender norms. Yet this view does not escape the problem inherent in anti-essentialism: in order to escape linguistic monism, or other forms of radical constructivism, Butler has to assume that there is something outside of discourse. What that outside is, and how to conceptualize it, cannot be reflected upon from a constructivist point of view.

Even though I find this way of perceiving the body unsatisfactory, I still want to hold on to some aspects of this notion of the body, because of its political implications. For Butler this extra-discursive outside is not delimited but is defined by the boundaries of discourse. It is from the outside, the "exterior regions of those boundaries" (1993, 12), in other words from the abjected bodies that fail to materialize that the logic of the heterosexual symbolic can be disrupted. Change is possible because some bodies, abjected or delegitimated bodies, fail to count as "bodies." They are produced in the reiterative practice as bodies that do not matter.

In describing an alternative view of the body, I would like to hold on to the fruitful implications of the constructivist approach of the body. So, what I aim at is sketching a notion of the body that escapes essentialism, that also doesn't fall into the trap of constructivism, and that has the political implications a constructivist notion has. Therefore I consider Irigaray's "phenomenological" account of the body inspiring.[7]

Before sketching this account of the body, another problem that rises in confronting Irigaray's notion of gender-identity with Butler's demands reflection namely the repetition of the gender binarity. Irigaray's conception "becoming one's gender" alludes to a conception of gender identity, which Butler criticizes. Becoming one's gender implies the construction of "man" for male bodies, and of "woman" for female bodies. Thereby Irigaray gives rise to new sorts of exclusion—namely of bodies that do not fall into the clear binary boundaries. Bodies that are somewhat masculine, and somewhat feminine, transvestite bodies, etc. Also, Irigaray privileges sexual difference above other differences. She does not take into account that privileging sexual difference above other differences is a cultural fact. Whereas sexual difference is not an essentialist notion, i.e., not a fixed meaning is given to masculinity or femininity; it still is a universal (see 1996, 43–48), and something that is inscribed in nature.

How to avoid that developing an identity means reiterating binary cultural norms? We have seen that in Irigaray's perspective binarity cannot and must not be avoided: the negative in sexual difference is a necessary condition for developing an embodied identity, which enables one to escape from chaos and disorientation. Yet, it is not this conception of the negative in itself that causes the trouble of binarity, but the idea that there are only two categories to which one can belong. The unsurmountability of sexual difference that Irigaray supposes is not necessarily related to the negative in sexual difference. The twofoldness of sexual difference is an ontological and metaphysical thesis that is not inevitably connected with Irigaray's phenomenological account of developing a gendered identity. Irigaray's philosophy combines a phenomenological account of embodied identity, with the presumption that nature is two. That creates a tension in her work and causes the problems of exclusion I just mentioned. However, thinking embodied identity in the way Irigaray's phenomenological account demonstrates to us does not necessarily imply prioritizing sexual difference and repeating the gender binarity.

In short, my aim is to describe a notion of the body that does not entail repeating the binary gender norms; that is not essentialist or naturalistic and that is open to individual, historical, and cultural differences in identity-formation - differences between, but also within individuals. Although Irigaray's references to nature may be read as presupposing a nature/culture dualism, I think we need to rethink our usual ideas of transcendence and the body/culture dualism itself. For the body this implies that it is not a static phenomenon, but a mode of intentionality. It is the condition for access to the world and to others, and thereby a being comported beyond itself. Living one's body, and developing an identity in correspondence with it, then means taking up and interpreting received interpretations, and being able to relate anew to a historical set of interpretations. This is a process that departs from the body: starting from our embodiment we repeat and interpret cultural norms.

In this view gender is a way of existing in one's body, which implies taking up and reinterpreting cultural possibilities and restraints. For the most part, these are still binary. However, other ways of experiencing the body exist, in other words: other ways of existing in one's body than becoming a heterosexual woman or man are already lived (for example: drag, transsexuality). Therefore possibilities of escaping the gender binarity already have a corporal form, which can and must be articulated. I do not suggest that this can be done easily; the normativity of the cultural order cannot and must not be underestimated. Analyzing and criticizing those binary and exclusive gender norms remains one of the tasks of feminist theory. What I suggest is that we could take a phenomenological look at the different ways of living our body in order to sketch other possible identities.

In this view, the body is not only formed in normative practices, but is a living, existing body that gives meaning to the world. This phenomenological account of the body[8] could lead to a conception of embodiment as not stable or a-historical, but as a constant process of redefining one's relationship to the world and to others.

Notes

1 In Irigaray's later works, she explicitly aims at developing a notion of identity for men also. Whereas in her earlier works, she focused more on creating the opportunities for women to develop subject positions, in her later works she aims at both sexes.

2. Not only Judith Butler, as mentioned earlier, but also Donna Haraway (1985, 1991) criticizes the nature-culture distinction. With her notion of the cyborg, Haraway more specifically criticizes the distinction between technology and "natural" body.

3. Following the definition of Naomi Schor, essentialism implies presuming that the body is the rock of feminism, mapping the feminine into femaleness, and not distinguishing sex and gender (1994: 59–60). My claim is not only that Irigaray is not an essentialist, but that her notion of the body is fruitful within an anti-essentialist context.

4. In Beauvoir's and Sartre's work, for instance, Butler finds several occasions of a Cartesian dualism of the body as mute facticity on the one hand, and immaterial consciousness on the other hand, which attributes meaning to that matter Furthermore, she opposes to Foucault's "bodies and pleasures" which he proposes as a counterattack to the disciplinary workings of sex-desire in *The History of Sexuality I* Butler is in full agreement with Foucault's analysis of the construction of sex: "To be sexed is to be subjected to a set of social regulations" (1990: 96). Yet she detects an unresolved tension: "On the one hand, Foucault wants to argue hat there is no 'sex' in itself which is not produced by complex interactions of discourse and power, and yet there does seem to be a 'multiplicity of pleasures' *in itself* which is not the effect of any specific discourse/power exchange" (1990, 97). These possible escapes that Foucault envisions for the drama of cultural inscription, are rejected by Butler in the same way as she rejects the Cartesian dualism of consciousness and body: they presume a body prior to that inscription, a materiality which is prior to signification.

5. See Merleau-Ponty (1962) for a notion of the body as open to the world, and as partly constitutive for perception.

6. See for instance Irigaray (1996, 35–42), where Irigaray claims that nature is two, instead of one, and writes about "the natural" as if existing in itself.

7 See also for Irigaray's phenomenological account of the body, my "Phenomenology in the Feminine. Irigaray's Relationship to Merleau-Ponty" (To be published).

8. See for a feminist reinterpretation of the phenomenological account of the body, I. M. Young (1990).

Bibliography

Benhabib, S., and J. Butler J., eds. *Feminist Contentions· A Philosophical Exchange* New York and London: Routledge, 1995.

Butler, J. "Variations on Sex and Gender: Beauvoir, Wittig, Foucault." Pp. 128–142 in *Feminism as Critique*, edited by S. Benhabib and D. Cornell. Cambridge: Polity Press, 1987.

————. *Gender Trouble Feminism and the Subversion of Identity*. New York/London: Routledge, 1990.

————. *Bodies That Matter. On the Discursive Limits of 'Sex'*. New York/London: Routledge, 1993.

————. *The Psychic Life of Power: Theories in Subjection*. Stanford: Stanford University Press, 1997.

Haraway, D. "A Manifesto for Cyborgs: Science, Technology, and Socialist Feminism in the 1980s" *Socialist Review* 80 (1985): 65-107.

————. *Simians, Cyborgs, and Women The Reinvention of Nature*. London: Free Association Books, 1991.

Irigaray, L., *Sexes and Genealogies*. Trans. G. C. Gill. New York: Columbia University Press, 1993. (Original: *Sexes et parentés*. Paris: Minuit, 1987).

————. *I Love To You. Sketch of a Possible Felicity in History*. Trans. A. Martin New York and London: Routledge, 1996. (Original: *J'aime à toi*, Paris: Grasset, 1992).

Merleau-Ponty, M. *Phenomenology of Perception*. Trans. C. Smith. London: Routledge and Kegan Paul, 1962.

Svhor, N. 'This Essentialism Which Is Not One. Coming To Grips With Irigaray', pp. 57-78 in *Engaging With Irigaray*, edited by C. Burke, N. Schor, M. Whitford. New York: Columbia University Press, 1994.

Oudshoorn, N. *The Making of the Hormonal Body. A Contextual History of Sex Hormones 1923-1940*. Enschede: Alfa, 1991.

Young, I. M. *Throwing Like a Girl and Other Essays in Feminist Philosophy and Social Theory*. Bloomington and Indianapolis, 1990.

Chapter 11

Butler's Sophisticated Constructionism: A Critical Assessment

Veronica Vasterling

During the last decade something like a new paradigm has emerged in feminist theory: the paradigm of radical constructivism. The work most closely linked to the new paradigm is probably Judith Butler's. On the basis of a creative appropriation of poststructuralist and psychoanalytical theory, Butler elaborates a new perspective on sex, gender, and sexuality. A well-known expression of this new perspective is Butler's thesis, in *Bodies That Matter* (1993), that not only gender but also the materiality of the (sexed) body is discursively constructed.

Since the publication of *Gender Trouble* in 1990 however, the emergence of radical constructivism as a new paradigm has not gone uncontested. One of the most focused critical assessments of this new paradigm takes place in the context of the discussion between Benhabib, Butler, Cornell, and Fraser on the merits and dangers of postmodernism in *Feminist Contentions* (1995). Especially Benhabib and Fraser formulate important critical objections and questions with respect to subjectivity, agency, and the political-normative force of Butler's work. Benhabib accuses Butler of a complete debunking of any concepts of selfhood, agency, and autonomy (21) and she doubts whether Butler's theory of performativity can explain not only the constitution of the self but also the resistance that this very self is capable of in the face of power/discourse regimes (111). According to Fraser, Butler's Foucaultian framework is structurally incapable of providing satisfactory answers to the normative questions it unfailingly solicits, for instance the question how to distinguish between better and worse practices of subjectivation (68).

Butler herself however, attributes most of the objections to a misunderstanding of radical constructivism and/or poststructuralism which tends to reduce both to linguistic monism and determinism. The claim for instance, that the subject is constituted by language does not entail that the subject is fully determined by language (1995, 135). Likewise, the notion of agency as the effect of discursive conditions does not entail that these conditions control the use of agency (1995, 137). Both in her second contribution to *Feminist Contentions* and, more explicitly and extensively, in *Bodies That Matter* Butler defends her position as a sophisticated version of radical constructivism that overcomes the charges of linguistic monism and determinism.[1]

These charges have indeed to be countered if radical constructivism is to be validated as a feasible or useful paradigm for feminist theory. A determinist theory, that is, a theory which does not allow a viable concept of agency, obviously debilitates the feminist project. Though the practical consequences of linguistic monism are less obvious, a theory which negates materiality by reducing it to "linguistic stuff" does not seem a good starting point for a feminist theory of the body. For this reason I will focus my discussion of radical constructivism almost exclusively on the ways in which Butler, in *Bodies That Matter*, tries to refute the charges of linguistic monism and determinism. *Bodies That Matter* is in my opinion, up to now, the most extensive and theoretically sophisticated account of the radical constructivist position. Following through and connecting diverse lines of argument in this book I consider as a better basis for critical assessment of this position than recapitulating and commenting the already very wide and varied discussion of Butler's work and its poststructuralist theoretical framework. Furthermore, as the arguments in *Bodies That Matter* are often intricate and sometimes quite impenetrable, an indepth discussion of several arguments will serve also the purpose of (partial) clarification of the radical constructivist position. I think there is some truth in Butler's suggestion that her position often is misunderstood, but this, I'm sure, is at least partly due to her style of writing. Daunting in its incessant use of highly abstract jargon, not seldom confusing in its rhetorical effects, and often implicit in its argumentation, Butler's text is one of the most difficult but also one of the most provocative texts I have read the last few years.

Linguistic Monism: The Question of the Body

How does the problem of linguistic monism arise? One of the aims of *Bodies That Matter* is the deconstruction of the notion of the body as a natural, pre-linguistic given. This is how Butler puts it, "The body posited as prior to the sign, is always *posited* or *signified* as *prior*. This signification produces as an *effect* of its own procedure the very body that it nevertheless and simultaneously claims to discover as that which *precedes* its own action. If the body signified as prior to signification is an effect of signification, then the mimetic or representational status of language, which claims that signs follow bodies as their necessary mirrors, is not mimetic at all. On the contrary, it is productive, constitutive, one might even argue *performative*, inasmuch as this signifying act delimits and contours the body that it claims to find prior to any and all signification" (30).

Butler's deconstruction of the body as a natural given results in the claim that the body is always already linguistically constructed. Obviously, it is this claim which evokes the charge of linguistic monism: doesn't the claim entail a sort of linguistic metaphysics of the body?[2] What needs to be examined, however, is the exact import of this claim: is it an ontological or an epistemological claim? Does the claim entail that the body is ontologically coextensive with its linguistic constructions, in other words, that the body *is* nothing but a collection of linguistic constructions? Or does it imply that the body is only epistemologically accessible as a linguistically constructed body? Only the former, not the latter, would justify the charge of linguistic monism.

I will examine two lines of argument which in Butler's opinion undercut the charge of linguistic monism. The first one, concerning the notion of referentiability, can be construed as a general epistemological argument about language and its relation to reality. The second argument is more complex. It starts from the claim that language is the condition of appearance of materiality. The import of this claim is ambiguous: it can be construed as either an ontological or an epistemological claim. Though my conclusion is that Butler succeeds in refuting the charge of linguistic monism, the way in which she solves this problem raises new questions. On the one hand, she seems to end up defending an epistemological position which is not only too restrictive, but which, in my opinion, also has negative consequences for a feminist and queer theory of the body. On the other hand, certain passages suggest another, more phenomenological approach which, though hardly elaborated, opens an interesting and more fruitful perspective on such a theory.

Referentiability

The claim that language constructs the body, does not mean that language originates, causes, or exhaustively composes that which it constructs. Rather, it means that there can be "no reference to a pure body which is not at the same time a further formation of that body"(10). In more general terms, instead of merely describing or referring to a body that is simply "there," the constative or referential use of language is "always to some degree performative" (11). This argument can be interpreted in the following way. Though referential or constative language seems to offer a direct connection to extralinguistic reality, it in fact depends on the prior semantic definition of the words used. The statement "this body is female", for instance, can only be uttered by a speaker who has acquired some knowledge of what these words mean. Referential or constative language is not only dependent on the prior semantic definition of the words used; precisely on the basis of that semantic definition, it also effects a certain delimitation of what is taken as extralinguistic reality. Apart from referring to extralinguistic reality, the statement "this body is female" at the same time delimits the body it refers to *as female*, with all the connotations this term carries. If the words "this body is female" appear to represent or mirror an extralinguistic reality, then only because, in everyday usage, we systematically forget that the possibility of referential or constative language depends on prior semantic definitions of the words used which delimit or highlight the reality that is referred to in certain ways.

Yet the fact that referential or constative language introduces a certain semantic construction of the reality that is referred to does not imply that there *is* nothing but these semantic constructions. That the body is linguistically constructed does not preclude that it has, as it were, a life of its own. Rather, Butler's argument implies that our knowledge of the body, of reality in general, always already is mediated by language: to have an idea of what a female body is, we need to know the meaning of the words "body" and "female." This epistemological argument does not, by itself, entail the ontological conclusion of linguistic monism that reality consists of or is reducible to "linguistic stuff." What, if any, ontological conclusions are to be drawn from this argument is in fact an open question.

Language as the Condition of Appearance of Materiality

In the context of a similar argument about referentiability, Butler proceeds with what looks like a much stronger claim: "Can language simply refer to materiality, or is language also the very condition under which materiality may be said to appear?" (31). Though put in the form of a rhetorical question the implied claim that language conditions the *appearance* of materiality is confirmed subsequently in Butler's discussion of Foucault: "'Materiality' appears only when its status as contingently constituted through discourse is erased, concealed, covered over. Materiality is the dissimulated effect of power" (251). The quotation marks around materiality indicate that Butler refers to the common, everyday notion of materiality as a given, extralinguistic reality. The long established discourse on the naturalness and givenness of material entities and bodies conceals the fact that language constructs material reality. Because of this erasure bodies and material entities are perceived as a given, extra-linguistic reality.

The import of the claim that language conditions the appearance of materiality differs from the one discussed above because of the introduction of the notion "appearance," an ambiguous notion with strong ontological and epistemological connotations. Depending on the interpretation of "appearance," the claim either implies linguistic monism or a very strict epistemological assumption.

In the phenomenological-ontological tradition the notion "appearance" is one of the key terms. For Heidegger "being" is synonymous with "appearing": only in so far as it appears, something can be said to exist, to be there.[3] In this sense reality is all that appears. According to Heidegger language enables the interpretation of what appears, it does not enable *that* things appear. Hence, reality is epistemologically dependent but ontologically independent of language. The ontological independence of reality is reversed into dependence if, according to the above claim, language conditions the possibility of appearance. In so far as it enables that things appear, language determines the limits of reality. As language is contingent and variable over time, so are the limits of what we call, and perceive as, reality. Though much more sophisticated and defensible than the rather absurd conclusion that reality consists of "linguistic stuff," in my opinion this position still amounts to linguistic monism for it precludes the possibility of an ontologically independent, extralinguistic reality. What appears or is perceived as extralinguistic reality is still a hidden effect of language or, in terms of Butler, the dissimulated effect of discursive power.

In the Kantian tradition "appearance" is an epistemological notion, albeit an epistemological notion with ontological repercussions. According to Kant knowledge of reality is restricted to appearances (*phenomena*). What things are in or by themselves (as *Ding an sich*) we cannot know. The upshot of this argument is that knowledge does not determine the ontological limits of reality. Hence, the ontological independence of reality is preserved even though it is epistemologically beyond our reach. Following this Kantian logic, Butler's claim can be interpreted as denying, not the possibility as such of an ontologically independent, extralinguistic reality, but the possibility of *access* to an ontologically independent, extralinguistic reality. In this Kantian context, the claim that language conditions the possibility of appearance means that language, as the epistemological condition of accessibility, determines the way in which reality appears to us. Thus, if materiality appears as a given, extralinguistic reality then this extra-linguistic reality is still an effect of language but materiality, qua reality, is not reducible to these linguistic effects, that is, to the semantic constructions of language.

May we conclude from the Kantian interpretation of Butler's claim that reality, in so far as it is not reducible to language, is ontologically independent of language, in other words, that language does not determine the ontological limits of reality? And, hence, that the charge of linguistic monism is refuted? I think we may because Butler, in a recent Dutch interview (1997), dispels the ambiguity that clings to many passages on this topic in *Bodies That Matter* by explicating her position as a "post linguistic turn" Kantian position: "the ontological claim can never fully capture its object, and this view makes me somewhat different from Foucault and aligns me temporarily with the Kantian tradition as it has been taken up by Derrida. The 'there is' gestures toward a referent it cannot capture, because the referent is not fully built up in language, is not the same as the linguistic effect. There is no access to it outside of the linguistic effect, but the linguistic effect is not the same as the referent that it fails to capture."[4]

In whatever way language constructs reality, no construction nor all constructions together can ever fully capture it. With a linguistic turn of Kant, Butler says that the reach of language and, hence, the reach of knowledge is limited: the signifying processes of language always leave, as it were, an ontological remainder. But if language does not determine the ontological limits of reality, it does determine the epistemological limits of access to reality. According to Butler, there is no access to reality without language. This epistemological assumption is more strict than the one which follows from the first claim I discussed for it implies that language conditions not only the intelligibility of reality but also its accessibility. I have my doubts about this assumption. Positing language in both cases as condition, it implicitly equates intelligibility and accessibility. Yet isn't the reach of the latter wider than the reach of the former? Can't we have access to phenomena we do not understand?

Intelligibility and Accessibility

Whereas everything that is intelligible to us is also accessible to us, the reverse is not true. Phenomena that are intelligible to us are phenomena we do understand in some way or other. At the most basic level, understanding something means being able to name or to refer to it. As the capacity to name or to refer or, in general, to articulate, implies that one has some notion of the meaning of the words used, understanding is always mediated by language. To equate intelligibility and accessibility would mean that we cannot have access to phenomena we do not understand, that is, phenomena we cannot articulate. That does not seem plausible. By following the hermeneutic model of understanding, I will try to show that we can have access to phenomena we do not understand, i.e., cannot articulate, though this access is not completely independent of linguistically mediated understanding.

In daily life, our behavior and actions are guided by a mostly implicit understanding of the world we inhabit, an understanding which is based upon the ways in which this world is semantically constructed. Even so, our daily routines are every now and then slightly, and sometimes profoundly, disrupted because we are confronted with people, situations, actions, images, texts, things, bodily sensations, et cetera that defy our understanding. These confrontations or encounters are enabled by the context of habitual understanding.[5] To become aware of something we do not understand, we need a context of what we do understand.[6] By giving access to what we do not understand, the context of habitual understanding does, as it were, indicate its own limits. We register these limits not simply as a lack of understanding but, more precisely, as a lack of our capacity to articulate. The nagging feeling or awareness of something we cannot put in words is nothing unusual. This fact of everyday life implies that the range of accessibility is wider than, though not independent of, the range of intelligibility. Whereas the latter more or less coincides with our linguistic capacities, the former indicates that these capacities do not (fully) determine our awareness of, and contact with reality.

The Body as "Demand in and for Language"

Mostly, in *Bodies That Matter*, I get the impression that Butler implicitly equates intelligibility and accessibility. However, there are some passages in *Bodies That Matter* that suggest a wider, more phenomenological notion of accessibility. The most intriguing one is to be found in the context of a subtle reinterpretation of Freud's notion of the bodily ego and Lacan's mirror stage. In this context, Butler examines the indissolubility of the psychic and the corporeal. The psyche is to be understood "as that which constitutes the mode by which [the] body is given, the condition and contour of that givenness. [But] the materiality of the body ought not to be conceptualized as a unilateral or causal *effect* of the psyche in any sense that would reduce that materiality to the psyche or make of the psyche the monistic stuff out of which that materiality is produced and/or derived" (66).

Butler's use of the phenomenological terms "given" and "givenness" reveals how we are to understand the indissolubility of the psychic and the corporeal. Givenness is always transitive, it is always givenness *to*. Hence, by itself, givenness implies the interdependence of two instances: something which gives itself and something to which this givenness is given. In more concrete terms, the body can only give itself if there is something, i.e., the psyche, to which it gives itself. But if the givenness of the body is dependent on the psyche, the converse is also true. The psyche cannot constitute the mode and contour of this givenness without the body giving itself. It would, as it were, have nothing to work upon. Thus, the indissolubility of the psychic and the corporeal refers to the mutual dependence, not simply of body and psyche but, rather, of a body which gives itself, that is, which somehow signals its presence, and a psyche which receives, translates, and transforms these signals.

The phenomenological conception of the body as that which gives itself or signals its presence, denotes, what might be called, the persisting dynamic materiality of the body. Now, with respect to the notion of the body as persisting materiality Butler has something very interesting to say: "We might want to claim that what persists . . . is the 'materiality' of the body. But perhaps we will have fulfilled the same function, and opened up some others, if we claim that what persists here is *a demand in and for language,* a 'that which' which prompts and occasions, say, within the domain of science, calls to be explained, described, diagnosed, altered or within the cultural fabric of lived experience, fed, exercised, mobilized, put to sleep, a site of enactments and passions of various kinds. To insist upon this demand, this site, as the 'that without which' no psychic operation can proceed, but also as that on which and through which the psyche also operates, is to begin to circumscribe that which is invariably and persistently the psyche's site of operation; not the blank slate or the passive medium upon which the psyche acts, but, rather, the constitutive demand that mobilizes psychic action from the start . . ." (67).

Persisting materiality or, in my terms, the body that signals its presence, is interpreted here as a demand in and for language. Though maybe strange at first sight, a plausible explanation can be given; an explanation moreover, that has some interesting practical consequences. The body that signals its presence is the accessible body, but not necessarily the intelligible body. In so far as they are not intelligible, these signals might be registered as a lack of the capacity to articulate. The feeling of lack however, often is accompanied by the urge to fulfill the lack: the lack of language turns into a demand for language. *In* language, that is, in our linguistic existence, a demand *for* language may manifest itself. This demand for language is the urge to articulate, hence understand, the unintelligible.

Thus, the body that makes itself felt as a demand in and for language is, in my explanation, the—as yet—unintelligible body. The body is unintelligible insofar as it exceeds not only, in general, the limits of the linguistically constructed body but, more specifically, the limits of the sexed, gendered, and sexualized body. This specification is important for sex, gender, and sexuality are anything but neutral categories. The construction of the sexed, gendered, and sexualized body is, at least partly, regulated by oppressive norms among which, as Butler rightly stresses, the norm of heterosexuality. If the intelligible body is a body that is sexed, gendered and sexualized according to (oppressive) norms, then not only our understanding but also our lived experience of the body will be permeated by these norms. What they prescribe often will be understood and lived as natural and, hence, inevitable "facts of human life." But lived experience is not restricted to the intelligible body. If it were, it would be hard to explain why and how, for instance, a teenager who has grown up in a community that considers heterosexuality as a natural fact feels desires that don't fit this fact. If accessibility were restricted to the intelligible body, it would be very hard indeed to explain phenomena like this. It is exactly because we have access to the unintelligible body with its, sometimes, unintelligible desires that we not only may come to feel ill at ease with the intelligible body but also may come to conceive of, for instance, heterosexuality as an oppressive norm.

The Unintelligible Body as Critical Force and Creative Resource

There are two reasons why I think it is important to distinguish between intelligibility and accessibility. First, we need this distinction in order to explain why aspects of the intelligible body may be experienced as not fitting and even oppressive. Experiences of this kind presuppose the awareness of an alternative. If accessibility were restricted to the intelligible body, access to an alternative experience of the body would simply be impossible. The second reason has to do with motives and resources for criticizing and changing oppressive aspects of the intelligible body. Access to what exceeds the intelligible body might be a powerful motive and resource for criticism and change. In other words, the unintelligible body may come to function as a creative resource and critical force. Manifesting itself as a demand in and for language, the unintelligible body may mobilize us to articulate new meanings and new discursive practices with respect to the body. The signals of the unintelligible body and their demand may, if we are responsive to them, initiate an effort of articulation that is not only creative but also critical insofar as it challenges oppressive norms that regulate the intelligibility of the body.

Though inspired by Butler's characterization of the body as a demand in and for language, this interpretation of the unintelligible body is incompatible with the epistemological position Butler, in general, defends. If language determines the limits of accessibility then access is restricted to what we can name, articulate, and, in a basic sense, understand. What it comes down to is that this epistemological position precludes the possibility of (pre)conscious experience of the unintelligible body. This conclusion is confirmed by the psychoanalytical interpretational scheme which dominates *Bodies That Matter*. According to this scheme, the normative standards of sex, gender, and sexuality which regulate the intelligibility of the body initiate the psychic operation of repudiating and abjecting the unintelligible body, thereby excluding it from the realm of (pre)conscious experience. Though this psychoanalytical interpretation makes sense in specific cases, as a generalized interpretational scheme applied to Western culture as a whole, as Butler tends to do, it is, in my opinion, both empirically implausible and politically self defeating.[7] The force of normative standards is not always and everywhere the same nor are the circumstances and backgrounds of individuals the same. Depending on these two variable factors, psychic reaction with respect to the unintelligible body may vary from, indeed, repudiation and abjection to acceptance and even celebration. The political consequences of the generalized scheme are more serious. Though Butler stresses the subversive potential of the abjected, unintelligible body, it is the kind of subversion that is not likely to change anything for the better. What is excluded from consciousness does not disappear, on the contrary, it haunts conscious experience and it does, indeed, exert a subversive pressure on intelligible reality. But to what good? Unless we can take control of it, its very subversiveness will lead either to defensive reactions, hence it will consolidate the normative standards which regulate the intelligible body, or, quite simply, to mental and/or emotional breakdown, hence to suffering instead of change for the better. Only if the unintelligible body is accessible to (pre)conscious experience and conscious efforts of articulation, its subversive potential may turn into the positive potential of critical force and creative resource.

To sum up, it is not only the resolution of the problem of linguistic monism but, rather, the phenomenological notion of accessibility which, in my opinion, validates Butler's theory of the body as a useful contribution to feminist and queer theory. However the tendency, reinforced by psychoanalytical interpretation, to equate accessibility and intelligibility or, in other words, to restrict (pre)conscious experience to the intelligible, is debilitating for such a theory. It leaves us with a body the intelligibility of which can neither be contested nor transformed by our own experiences of the body. That, to me, does not only seem implausible but also depressing.

Determinism: The Question of Agency and Power

It is clear from certain passages in *Bodies That Matter* that Butler *assumes* a viable and defensible conception of agency, but the theoretical framework on the basis of which this conception of agency can be accounted for is plainly deficient in at least one respect and very obscure in other respects. What is the conception of agency Butler assumes? In chapter four she says that "drag is subversive to the extent that it reflects on the imitative structure by which hegemonic gender is itself produced and disputes heterosexuality's claim on naturalness and originality"(125). In the last chapter she describes queer politics as a laying claim to terms "through which we insist on politicizing identity and desire" and as "a self-critical dimension within activism" (227).

"Reflection," "dispute," "laying claim to terms," and "self-criticism" require an intentional and reflective subject, a subject that is capable of deliberate and purposive action. An explicitly elaborated conception of such a subject, however, is not to be found in *Bodies That Matter*. The reason for this omission, it seems to me, is that Butler apparently fears that this conception of the subject will reintroduce the ghost of the humanist subject, fully capable of self-determination and self-creation. The latter, however, does not necessarily follow from the former. On the contrary. The conception of an intentional, reflective subject, capable of deliberate and purposive action, can be fully compatible with the poststructuralist notion of a subject implicated in chains of signification and relations of power that it cannot (fully) control, i.e., the notion Butler works with. The general problem with Butler's theoretical framework is that its conceptualization of the relation between language and subject is too restrictive. The relation typically is described as a unilateral one, in which the subject appears as being formed and constructed by language. Consequently, it is difficult to see how this subject can be capable of the kind of action Butler, typically, attributes to it, namely resignifying the significations that have formed this subject.

Apart from poststructuralist linguistic theory, another important theoretical source of Butler's notion of agency is Foucaultian theory of power. Inspired by this theory, Butler characterizes agency as a practice of rearticulation or resignification that is "immanent to power" and not in "a relation of external opposition to power" (15). Agency is "*implicated* in the very relations of power it seeks to rival," it is a "turning of power against itself to produce alternative modalities of power, to establish a kind of political contestation that is not a 'pure' opposition, a 'transcendence' of contemporary relations of power, but a difficult labor of forging a future from resources inevitably impure" (241). Apart from the question how to interpret it, the reader cannot but be struck by the relentless "antihumanist" idiom (Fraser, 1995, 67) in which Butler's conception of agency is couched. Despite its opposite rhetorical effect, however, the antihumanist idiom should not be taken as a symptom of the, maybe unwitting, reduction or evacuation of agency. Though the Foucaultian framework tends to obscure the role of agency, it is possible to distill a politically engaged account of agency from Butler's text.

Language and Subject

Butler conceives of language as a process of reiteration carried forward, as it were, by the (re)citations of subjects. The speaking of subjects is recast as citing. There is nothing bizarre about this for every word we utter is, quite literally, a citation. As nobody, no single subject, invents by itself the language it speaks, its speaking is rather like a borrowing, a citing, from an already existing vocabulary. To be able to speak, however, does not simply mean that one is able to cite words but rather that one is able to apply the rules or conventions that regulate the use, i.e., the meaning, of words. Thus, while citing words, we at the same time cite the conventions that regulate the use of those words.

In *Bodies That Matter*, the possibility of agency is consistently, and correctly I think, located in the process of reiteration: recitations can be resignifications. Yet, if we look more closely into the way the process of reiteration is conceptualized, the possibility of agency seems to evaporate. The process of reiteration, as Butler time and again insists, can be both stabilizing and destabilizing, in the latter case opening up possibilities of agency. The idea of destabilization may look promising, but what exactly does it mean? The process of reiteration is not a process of simple repetition. Derrida, from whom Butler borrows her notion of iterability, is very clear on this. Every citation implies, by itself, a shift: the words I am citing here and now, are cited in a temporal and spatial setting that is necessarily different from former or later citations elsewhere of the same words. These inevitable temporal and spatial shifts, in short: contextual shifts, are at the same time shifts of meaning.[8] The citation of the word "woman" in one context can signify something completely different, slightly different, or anything in between, but never *exactly* the same, as the citation of the same word in another context. Because of the continuous shift of meaning, the process of reiteration is a process of change which can be either stabilizing or destabilizing, that is, reinforcing or undermining signifying conventions. Yet, the point is that the continuous (de)stabilizing shift of meaning is completely independent of any acts or intentions on the part of the subject who does the citing. It inheres in the very movement of language itself, its "temporalization" and "spatialization" as Derrida calls it, a movement that is carried forward but not controlled by the citations of subjects.[9]

Though the question of agency is, at best, still open, what this conception of language does achieve is the deconstruction of certain determinist consequences of the structuralist conception of language. The latter typically identifies certain structures, for instance the structural interplay of castration and phallus in Lacan, as invariable, unchanging structures that determine to a certain extent the shifting signifying chains of language. As the movement of the signifying chains of language is always completely contingent, Butler's Derridean conception of language effectively undermines the determinist result of the structuralist conception.[10] But deconstruction of structuralist determinism does not, by itself, imply that room is made for a viable notion of agency. This requires at least that the subject is not only the carrier of the process of reiteration, but also a possible participant in this process.[11] The trouble with Butler's account of the relation between language and subject is, as I said above, that almost invariably the subject is cast as being constructed and reconstructed by the signifying chains of language. The subject is not completely passive, for its activity of citing is a necessary condition of its (re)construction. Therefore Butler legitimately can claim that the process of (re)construction is not simply undergone by the subject (3). Yet again, this does not add up to a viable notion of agency.

Butler's Derridean conception of language does not simply exclude the possibility of agency. Though often it is understood as precluding the possibility of intentionality,[12] it, in fact, does not imply that we do not intend certain meanings when we speak or act. The point is rather, that our intentions do not effectively control or *decide* the meaning of words and (speech)acts. The individual subject does not, and cannot, decide the meaning of words and (speech)acts, including its own, for two reasons. On the one hand, the subject always already finds itself in a language with more or less established signifying conventions. When we learn to speak, we learn to apply those conventions and when we have become proficient speakers, our speech still has to be more or less compatible with those conventions in order to be intelligible, not only to others but also to ourselves. Yet, there is room for initiative here: we can, intentionally, try to deflect or guide the signifying conventions or chains we are citing in a certain direction, aiming at the resignification, the shift of meaning, that is our goal. This initiative, on the other hand, does not imply that our intentions can control the future course of these signifying chains, can decide the future meaning of the words that are being cited. But neither does it imply that the initiative or intervention on the part of the subject never leaves a trace. It does leave a trace, and it may be effective in the long run, when the initiative is picked up by other subjects who continue the deflecting course of the signifying chain.

Explicated thus, the Derridean, i.e., Butlerean, conception of language is fully compatible with a, in my opinion, realistic notion of agency. While doing away with the misguided idea that the subject is capable of complete self-determination and full control over language, it retains what I take as the quintessence of agency: the possibility of initiative or intervention; a possibility that is both dependent on the past, i.e., established conventions, and at mercy, as it were, of the future, but nevertheless a possibility that may effect desired changes if—and this "if" indicates a necessary condition—the initiative is picked up by others.[13]

Power and Agency

Agency, Butler says, is implicated in the very relations of power it seeks to rival. Though it is not easy to get a clearer picture of the, in a literal sense, ambivalent relation of agency and power, a discussion of the main characteristics of power in Butler's text may shed some light both on her concept of power and its relation to agency.

Schematizing, one can discern four related characteristics: power is discursive, reiterative, productive, and exclusionary. Roughly speaking, the first two characteristics locate the domain of power and specify the way it works, whereas the last two explicate the effects of power. Power is located in discourses and discursive practices, more specifically in the conventions that constitute and regulate these discourses and practices. In terms of agency this implies the following. In order to speak and act intelligibly, I will have to comply, to some extent, with the conventions that regulate the use, i.e., the meaning, of words and that constitute the particular practices in which I participate. I cannot, for instance, act intelligibly as a teacher without, to some degree, following the conventions that constitute the practice of teaching. Precisely because one has to comply with, in Butler's terms: recite them in order to speak and act intelligibly, conventions are binding or normative. As such, conventions are both constraining and enabling: they enable us to speak and act intelligibly *exactly in so far* as they constrain us.[14] Thus, in so far as it is enabled and constrained by the conventions that constitute and regulate the domain of intelligible discourse and practice, agency is enabled and constrained by discursive power.

The Derridean notion of iterability highlights the temporal and contingent aspect of discursive power. Iterability is a necessary condition of conventions: conventions are only conventions in so far as they are not unique but, on the contrary, reiterated or recited over and over again by many people. Hence, if conventions are reiterable, so is discursive power. More precisely, power is located not so much in the conventions themselves, i.e., in their content, but rather in their reiteration. We have seen already that reiteration is a process, not of repetition, but of perpetual and contingent shifts. These shifts are contingent in so far as they inhere in the reiterative process itself and, hence, are not due to purposive, intentional agency. Because of (the accumulation of) contingent shifts in its reiterative course, conventions may either get consolidated or extenuated, stabilized or destabilized. Thus, whatever the content of a specific convention, its power increases or decreases as its reiteration consolidates or extenuates the convention in question. In terms of agency, the reiterative aspect of power implies, first, that we will be able to influence the power of conventions only in so far as we participate—instead of merely being implicated—in its reiterative course for only then we have a chance to intervene; and, second, that the success of our interventions always will remain dependent on the, in principle, incalculable future course of the reiterative chains or, in general, on the incalculable effects of our interventions.

Whereas in liberal politics and also in everyday usage the term "power" is associated with the effects of prohibition and repression, Butler stresses the productive and exclusionary effects of power. Power is productive in the sense that the reiteration of conventions brings into being or materializes what these conventions specify: we perceive reality through the sedimented "grid" of signifying conventions. For instance, the reiterative power of the convention or norm of binary sex/gender differentiation produces or materializes bodies that are either male or female.[15] Yet, in so far as it is productive, power is also and at the same time exclusionary. If the reiterative power of the sex/gender norm produces bodies that are either male or female, then, simultaneously, it excludes any other type of body from the domain of social and symbolic intelligibility. Generally speaking, the reiteration of conventions both produces the intelligible and, at the same time, excludes the unintelligible. Hence, reiterative discursive power constitutes both the intelligible and the unintelligible. Explicated in terms of agency, the import of the productive and exclusionary effect of power is more or less tautological. If reiterative discursive power enables and constrains speech and action, i.e., agency, then another way of saying this is that it produces intelligible speech and actions while excluding those actions and utterances which are unintelligible.

The explication of the role of agency I have given thus far is meant to demonstrate that Butler's reliance on poststructuralist Foucaultian theory and its antihumanist idiom does not lead to the reduction or evacuation of agency. What is not yet clear, however, is why we would seek to rival the power in which we are implicated. Why would we try "to turn power against itself"? For what reasons or motives would we contest (the effects of) discursive power?

Political Contestability

On first sight the above explication of power does not seem to give any clear indications whether or why power may be politically contestable. The mere fact that discursive power is constraining and exclusionary cannot be held against it,[16] for if it were not it would not be enabling and productive either. Constraint and enablement, exclusion and production, are, as it were, two sides of the same coin. Discursive power enables intelligible speech and action only in so far as it constrains agency, i.e., excludes the unintelligible. Unless the distinction between the intelligible and the unintelligible is given up altogether, both sides belong together. To criticize this distinction simply because of its constraining and exclusionary implications does not really make sense for it is constitutive of agency. At least, I do not see how any realistic account of what it means to be able to speak and act can do without it.

Yet, even though the distinction *itself* between the intelligible and the unintelligible is irreducible, every specific instance of it is contingent and, hence, contestable. Any specific demarcation of the intelligible from the unintelligible is contingent because it cannot but rely on conventions which are contingent or arbitrary themselves. Apart from the contingency inherent in the process of reiteration, from the viewpoint of reflective agency as well, conventions are, in principle, arbitrary: we cannot provide them with a conclusive foundation or justification. No matter how well established or how well argued, no foundation or justification can ever succeed in turning conventions into necessary rules without alternative. It is always possible, in principle, to conceive of an alternative to any specific convention, and consequently to contest its constraints and exclusions and to reinterpret its demarcation of the intelligible and the unintelligible. For example, despite its long tradition and its scientific justification, it is not difficult at all to think up several alternatives to the convention of binary sex/gender differentiation: plural sex/gender differentiations are conceivable or, conversely, the conception of just one sex or gender. These alternative conceptions involve a reinterpretation of the body as we know it. What is unintelligible now might become intelligible and vice versa. Heterosexuality for instance, would lose its self-evident and maybe also its intelligible character whereas bodies that are neither male nor female would become intelligible.[17]

Thus, because of the irreducible contingency of any specific convention discursive power is, in principle, always contestable. The question, however, why we would contest the power of any specific convention is still open. Merely its contingency, i.e., the mere fact that it is possible to contest a convention, is no reason to actually contest it. Butler's discussion of the so called "law of sex" suggests that it is the *hegemony* of a convention which provides a reason to contest it. She uses the expression "law of sex" to indicate the hegemonic status of the conventions or norms that make up this law, i.e., heterosexuality and binary sex/gender differentiation. The introduction of the term "hegemonic" implies a certain hierarchy with respect to the relative force of conventions, namely hegemonic or dominant conventions as the most forceful and minor or subordinate conventions as the weakest. The relative force of a convention affects its power. Whereas the power of hegemonic conventions tends to be *compelling*, the power of minor conventions leaves more room for choice.

From Butler's discussion of the law of sex throughout *Bodies That Matter*, I infer that the power of hegemonic conventions is compelling in so far as it determines subject status. In order to qualify for and maintain the status of subject, one has to comply with, i.e., recite, the law of sex. In other words, compliance with the law of sex is a necessary condition for subject status.[18] Whereas noncompliance with minor conventions, for instance the conventions which regulate the practice of teaching, will not disqualify me as a subject but, in this case, as a teacher, non-compliance with the law of sex results in deprivation of subject status. Those who do not comply are degraded to the status of "abjects": "those who do not enjoy the status of the subject" (3), who do not qualify as "fully human" (16), and whose bodies do not matter.

Whereas hegemonic conventions specify the necessary conditions of subject status, nonhegemonic conventions specify the many variations and forms of subjecthood. Within the confines circumscribed by hegemonic conventions, the wide variety of nonhegemonic conventions allows many different ways to shape our identity as a subject or actor. As long as we comply with hegemonic conventions our words and deeds will be acknowledged, even if they are unintelligible. Not the mere fact that every now and then my words and actions are unintelligible disqualifies me as a subject but, rather, the persistent failure to embody and realize those features of subjecthood or humanness which are deemed to be "essential." To be disqualified, to be an "abject," means that one's words and deeds will be ignored or dismissed, not because they are in or by themselves unintelligible, but because they "emanate" from an unintelligible, unthinkable, and even threatening being; a being whose claim to intelligibility and subject status I cannot acknowledge without jeopardizing my own secure status as a subject.

As it results in deprivation of subject status, the exclusions effected by hegemonic conventions are dehumanizing and violent. It is the very violence of their exclusionary power that provides a good reason to contest and oppose hegemonic conventions. But what exactly can we achieve, given Butler's concept of power and agency, if we contest and oppose the power of hegemonic conventions, in this case the norms that make up the law of sex? Agency is a "turning of power against itself to produce other modalities of power," that is, it cannot annihilate power. We cannot simply abolish these norms, we can only undermine their hegemony by resignifying them in such a way that neither heterosexuality nor binary sex/gender differentiation designate natural or essential humanness. What we may achieve through resignifications of this kind is a less exclusive definition of subject status, a definition which includes the "abjects." Never however, can we achieve a totally inclusive definition for "the ideal of a radical inclusivity is impossible" though Butler adds that "this very impossibility nevertheless governs the political field as an idealization of the future that motivates the expansion, linking, and perpetual production of political subject-positions and signifiers"(193).

The Political Ideal of Radical Inclusivity

Butler's argument concerning the political ideal of radical inclusivity is somewhat paradoxical: we have to strive for something we will never achieve. Why is radical inclusivity impossible? Why would we be motivated by an ideal we cannot realize? In what sense does radical inclusivity function as a positive political ideal?

Total or radical inclusivity is impossible because no category can be all-inclusive. Unless they are completely empty or meaningless, categories cannot but have exclusionary effects. To be intelligible at all, the category of "the subject" or "the human" has to be interpreted, i.e., assigned some meaning, and it is this very interpretation which will produce exclusionary effects. Even when it is very broad or abstract, no interpretation can ever be all-inclusive. It always will foreground one or several signification possibilities at the (implicit) expense of other possibilities. However, "even if every discursive formation is produced through exclusion, that is not to claim that all exclusions are equivalent" (207). Only the violent ones are problematic, that is, the exclusions produced by hegemonic conventions, i.e., interpretations. If we cannot simply abolish discursive power and its exclusionary effects, we can, Butler suggests, change its modality or force. In the process of resignification we may undermine the compelling force of hegemonic conventions or interpretations and, consequently, reduce the violence, if not the exclusionarity, of discursive power.

Moreover, it would be politically undesirable to reduce the exclusionary effects of noncompulsive discursive power. As I indicated above, it is the non-hegemonic conventions which enable the differentiation of specific subject-positions or identities. These differentiations are in a neutral, almost tautological way exclusionary: being a teacher, philosopher, and feminist for instance, excludes numerous other possible positions or trajectories I could, in principle, have chosen or in which I could have happened to end up. Actually, because of the negative connotations of the term "exclusion(ary)," it would be more helpful and adequate to speak of the *differentiating*, instead of exclusionary, effects of noncompulsive discursive power. It is obvious that radical inclusivity in the sense of a complete reduction of all differentiations would make for a very dubious political ideal. The political condition that comes closest to realizing radical inclusivity in this sense is, in fact, totalitarianism. In the definition of Hannah Arendt totalitarianism refers to the destruction of plurality, i.e., the differences constituted by speech and action. I suppose it is this totalitarian reduction of plurality that Butler has in mind when she says "that there can be no final or complete inclusivity . . . and that, for democratic reasons, ought never be" (221).

Butler nevertheless offers radical inclusivity as a positive political ideal. But she does this in the context of a critical political diagnosis of the world we live in: a world in which hegemonic conventions determine who is to count as a subject and who is not. In this context, to strive for total inclusivity means to strive for a radical democratic world, that is, a world that is not regulated anymore by hegemonic conventions, in which everyone is entitled to the status of subject. Yet, even though it is a positive political ideal, Butler is wary of presenting radical democracy simply as an achievable goal. To become an achievable goal, the ideal of radical democracy has to be translated in a political program or movement: the abstract, as it were, empty universality of total inclusivity is translated into a concrete, meaningful universality, for instance the concrete universality of human rights. Though inevitable if the ideal is to be effective, the translation has its price for it cannot fail to be exclusionary and contestable. If radical democracy is simply taken as an achievable goal, ideal and translation get conflated. What gets lost in the conflation is the irreducible and critical distance between abstract and concrete universality, between the idea (l) of total inclusivity and its inevitably exclusionary and contestable translation. Because of the lack of critical distance the translation becomes self-evident, uncontestable, in short: hegemony, and the violence of its exclusions, will be ignored, excused, or, most likely, remain invisible. In other words, without the critical distance between ideal and translation, the ideal of radical democracy, like any other ideal of a "perfect world," may turn into its opposite.[19] To prevent the conflation of ideal and translation, radical democracy should be taken, not as an achievable goal but, rather, as a regulatory idea in the Kantian sense. As such it enjoins us to both act *as if* total inclusivity is realizable in the future and, at the same time, contest here and now any (violent) exclusions effected in its name.

From the general argument concerning radical inclusivity a valuable lesson can be drawn for feminist politics. In so far as it invokes the category of "women" feminist politics seems to face a dilemma. On the one hand, it cannot but rely on this category if it is to have a basis for solidarity and empowerment. On the other hand, not even the most politically correct, multiculturalist specification of identities can fulfill the promise of inclusivity this category holds out. On the contrary, if anything, politically correct identity politics seems to evoke rather than assuage recriminations of exclusion and lack of recognition. Instead of empowerment and solidarity, a "politicing of identity" (117) is the result. We seem to be confronted with the dilemma of either giving up the category of "women" and, hence, the basis of feminist politics or resigning ourselves to proto-totalitarian identity politics. However, if we take the category of "woman" as a regulative idea (l) rather than an actual representation of all women, the dilemma is resolved. This means that we have "to learn a double movement: to invoke the category and, hence, provisionally to institute an identity and at the same time to open the category as a site of permanent political contest" (222). Only if we do not forget that the idea of total inclusivity is not realizable as such and, hence, that the category of "women" is permanently open to different interpretations, the invocation of this category may enable solidarity and empower feminist politics.

Notes

1. Cf. the Introduction of *Bodies That Matter* (1993, 1–23).

2. Cf. Susan Hekman's characterization of *Bodies That Matter* as a "theoretical metaphysics of the body" (1995, 151). With respect to the charge of linguistic monism, this characterization can be specified as a linguistic metaphysics of the body.

3. Cf. *Sein und Zeit*, paragraph 7, especially section C (Heidegger, [1927], 1977)

4. Cf. Costera Meijer and Prins (1997, 26). I have quoted the original English version of the interview which was published in the Dutch *Tijdschrift voor Vrouwenstudies* (Journal of Women Studies). In 1998 an English version of this interview appeared in *Signs*.

5. I am following here one of the basic presuppositions of the hermeneutic tradition as established by Heidegger ([1926] 1977) and taken up, in different ways, by Gadamer ([1960] 1975) and Habermas ([1981] 1988). According to Heidegger, implicit habitual understanding—which, to a large extent, he considers to be of a practical nature in the sense that it is a "knowing how" rather than "knowing that"—of the world we inhabit provides the context, not only of our explicit, i.e., for instance scientific or philosophical, understanding, but also of our encounter with phenomena we don't understand.

6. This does not mean that phenomena which are without context in this sense, hence, which are in no way linguistically mediated, are completely inaccessible. Rather, I consider them as limiting cases. Especially with respect to the body, one can think of the following examples. The infant who lacks language, c.q. linguistically mediated understanding, still has access to its body in a variety of ways. Though this access is not without context, it is a sensory rather than a linguistically mediated context. Another, related example is our sensory experience of the matter of bodies or other material things. Matter can be touched, sniffed, or tasted and sometimes it is quite difficult to articulate our sense of smell, taste, or touch. Though these senses definitely give us access to matter, they function partially independent of language. As numerous biologists and psychologists have pointed out recently, the reason for this lies in different evolutionary stadia of development of brain capacities. In evolutionary terms, these senses are much older than the capacity to speak. They are regulated by the old part of the brain whereas linguistic capacities are located in the cortex, the new part of the brain.

7. I am referring here to Butler's theory of subject constitution which is based on a politicized reinterpretation of Lacanian theory. According to Butler "the forming of a subject requires an identification with the normative phantasm of "sex," and this identification takes place through a repudiation which produces a domain of abjection, a repudiation without which the subject cannot emerge." (1993, 3) The repudiation concerns the body in so far as it does not qualify "for life within the domain of cultural intelligibility" (1993, 2), i.e., is not intelligible according to the normative standards of heterosexuality and binary sex/gender differentiation. As far as I can see, this view implies that one cannot be a subject without being homophobic. Apart from the psychoanalytical context, the question of abjection has important political implications to which I will return in the next section.

8. Derrida does not rely on the Wittgensteinian notion of rules or conventions, but on the (adapted) Saussurian paradigm that meaning is generated by the differences between signs (words) Thus, context shifts will result in shifts of meaning. From a

Wittgensteinian viewpoint however, you also can reach this conclusion. As the relation between rules, c q conventions, and instances is anything but determinate, the idea of contextual shifts of meaning is as much part of Wittgenstein's theory of language as it is of Derrida's.

9. Cf. Derrida, "*La différance*" in *Marges de la philosophie* (Paris, 1972), 3–29, esp. 8. The neologism *différance* refers to the temporalizing and spatializing movement of language, a movement that differentiates signs and consequently generates meaning. Meaning therefore, is not a mental image or, in general, a creation of consciousness, but rather the uncontrollable, ephemeral product of the differentiating movement of language itself.

10. Cf. for instance chapter two ("The lesbian phallus") of *Bodies That Matter* for a convincing deconstruction of the phallus as the privileged signifier of the symbolic order.

11. Cf. Allison Weir who makes a similar point in *Sacrificial Logics. Feminist Theory and the Critique of Identity* (New York and London 1996), 127.

12. Like Derrida, Butler does not exclude intentionality but she fails to explicate its function with respect to agency. Commenting a quotation in which Derrida mentions the place of intentionality, Butler says: "In other words, when words engage actions or constitute themselves a kind of action, they do this not because they reflect the power of an individual's will or intention, but because they draw upon and reengage conventions which have gained their power precisely through a *sedimented iterability*. The category of 'intention' indeed, the notion of 'the doer' will have its place, but this place will no longer be 'behind' the deed as its enabling source. If the subject . . . is performatively constituted, then it follows that this will be a constitution *in time*, and that the 'I' and the 'we' will be neither fully determined by language nor radically free to instrumentalize language as an external medium " (Butler, 1995, 134–135).

To suggest that "the place" of the intentional subject should be located somewhere between being fully determined by language and being radically free to instrumentalize language is stating the obvious. What I have not found in Butler is an explication of, precisely, this (limited) place and function of intentionality within the context of her theory of language.

13. This notion of agency is in fact inspired by Hannah Arendt's conception of (political) action. The two distinguishing features of action Arendt (1958) stresses are spontaneity or initiative, and, what she calls, "acting in concert." An act performed completely by myself, without any witnesses, will simply disappear. That is why we, as actors, always need others: as witnesses and co-actors.

14. The observation that conventions enable only in so far as they constrain I owe to Fraser who elucidates this point in her admirable—for its clarity—analysis of Foucault's concept of power (Fraser, 1989, 31)

15. The productive effect of power is emphasized in Butler's newly coined notion of performativity. Performativity should be understood "not as the act by which a subject brings into being what she/he names, but, rather, as that reiterative power of discourse to produce the phenomena that it regulates and constrains" (1993, 2). Instead of performance in the theatrical or restricted linguistic sense (i.e., speech act theory), the notion of performativity refers to the discursive, reiterative, and productive aspect of power.

16. Cf. Fraser, 1989, 31.

17 One might of course object that the biological facts concerning reproduction provide conclusive evidence for binary sex differentiation. I would like to counter that objection with the following claims. First, facts are not, as it were, discovered "in the wild." Facts are constructed on the basis of selected and interpreted data; to be able to select and interpret data one needs a framework of established or paradigmatic conventions which enables and guides the selection and interpretation. Hence, if the

framework changes, so do, ultimately, the facts. Second, by themselves the scientific facts concerning reproduction provide evidence of only a specific sexual binarity, not of the overall binary differentiation of bodies and identities.

18. I am not referring to a necessary condition in the classical philosophical sense of term for hegemonic conventions, like any other convention, are still contingent. Therefore the necessity they entail is not absolute but relative or contin-gent: it is only effective during a certain period of time and within a certain social-cultural space and in comparison with other, nonhegemonic conventions.

19. The dangerous, in so far as it is uncritical, logic of political utopianism is a recurrent theme in the work of Arendt and Lyotard. Both point out that in the course of Western history the ideal of a heaven on earth, of a perfect world, invariably has ended in hell, in terror, or violence. The most (in)famous example is the Marxian ideal of an egalitarian and free society which turned into its totalitarian opposite in the communist states of Eastern Europe. Though their political theory differs in many other respects, both Arendt (1977) and Lyotard (1983) follow in the footsteps of Kant in explaining the loss of critical distance as the failure to recognize the heterogeneity of thinking and acting, of idea and reality. While it is possible to think the absolute, the perfect, the total, these ideas are not realizable as such for agency and the reality it constitutes are always bounded by contingency and plurality

Bibliography

Arendt, Hannah. *The Human Condition*. Chicago: University of Chicago Press, 1958.
————. *The Life of the Mind*. New York: Harcourt Brace Jovanovich Publishers, 1977.
Benhabib, Seyla. *Feminist Contentions. A Philosophical Exchange*. New York: Routledge, 1995.
Butler, Judith. *Gender Trouble. Feminism and the Subversion of Identity*. New York: Routledge, 1990.
————. *Bodies that Matter On the Discursive Limits of "Sex."* New York: Routledge, 1993.
Cornell, Drucilla.. *Feminist Contentions. A Philosophical Exchange*. New York: Routledge, 1995.
Costera Meijer, Irene. *"'Ik wil het bestaansrecht van abjecte lichamen afdwingen' Een interview met Judith Butler " Tijdschrift voor Vrouwenstudies* 18, no. 1 (1997): 22–33.
————. "How Bodies Come to Matter: An Interview with Judith Butler." *Signs* 23, no. 2 (1998): 275–286.
Derrida, Jacques. *Marges de la Philosophie*. Paris: Les éditions de Minuit, 1972.
Fraser, Nancy. *Unruly Practices Power, Discourse and Gender in Contemporary Social Theory*. Minneapolis: University of Minnesota Press, 1989.
Gadamer, Hans-Georg. *Wahrheit und Methode*. Tübingen: J.C.B. Mohr, [1960] 1975.
Habermas, Jürgen. *Theorie des Kommunikativen Handelns*. Frankfurt am Main: Suhrkamp Verlag, [1981] 1988
Heidegger, Martin. *Sein und Zeit*. Tübingen: Max Niemeyer Verlag, [1927] 1977.
Hekman, Susan Review of *Bodies That Matter*. *Hypatia* 10, no. 4 (1995): 151–156.
Kant, Immanuel. *Kritik der Reinen Vernunft*. Hamburg: Felix Meiner Verlag, [1781] 1971.
Lyotard, Jean-Francois. *Le Différend*. Paris: Les éditions de Minuit, 1983.
Prins, Baukje. *"'Ik wil het bestaansrecht van abjecte lichamen afdwingen.' Een interview met Judith Butler " Tijdschrift voor vrouwenstudies* 18, no. 1 (1997): 22–33.

————. "How Bodies Come to Matter: An Interview with Judith Butler." *Signs* 23, no. 2 (1998): 275–286.

Weir, Allison. *Sacrificial Logics. Feminist Theory and the Critique of Identity.* New York: Routledge, 1996.

Chapter 12

A Critique of Feminist Radical Constructivism

Saskia Wendel

There is hardly any experience as natural as experiencing the difference between the sexes and it was long considered utter nonsense to doubt its reality. Today, however, it can no longer be taken for granted. Simone de Beauvoir's famous saying "One is not born a woman, one becomes one" referred principally to socialization patterns and the assignment of roles, in other words to gender roles and not to sexual identity. In the meantime, radical constructivists such as, for example, Judith Butler have taken different paths: for them, sexual identity is also a product of a social and cultural construction process, and not gender roles alone.

In this essay I would like to show that constructivist theory, and thus the gender discussion, is not as new as it seems. I would like to illustrate this using Judith Butler's approach. Butler herself, her recipients, and her critics may quote, for example, Foucault, Nietzsche, and Kant as sources of her approach, but connecting lines can be drawn to a field of philosophical discussion that reaches even further back into the philosophical past. I am thinking of the nominalist-realist controversy. For sex was traditionally considered to be a general definition, a "universal." But what status does this general term have? Does it correspond to a reality independent of the mind? Or is it only a construct? This questioning of the reality of universals was at the core of the nominalist-realist controversy, and the debate on the status of sex and gender can accordingly be considered to be a continuation of the nominalist-realist controversy, with all the open questions and problems that this dispute involves. Butler's constructivist position can be compared to the nominalist position in the debate on universals. I would like to provide evidence for this hypothesis by comparing Butler's central themes with those of William of Ockham, the main exponent of nominalism in the middle ages. In the process I will briefly touch on George Berkeley's idealistic approach. I will close with a critical summary.

The Fundamentals of Ockhamian Nominalism

We know that the two "sides" in the debate on universals were described as "realism" and "nominalism." Ockham assumes a moderate and differentiated form of nominalism, that can be summarized as follows. Ockham commits himself ontologically to an identification of realities with singularity or individuality, only individual objects exist, individual substances: *"omnis substantia est una numero et singularis, quia omnis substantia vel est una res et non plures vel est plures res."*[1] This ontological commitment by Ockham conforms to his famous principle of economy, the so-called "Ockham's Razor": "Entities should not be multiplied without necessity" is how the principle of economy is often quoted.[2] The recognition of the reality of individual objects implies the fundamental recognition of materiality independent of the mind. Ockham's moderate nominalism is thus by no means synonymous with an extreme idealism as espoused by, say, Berkeley. We will briefly consider this difference again later [2]

We immediately recognize the reality of individuals by using intuitive recognition (*notitia intuitiva*) which Ockham differentiates from abstractive recognition (*notitia abstractiva*): *"notitia intuitiva rei est talis notitia, virtute cuius potest sciri, utrum res sit vel non, ita, quod, si res sit, statim intellectus iudicat eam esse et evidenter cognoscit eam esse, nisi forte impediatur propter imperfectionem illius notitiae."*[3] All recognition begins with intuitive recognition.[4] The stimulus for this intuitive recognition comes directly from the individual objects, without mediation by any *"species intelligibilis."*

Now the question of whether universals also exhibit a reality independent of the mind arises—beside or in individual objects. Ockham rejects this[6] and gives several reasons for this. For one thing, no individual can be made up of universals, because if it were so composed it would, strictly speaking, no longer be an individual.[7] For another thing, the assumption of universal entities leads not only to a simple doubling of the world but also to an unending regress. It therefore follows that universals are not objects, but designations and thus functions in predications. They fulfill this function within the framework of "abstractive recognition" that must be differentiated from the immediate, intuitive recognition of the reality of individual objects. For Ockham, realists have fallen into the language trap. General definitions may logically be necessary, but their essential function in predications in no way results in their reality or substantiality. General terms do not constitute objects independent of the mind, but are instead supposition termini, that can be representative of several individual objects.[8] Similarly, they cannot be, so to speak, "singled out" from sensory perception by abstraction. Thus Ockham breaks away from both representation and abstraction theories. Universals are given meaning through their use in language and not by corresponding to an object independent of the mind. However, universals are no *"ficta,"* as *"intentiones animae"* they possess a mental existence, an "*esse subiectivum*" as a quality of the intellect or soul. So they do indeed possess a reality, though only as an existence in the mind and not in the objects outside the mind.[9] So much for Ockham's position. Some consider George Berkeley's idealism and conceptualism to be the successor to Ockham's theory. Judith Butler is now often accused of idealism, and therefore I would like to briefly discuss Berkeley's idealistic position—though only with regard to Ockham's nominalistic position. Later I will show that Butler initially identifies more with Ockham's ideas than with Berkeley's extreme idealism, but that she subsequently came disturbingly closer to it with her negation of subjectivity, and the allied monopolization of discourse.

The Extreme Idealism of George Berkeley

Many connecting lines have been drawn between Ockham and Berkeley, some historians of philosophy ascribe conceptualism to both of them. Areas of common ground do, indeed, exist. For example, like Ockham, Berkeley criticized representation theory.[10] However, I believe there is a central difference: whereas Ockham saw only universals as mental realities but individual objects as realities independent of the mind, Berkeley came to deny the reality of individuals independent of the mind, too.[11] This leads to an idealistic monism, because for Berkeley the spirit is the only substance. Accordingly, Berkeley identifies things with ideas, for ultimately they are nothing other than ideas of the spiritual substance.[12] It's true that Berkeley also wrote that he had no doubt that the things really exist,[13] but however, he questioned the existence of material or corporeal substance.[14]

I am of the opinion that Butler's constructivism borrows parts of Ockham's nominalistic theory—without, however, admitting to it, perhaps even without being aware of it. For this reason I describe Butler's constructivism as a variant of nominalism, and accordingly I identify the debate on the construction of gender as the reincarnation of the nominalist-realist controversy within the framework of feminist theory. I would like to make this clear in the following section. It must be said, however, and I will try to clarify this too, that Butler radicalizes the nominalist position and, therefore, despite her attempts to dissociate herself from them, winds up in the domain of Berkeley's idealism.

Butler's Constructivism—a Theory between Nominalism and Idealism

While Ockham emphasizes that universals have no reality independent of the mind, Butler stresses that "gender" has no reality independent of language. Thus Butler clearly adopts a nominalist position vis-a-vis the nominalist-realist controversy. Critics of Butler, such as Barbara Duden, object to the negation of the body and corporeality.[15] Butler's argument against this criticism is that she does indeed assume the reality of individual bodies in order to avoid linguistic idealism or monism: "The body is not produced as a consequence of discourse or culture or any other monolithic source of 'construction' if by 'produced' we mean: 'caused by' or 'made from.' That a body lives, dies, breathes and ages is not disputed. The notion that these are all social and discursive practices does not, however, mean that these phenomena are fundamentally to be denied. It would be wrong if one were to equate 'construction' with what is 'artificial' or 'dispensable.'"[16] Or in another passage: "For surely bodies live and die; eat and sleep; feel pain, pleasure; endure illness and violence; and these 'facts,' one might skeptically proclaim, cannot be dismissed as mere construction. Surely there must be some kind of necessity that accompanies these primary and irrefutable experiences. And surely there is."[17]

On the other hand Butler also talks of the creation of the materiality of sexed bodies.[18] That could be interpreted as meaning that in the end Butler really does deny the reality of individual bodies, if she understands "materiality" to mean manufactured. But what does she really mean by "materiality"? Does she really mean the reality of individual objects or individual bodies? Or does she mean "material" in the sense of a general term as opposed perhaps to "spirit"? Butler's problem here is that her inexact use of terms leads to confusion. On the one hand, she calls for a complete return to the concept of material, but on the other hand material not imagined "as site or surface but as a process of materialization that stabilizes over time to produce the effect of boundary, fixity, and surface we call matter. That matter is always materialized has, I think, to be thought in relation to the productive and, indeed, materializing effects of regulatory power in the Foucaultian sense."[19] One cannot, according to Butler, postulate a materiality located outside language.[20]

In this passage I understand Butler to mean that she really does assume the reality of individual bodies that one could also describe as "materiality." But this materiality of individual bodies must be distinguished from what Butler understands as "material" in the sense of "materialization": "materialization" as a process, as something that "happens" to individual bodies. Accordingly, "the" material, as a monolithic substance that we perceive, does not exist, rather we "produce" "material" in this sense. In this it is important to differentiate between "materiality" as the reality of individual objects and "materialization." To quote Butler: "Neither of these essays [in *Bodies That Matter*] is meant to dispute the materiality of the body; on the contrary, together they constitute partial and overlapping genealogical efforts to establish the normative conditions under which the materiality of the body is framed and formed, and, in particular, how it is formed through differential categories of sex."[21]

In my opinion, this understanding of materiality conforms to Ockham's ontology of individual objects: individual bodies exist. Universals, on the other hand, and gender is one, are not entities, either detached from these bodies or in them. The materiality of gender is manufactured and not part of the materiality of the individual. Thus Butler initially shares the ontological commitment of nominalism toward the reality of the individual. In contrast to Ockham, however, no considerations on the form of the recognition of individual objects can be found in Butler; intuitive recognition of individual objects is of as little interest to her as abstractive recognition by means of universals.

Butler also shares Ockham's criticism of representation theory: sexed bodies do not predate recognition or language, they are created by language. And in the same way that Ockham, ultimately, finds that universals are not fictions but, as *"esse subiectivu,"* do indeed possess mental reality, so Butler also emphasizes that gender is no fiction but a linguistically created reality.

This nominalistic position is different from an extreme idealism, such as is found in Berkeley. Accordingly, it is only too understandable when Butler defends herself against the allegation that her approach is "linguistic idealism" or "linguistic monism." I believe, however, that Butler reverts to just such a linguistic monism or idealism and this is indicated by an important difference between Butler's and Ockham's approaches. Ockham speaks of a mental existence of universals and connects this to the intellect of the subject doing the recognizing. Thus for Ockham the recognition process presupposes an actively recognizing subject, in other words a bearer of the recognition process. We recognize the existence of individual things intuitively, and we provide them with predicates through the universals that are unique to our understanding. For Butler, on the other hand, universals are not immutable realities of the mind. And a subject as bearer of the recognition process is just as nonexistent. Universals are historically developed lingual definitions, just as historic as the language through which, according to Butler, they are created by means of performative acts. They are effects of discourse and, like it, are socially, culturally, and economically conditioned. The classification of individuals always takes place in conjunction with cultural standardization.[22] Similarly, there is no subject of recognition that is independent of discourse, on the contrary: it is brought about just as discursively as the universals. Butler considers the idea of an active or recognizing subject an illusion, the subject is part of the discursive designation process and not its bearer.[23] Butler thus radicalizes Ockham's nominalism that clings to a recognizing subject. Simultaneously, she is again approaching Berkeley's position. For his basic principle *"esse est percipi"* has certain clear similarities to Butler's "reality is created through performance." For Berkeley the spirit claims existence through perception, for Butler reality exists through the performed act. Unlike Berkeley, however, Butler considers that it is not the spirit or the recognizing subject that is the bearer of these acts, but ultimately the discourse itself, of which the subject is a part. It is precisely here that Butler's nominalist position mutates into extreme idealism. And it is here, too, that my criticism of Butler's approach begins.

A Critical View: Feminist Constructivism in a Cul-de-Sac

Despite its undeniably accurate criticism of an unbroken universal realism regarding sexual understanding, the constructivist approach raises fundamental questions that, to some extent, turn out to be problems associated with the still unsolved problem of universals. I would like to touch on these briefly in note form.

First, even if Butler would like to distance herself from extreme idealism, her surrender of subjectivity and her treatment of the discourse as absolute leads to just such an idealism. Instead of the spirit-substance of Berkeley it is the discourse that "constructs," that sets reality by means of performative acts. This causes a breaking down of the difference between the extradiscursive reality of individual things and the discursive construction of universals. If the discourse is ultimately "all," how can something like an extradiscursive reality of individuals then exist? If even the self is only a part of the discourse, when subjectivity itself is ultimately an effect of the discourse, like gender and other universals, then how can a dividing line be drawn between extra-discursive reality and discursive reality in the sense of a construction? Furthermore, universals are even denied a mental being, they are simply epiphenomena of the discourse, in historic form, created in the never-ceasing flow of language. The result of Butler's theory is thus precisely the "linguistic monism" that should be avoided, and thus the radicalization of a nominalistic to an idealistic position of a Berkeleyan shade.

Second, added to this we have Butler's unclear term "materiality." If the border between the extradiscursive reality of individuals and the discursive "reality" of universals breaks down, then so too must the border between the extradiscursive reality of materiality in the sense of individual reality, and the discursively constructed term "materiality" or "material" as a universal term as opposed to "spirit." This results in terminological confusion on the part of the reader and constant efforts at justification on the part of Butler (something like: "No, I do not deny that . . . , but in my opinion . . .").

Third, should not "sex" also, like all universals, have a hold on reality, a kind of realistic "rest"? Doesn't our recognition need a reference to reality independent of the mind, that extends beyond reference to individual things?[24] Otherwise, our recognition would turn on itself all the time and reality would degenerate into a simple conglomerate of isolated individuals. Thought and language are monopolized or made absolute, and reality independent of the mind would simply be degraded to a weapon of terminological-discursive thinking, a form of thought that heaps the universals on the individuals and thus debases them just as much as a metaphysical, universal-based orderly way of thinking. It is precisely here that the insolubility of the problem of universals crops up: if there are good arguments against a universal realism (doubling of the world, infinite regress, dissolution of the unit of the individual, function of language in the process of recognition, primacy of singularity as opposed to universals), then the arguments for it are just as good (monopolization of the mental and discursive and the resulting dissolution of nonmental and nondiscursive reality, recognition turning on itself, "arming" reality provided by the senses with terminological thinking, reduction of reality to isolated individual objects by radical nominalism). Butler's gender constructivism reproduces this insolubility instead of overcoming it. The negation of "sex" as an ontological measure leads to a negation of the whole physical experience, insofar as "sex" and "body" are indivisibly united. For if "everything is discourse," then there is no room left for a nondiscursive experience of one's physicality or sex. And further: physical experience becomes simply an object of discursive designation, a *"tabula rasa"* without quality. In this way the extreme idealistic dualism of body and spirit is not overcome but extrapolated. It is not the spirit that sets or defines things perceived by the senses, but the all-too-powerful discourse.[25]

What now? Must we accept that the question of the status of sex and gender is just as insoluble as the problem of universals? Even if the problem of universals is ultimately as insoluble as the gender debate, it seems to me that it is still necessary to look for a half-way practicable solution that can perhaps at least defuse the issue or make it more "bearable." In my opinion, this can only be achieved in terms of moderate realism. Taking a narrow view, I would like to finish with a sketch of what such a moderate realism with regard to the question of the status of sex and gender could look like.

The discussion on the status of sex and gender has up to now concentrated, on the one hand, on an understanding of "sex" as a general term and, on the other hand, on an identification of sex within a system of two sexes. In addition, Butler interprets "sex" as a term of substance, as an ontological designation, and in her criticism of substance ontology argues consistently against the reality of "sex" as an ontological measure. And both "fractions" of the gender discussion, realists as well as constructivists, ultimately connect "sex" with the body, one with the constructed body and the other with the body existing before language. I prefer to determine sex as a way of existence, an existential, that is an existential of the corporeal self. I would like to continue by going deeper into this way of thinking, but I can only present here the logical sequence in note form.[26]

First, despite the legitimacy of some critics of traditional subject terminology, there really is a central insight of subject philosophy to hold on to: the evidence of the singularity (*Jemeinigkeit*) of my whole spectrum of experience. Such a singularity (*Jemeinigkeit*) can also be interpreted as an immediate and passive awareness of the existence of myself, for if I did not exist, so there would not be any imagination, any experience. This awareness is beyond a terminological, discursive, and identifying way of thinking: the "I" is neither a thing, nor just a term, it is prediscursive and prereflexive, and so it is fundamentally and radically open for reflection, for discursive practices, socio-cultural characterization, for historical registration and designation.[27]

Second, the recognition of singularity (*Jemeinigkeit*) does not take place in "*cogitare*," this in conflict with the reductionism of traditional subject philosophers, but in "the awareness of one's own body" (*eigenleibliches Sp, ren*) to borrow a term from the phenomenologist Hermann Schmitz.[28] The body in this context is not to be understood as the external surface of an "inner subject," I do not have a body like I have a pair of shoes or glasses. My self-being is body-being, I would be nothing if I were not corporeal. Body-being is an existential, without which human existence would simply be unthinkable.[29] Thus the body is not just a medium of intentionality and experience of the world, in other words part and medium of my in-the-world being (*In-der-Welt-sein*), but is simultaneously a precondition of the possibility of experiencing the world, the "to-the-world being" (*Être-au-monde*) as Maurice Merleau-Ponty said.[30] Looked at this way, my body-being is an asset of my openness to the world.

As the body-being and the self-being are indivisibly joined to one another, the "I am" is immediately illuminated by the immediacy of my "awareness of my own body" (*eigenleibliches Sp, ren*). Therefore, the recognition that "I am" does not result from an abstract "*cogito*," but from the concrete singularity (*Jemeinigkeit*) of the body-being.

Third, this awareness of my own body (*eigenleibliches Sp,ren*) is prediscursive and prereflective: the corporeally constituted self is thus open to reflection and discursiveness but does not get dissolved in it. Nevertheless, the corporeality in its openness is also always interpreted experience if and insofar that it is intentional, for in its intentionality it also shares in the domain of the reflective and discursive.[31] At this point it is useful to refer back to the phenomenological tradition of the separation of the spiritual body and the physical body: the spiritual body is the prereflective body, the immediate body-experience, the physical body, however, is the objectivised body that has been transformed to an object, that is subjected to discursive practices and thus the generated and interpreted images that we build up from the spiritual body and its experiences, in other words from bodily functions, bodily patterns, bodily structures, etc.[32]

Fourth, the body-being as an asset of openness to the world distinguishes itself in various ways of living my body-being. One of these ways of existence is the physical desire that can, in turn, be differentiated into numerous cravings, and one of them is the erotic-sexual desire. Thus sexuality is a human way of existence that belongs to the existential of body-being. Desire, too, can be thought of as intentional: I desire a particular object or aim, a good. Seen thus, desire is part of the discursive and never undisguised and immediately experienced but has always already been interpreted, "constructed." On the other hand, desire can also be considered an asset, the ability to desire and enjoy something at all. Seen like this it is initially free of intention, it is "naked" desire. This also applies to erotic-sexual desire: it is, initially, the ability to feel and exercise anything like an erotic-sexual attraction at all. Only through this kind of desire can another person in the world appear erotically attractive to me.

Fifth, desire is just as prereflective as physical being, to which it belongs, because I live from this asset, but I do not control it. I deal from and with it, but I cannot grasp it in real terms. Accordingly, sexual desire cannot be assigned to the objectivised body alone, but to the body-being, too. I think that this erotic-sexual desire can indeed be identified with sex. Sex is accordingly primarily and above all not an anatomical feature of the body, it is far more a way of existence, namely that of each individual erotic-sexual desire. Thus it possesses a material-somatic reality and is accordingly to be seen as an ontological measure and not as a substantive ontological measure, meaning that here "sex" is indeed no substance or definition of the being of mankind. At the same time it is also not simply a classification of individual things or individual bodies, it is therefore not a general term in this regard. It is, however, thoroughly "universal" in view of the fact that "sex" as a way of existence of the corporeal self is just as universal as singularity (*Jemeinigkeit*). I describe this position as moderate realism because "sex," as an existential, has a "*fundamentum in re*" and is not just mentally or linguistically generated.

Sixth, sex as an existential of the corporeal self is an ontological measure, but at the same time it is fundamentally open for descriptive practices and can thus also be normalized and shaped discursively. And so sex is also gender—as a discursively definition and determination of the prediscursive and prereflective sex as a erotic-sexual desire. As part of this process the variety of desires must necessarily be limited. This attempt at classification is the system of two sexes or better: two genders that define desire as well as the body that the desire is part of, and which ignites the desire. That ultimately means: I do indeed cling to the separation of "sex" and gender, though I no longer identify "sex" with a pre-existing sexual body, but with the erotic-sexual desire felt by an individual body. And I no longer identify gender with social roles, but with social-cultural classifications of desire as well as the body in the sense of objectivized bodies, in which this desire is ignited.[33]

Notes

1. William of Ockham, *Summa Logicae* (SL) I, 15, 3.

2. C f Jan P. Beckmann, *Wilhelm von Ockham* (Muenchen, Md.: Beck, 1995), 42.

3. William of Ockham, *Scriptum in librum primum Sententiarum* (OT I), Prologus, q.I, a.1, 21.

4. C f OT I, q.I, a.1, 25.

5. C.f. William of Ockham, *Quaestiones in librum secundum sententiarum* (OT V), 276. Quote from Beckmann, 54.

6. C.f. SL I, 15, 2ff.

7. C.f. SL I, 15, 6.

8. C f. SL I, 14.

9 "*Universale est aliqua qualitas exsistens subiective in mente, quae ex natura sua. . . est signum rei extra*   " (William of Ockham, *Scriptum in librum primum sententiarum Distinctiones* II et III (OT II), 289. Quote from Beckmann, 119).

10 C.f George Berkeley, *Eine Abhandlung ueber die Prinzipien der menschlichen Erkenntnis Nach der Uebersetzung von Friedrich Ueberweg mit Einleitung, Anmerkung und Registern neu herausgegeben von Alfred Klemmt* (Hamburg, Md.: Meiner, 1979), 18ff.

11. C f. Berkeley, *Abhandlung*, 26f.

12 C.f Berkeley, *Abhandlung*, 28.

13. C.f. Berkeley, *Abhandlung*, 43.

14. C f. Berkeley, *Abhandlung*, 43 and 76.

15. C f, e.g., Barbara Duden, "*Die Frau ohne Unterleib Zu Judith Butler's Entkoerperung*," *Feministische Studien* 2/1993, 24–33.

16 Judith Butler, "*Ort der politischen Neuverhandlung. Der Feminismus braucht 'die Frauen,' aber er muss nicht wissen, 'wer' sie sind,*" translated by Richard Dennis. *Frankfurter Rundschau*, 27.7.1993.

17 Judith Butler, *Bodies That Matter. On the Discursive Limits of "Sex,"* (New York and London: Routledge, 1993), xi.

18. Butler, *Bodies*, xi.

19. Butler, *Bodies*, 9f

20. C.f. Butler, *Bodies*, 9f

21. Butler, *Bodies*, 17.

22. C.f., e.g., Butler, *Bodies*, 67ff.

23. C.f. Butler's subject criticism, above all: "*Kontingente Grundlagen Der Feminismus und die Frage der 'Postmoderne.'*" In *Der Streit um Differenz Feminismus und Postmoderne in der Gegenwart*, ed. Seyla Benhabib et. al. (Frankfurt am Main, Md.: Fischer, 1993), 31–58.

24. C.f. Gudrun-Axeli Knapp, "*Politik der Unterscheidung,*" in *Geschlechterverhaeltnisse und Politik*, ed. *Institut fuer Sozialforschung* (Frankfurt am Main, Md.: suhrkamp, 1994), 277.

25. C.f. the critics of Landweer and Maihofer in Hilge Landweer, "*Generativitaet und Geschlecht. Ein blinder Fleck in der sex/gender-Debatte,*" in *Denkachsen Zur theoretischen und institutionellen Rede von Geschlecht*, ed. Theresa Wobbe/Gesa Lindemann (Frankfurt am Main, Md.: suhrkamp, 1994), 163; Andrea Maihofer, *Geschlecht als Existenzweise Macht, Moral, Recht und Geschlechterdifferenz* (Frankfurt am Main, Md.: Ulrike Helmer, 1995), 48.

26. C.f. to this my detailed considerations in: Saskia Wendel, "*Leibliches Selbst— geschlechtliches Selbst?!*" in *Kultur—Geschlecht—Koerper*, ed. Genus (Muenster, Md.: Agenda, 1999), 77–100; *Affektiv und inkarniert. Ansaetze Deutscher Mystik als subjekttheoretische Herausforderung* (Regensburg, Md.: Pustet, 2002); "*Der Koerper der Autonomie,*" in *Endliche Autonomie*, ed. Antonio Autiero et. al. (Muenster, Md.: LIT, 2004).

27. C.f. to this Dieter Henrich's and Manfred Frank's considerations to the pre-reflexivity of the self, for example in Dieter Henrich, "*Selbstbewusstsein. Kritische Einleitung in eine Theorie,*" in *Hermeneutik und Dialektik* (FS Hans-Georg Gadamer), *Aufsaetze* I, ed. Ruediger Bubner, Konrad Cramer, Rainer Wiehl (Tuebingen 1970), 266ff.; Manfred Frank, *Die Unhintergehbarkeit von Individualitaet. Reflexionen ueber das Subjekt, Person und Individuum aus Anlass ihrer postmodernen Toterklaerung* (Frankfurt am Main, Md.: suhrkamp, 1986).

28. C.f. Hermann Schmitz, "*Phaenomenologie der Leiblichkeit,*" in *Leiblichkeit Philosophische, gesellschaftliche und therapeutische Perspektiven*, ed. Hilarion Petzold (Paderborn 1985), 71

29. C.f. Maurice Merleau-Ponty, *Phaenomenologie der Wahrnehmung* (Berlin, Md.: De Gruyter, 1966), 167ff.

30. C.f. Merleau-Ponty, *Phaenomenologie*, 10.

31 C.f. to this also Elisabeth List, "*Das lebendige Selbst. Leiblichkeit, Subjektivitaet und Geschlecht,*" in *Phaenomenologie und Geschlechterdifferenz*, ed. Silvia Stoller/Helmuth Vetter (Wien: WUV-Universitätsverlag 1997), 292–318; "*Wissenskoerper Von der Theorie des Subjekts zur Politik symbolischer Repraesentationen,*"in *Die Praesenz des Anderen. Theorie und Geschlechterpolitik* (Frankfurt am Main, Md.: suhrkamp, 1993), 111–122. In the difference from List I think that it's necessary to connect this phenomenological approach with the approaches of Henrich and Frank. List, however, rejects these as idealistic theories of the subject (c.f. List, *Das lebendige Selbst*, 294). C.f. also Wendel, *Affektiv und inkarniert*, 243–313.

32. C f. Hermann Schmitz, "*Der gespuerte Leib und der vorgestellte Koerper,*" in *Wege zu einer volleren Realitaet Neue Phaenomenologie in der Diskussion*, ed. Michael Grossheim (Berlin: Akademie Verlag 1994), 91; Gernot Boehme, *Natuerlich Natur*

Ueber Natur im Zeitalter ihrer technischen Reproduzierbarkeit (Frankfurt am Main, Md.: suhrkamp, 1992), 80, 89.

Thanks to Richard Dennis for his help in translation.

Bibliography

Axeli-Knapp, Gudrun. *"Politik der Unterscheidung."* Pp. 262–287 in *Geschlechterverhaeltnisse und Politik* Ed. *Institut fuer Sozialforschung*. Frankfurt am Main: suhrkamp, 1994

Beckmann, Jan Peter. *Wilhelm von Ockham*. München: Beck, 1995.

Berkeley, George. *Eine Abhandlung ueber die Prinzipien der menschlichen Erkenntnis. Nach der Uebersetzung von Friedrich Ueberweg mit Einleitung, Anmerkung Und Registern neu herausgegeben von Alfred Klemmt*. Hamburg: Meiner, 1979.

Boehme, Gernot. *Natuerlich Natur. Ueber Natur im Zeitalter ihrer technischen Reproduzierbarkeit*. Frankfurt am Main: suhrkamp, 1992.

———. *Bodies that Matter On the Discursive Limits of "Sex"*. New York and London, 1993.

———. *"Kontingente Grundlagen Der Feminismus und die Frage der Postmodern"* Pp. 31–58 in *Der Streit um Differenz Feminismus und Postmoderne in der Gegenwart*, edited by Seyla Benhabib et. al. Frankfurt am Main: Fischer, 1994.

———. *"Ort der politischen Neuverhandlung Der Feminismus braucht 'die Frauen,' aber er muss nicht wissen, 'wer' sie sind."* *Frankfurter Rundschau*, 27.7.1993.

Duden, Barbara. *"Die Frau ohne Unterleib Zu Judith Butlers Entkoerperung."* *Feministische Studien* 2 (1993): 24–33

Frank, Manfred. *Die Unhintergehbarkeit von Individualitaet Reflexionen ueber das Subjekt, Person und Individuum aus Anlaas ihrer postmodernen Toterklaerung*. Frankfurt am Main: suhrkamp, 1986.

Henrich, Dieter. *"Selbstbewusstsein Kritische Einleitung in eine Theorie."* Pp. 257–284 in *Hermeneutik und Dialektik*, FS Hans-Georg Gadamer. *Aufsaetze* I. Ed Ruediger Bubner, Konrad Cramer, Rainer Wiehl. Tuebingen, Mohr Siebeck, 1970.

Landweer, Hilge. *"Generativitaet und Geschlecht. Ein blinder Fleck in der sex/gender-Debatte."* Pp. 147–176 in *Denkachsen. Zur theoretischen und institutionellen Rede von Geschlecht*, edited by Theresa Wobbe/Gesa Lindemann. Frankfurt am Main: suhrkamp, 1994.

List, Elisabeth. *"Wissenskoerper Von der Theorie des Subjekts zur Politik symbolischer Repraesentationen."* Pp. 111–122 in *Die Praesenz des Anderen Theorie und Geschlechterpolitik*. Frankfurt am Main: suhrkamp, 1993.

———. *"Das lebendige Selbst Leiblichkeit, Subjektivitaet und geschlecht."* Pp. 292–318 in *Phaenomenologie und Geschlechterdifferenz*, edited by Silvia Stoller and Helmuth Vetter. Wien: WUV, 1997.

Maihofer, Andrea. *Geschlecht als Existenzweise Macht, Moral, Recht und Geschlechterdifferenz* Frankfurt am Main: Ulrike Helmer, 1995.

Merleau-Ponty, Maurice. *Phaenomenologie der Wahrnehmung*. Berlin: de Gruyter, 1966

Schmitz, Hermann. *"Phaenomenologie der Leiblichkeit."* Pp. 71–106 in *Leiblichkeit Philosophische, gesellschaftliche und therapeutische Perspektiven*, edited by Hilarion Petzold. Paderborn: Junferman, 1985.

————. "Der gespuerte Leib und der vorgestellte Koerper '' Pp. 75–91 in *Wege zu einer volleren Realitaet Neue Phaenomenologie in der Diskussion*, edited by Michael Grossheim. Berlin, 1994

Wendel, Saskia. *"Leibliches Selbst–geschlechtliches Selbst?!''* Pp. 77–100 in *Kultur–Geschlecht—Koerper*, edited by Genus. Muenster: Agenda, 1999.

————. *Affektiv und inkarniert Ansaetze Deutscher Mystik als subjekttheoretische Herausforderung.* Regensburg: Pustet, 2002

————. *"Der Koerper der Autonomie Anthropologie und Gender.''* In *Endliche Autonomie*, ed. Antonio Autiero et. al. Muenster: LIT, 2004.

Chapter 13

Applying Time to Feminist Philosophy of the Body

Lanei M. Rodemeyer

Introduction

Since Aristotle's provocative consideration that there might be no time if there were no 'psyche' (soul) or 'psyche's nous' (the mind of soul)[1]—if not even earlier—philosophical analyses of time have regularly, and famously, focused on human consciousness (or the "mind" or "soul") as both the source of and the vehicle to understanding time. Descriptions such as these have encouraged philosophers to abstract time from space (and from the body), even to give time priority over space: time is (supposedly) the active apprehension of a static or passive space. Further, time-consciousness, as associated with activity and individuality, became a description of the masculine; thus, consciousness itself was also associated with the masculine (while corporeality was associated with the feminine), and this distinction of time from space contained a political or social nuance (whether intentional or unintentional of its propagators). Within the history of the philosophy of time, therefore, there arises a tendency to give preference to the individual over the intersubjective, to the mind over the body, and inherently, to the active masculine over the passive feminine—sometimes to the point of dismissing, or at least never addressing, the intersubjective and/or corporeal. This tendency is accurately and pointedly noted by Luce Irigaray: "Time becomes *interior* to the subject, and space *exterior* (this is developed by Kant in the *Critique of Pure Reason*). The subject, the master of time, becomes the axis, managing the affairs of the world."[2]

In response to this problem, a number of feminist philosophers turned away from time to analyses of space, place, corporeality, and the body. Some argue that when the body in *lived* space serves as the basis of phenomenological experience, philosophers can avoid a purely subjective starting point, as well as the associated assumptions of a masculinist, cognitive subjectivity. Other feminist works show us the associations of corporeality and passivity with the feminine (when not already to "woman"), and the effects such philosophies have had on societies, especially the women living in them. Still other works have shown us the active nature of the body, corporeality, or female desire, providing a counter to assumptions of its passivity.[3] These and similar analyses, by beginning with the body, are originally open to discussions of intersubjectivity because of their assumption of lived, shared space, and thus they render certain threats which surface regularly in "traditional" philosophy—such as solipsism—impotent. In this way, feminist philosophers have brought critiques to the aforementioned (and other) assumptions about temporality and corporeality.

The problems that have led feminist philosophers to turn away from time toward space and the body, however, are generated not by time itself, but by such analyses of time that limit it to the individual subject and to the pure activity of mental life. The goal of this paper is therefore to re-introduce temporality into feminist discussions of corporeality by revealing the *passive* and *intersubjective* aspects of time. In the first part, I will indicate the passivity apparent in temporality, based upon the phenomenological temporality of Edmund Husserl.[4] Husserl's phenomenology is both evidence for the masculinist tendencies noted above and a method that is open to recognizing the passive and intersubjective aspects of temporality. In the second part of this paper, I will use Susan Bordo's "slender body" as the locus for a discussion of the interrelations of temporality and corporeality.[5] As eating disorders exhibit an extreme manifestation of our culture's "battle" between mind and body, and therefore between temporal consciousness and corporeality, they put this interaction into relief for us. Although I am using the quite limited example of the eating disordered "slender" body, I would like this paper to stand as an introduction to a larger project, one which brings time back to the body, re-integrating the two concepts for further feminist philosophical discussion.

The Activity and Passivity of Temporality

Husserl's favorite example in his analyses of time is the perception of a musical tone or set of notes. The choice of a musical tone helps him to separate out the dimension of space from the question of time and thus allows Husserl to examine more directly how an object exists in time.[6] The musical tones are perceived in an ordered flow—not all at once, nor constantly remaining in present perception (even if the same note is being held for several moments, its quality changes, or we notice that it is being "held"). In addition, these notes influence one another; they are not a series of individual, independent notes that happen to be played and heard separately, but instead they modify each other in our experience of the series of their sounds. In other words, our perception of these notes is not simply of each individual note while it is in the present (otherwise we would have what could be called a constant form of "instant amnesia," always immediately forgetting what just came before). Rather, we perceive several notes at once, in a sense: the last few that have been played, the one(s) being played at the present moment, and even our anticipation of the next few notes to come. The past notes harmonize with the present ones, as well as lead to them, and we can only appreciate this harmony and order if we are able to "perceive" *more* than what is in the single present moment. Therefore, Husserl concludes, the "now" of consciousness is actually a "phase" which includes perceptions that have just passed and the expectation of those possibly to come. These are called the *retention* of experiences just-passed and a *protention* toward experiences that might be just coming. Supporting these two "tails" is the notion of an "impressional now," which identifies those perceptions of experiences which are *immediately* present.

The impressional now names that "opening" in phenomenological consciousness which reveals our immediate and constant flow of impressions. This impressional flow provides us with the "direction" in which time "moves" (i.e., into the "future"), as well as the content for retention and protention.[7] Temporality is based upon our flow of experiences, and our activity of retaining and anticipating them. Of course, these experiences could also be the activities of our own imagination, our own feelings, the "movements of our mind"; for phenomenologists, however, the temporal flow and the consciousness that constitutes it are most often discussed in relation to perceptual experience. And when we examine such experience, we find that we require the activity of retention and protention, of retaining and anticipating, for any of our experiences to make sense. In other words, we never experience an "instant" without the context of the others that surround it. Thus any focus on the impressional now can only be done hypothetically or abstractly and can only reveal a limited amount of information. A wealth of information, however, results from an examination of the "living present," which is the "now-phase" of consciousness that includes retention and protention.[8]

We have already mentioned that much of the activity of consciousness's living present lies in its retention and protention. With regard to the musical melody, the retentional aspect of consciousness is that which "holds on" to the melody as I take in the next coming notes. Retention links what is immediately present to what has just passed, so that I can understand what the present means. We pointed out before that, if the impressional now were not to be "stretched" beyond itself, we would not be able to appreciate the harmonies and phrases in a melody, because we would no longer know what we just heard. Another example is when I speak a sentence: if I were unable to actively hold the meaning of the first part of my sentence in my present consciousness, I would never know what I had just said, and thus would be unable to finish my thought.

Protention is also essential to this relationship. Through protention, I am able to "look forward" to the next notes in the melody, giving the musical phrase a sense *while* I am hearing it rather than only afterward. In other words, I know "where the melody is going" while I am listening to it; I do not wait until I have heard an entire piece and then reconstruct it so that it makes sense only after I have heard it. Of course, I may be wrong in my expectations, but protention is what allows me to have a sense at all in my flowing, temporal intuitions. When I am speaking a sentence—to return to our second example—I must have an idea "where I am going" as I speak, and I must hold this actively in my consciousness, in order to be able to voice my ideas. I cannot speak a sentence without having some part of my consciousness "ahead of me," as it were.

This now-phase as a whole, i.e., the living present, is essential to the constitution of objects. Without the retentional and protentional aspects of consciousness, we would be unable to recognize objects as identical, and more fundamentally, as persisting through time. If we could not hold the past few moments "in view," for example, we would keep hearing the note "C" being played anew, never knowing that the one note was just being held for a longer period of time. We would constantly be surprised at hearing the note ("instant amnesia" again). In fact, we would not be able to recognize the note "C" as such—it would always be a completely new experience and thus could never be given the name "C." Temporal consciousness allows us to recognize, to constitute, the note "C" as an object in itself because retention makes possible the recognition of an object's persistence through time. More importantly, we do not constitute these objects as "neutral" objects, but, through retention, we see them as having a temporal context; for example, the note "C" might be part of a melody, a harmony, or a discussion on music. It may be abstracted afterward from context, but it can never be understood originally as such. Thus, the living present connects all the "moments" of my experiences and unifies them so I can recognize objects and experiences as they relate to each other over time. Objects, both temporal and spatial,[9] are thus constituted through the function of the living present of consciousness.

This living present reveals the *active* nature of temporality through its function of constitution. Protention and retention reach out, retain, organize, and order all of the impressions that flow through consciousness, playing an active role in our perception and understanding of the world (and acting in conjunction with the world as well, which we will see later). Temporal consciousness is active because it grounds my perception of the world and the objects and meanings in it. But the foundation of this activity may also include what Husserl calls a "hyletic flow." This is the "stuff" or "sensory information" which makes up the material of my experiences. This flow of sensual "data," "prior" to its constitution as temporal objects, is still an aspect of temporality through its flowing—but temporality as *passive*. It is the "sensory input" over which I have little to no control. "Prior" to temporal constitution, which takes place through the activity of retention and protention, temporality is a passive flowing of unconstituted sensations, of the information that makes up my experiences. Thus, one might say that passivity is the "ultimate" foundation of temporal experience, in this hyletic flow. However, it is only through our abstraction to the impressional now that we are able to recognize the hyle as unconstituted flow at all, and thus this "ultimate" foundation can only be hypothetical. Since this passive aspect of temporal consciousness can only be understood abstractly, we cannot assume that it is the sole foundation of our experiences in itself. Rather, the combination of passive information and the active constitution of it would more likely be the cofoundations of our experiences together.[10] No matter how temporal consciousness is founded, though, we can see that it clearly has aspects of *both* activity and passivity.

We must remind ourselves that what we have been calling "passive temporality" is merely an abstract notion; we have no direct access to an "unconstituted" or "pre-temporal" region. Everything we experience is already constituted and in time. This would explain the focus in philosophy on the active and individual nature of time, as all experience is usually, eventually related to my ego. According to the traditional relation of temporality to the subject, my temporal consciousness, which unifies all the objects of my experiences as objects, also unifies them as belonging to *my* experiences. Temporal consciousness, accordingly, is both active and *mine*. But, given this, what prompts consciousness to move from the passive flow of sensations to an active constitution of objects? The answer to this question introduces another "passive" aspect to temporal consciousness, as the motivation for constitution actually comes from *outside* of consciousness itself. Husserl argues that objects are themselves somewhat involved in our constitution of them. In fact, he coins the term "affectivity" to describe the effect, the pull, that the individual object can have on me. For example, I am drawn to constitute a series of notes as a harmonious melody. It calls to me to appreciate it, to separate it out from the other notes, to attend to its repetitions and variations. But the way we constitute objects also involves the intersubjective world in which we live. I cannot always constitute the melody merely from itself; in fact, I usually have already been given a structure by which I can interpret it. The community of subjects around me strongly influences the meaning and the constitution of the objects I encounter in the world. Thus, the dynamic interplay between consciousness and intersubjective world reveals an interdependence between them, and as such, a different kind of passivity is integral to temporal consciousness.

One of phenomenology's main projects is an analysis and description of the structure of perception, i.e., how we, and how we are able to, experience the world. One of Husserl's most telling discoveries is that our perception of an object always includes that which we do not actually perceive as part of the perception. The other side of the desk, for example, is as positively "there," is as necessarily part of the perception, as the side facing me. We do not perceive merely a flat front side of the desk; the back side is already there for us, even though we may have never perceived it, and perhaps never will. This aspect of our perception is described by the term "appresentation," which requires a brief explanation: the perceptual impression I have in any moment, and taking place in the present moment, is called a *presentation*. A presentation, being contained in a fleeting moment, obviously passes over into another presentation, then another, and so on. My ability to go beyond a presentation, to link it (temporally) to either past or future moments or (spatially) to angles of objects that are not in my direct view, Husserl tells us, is called *appresentation*. An appresentation is a possible presentation that is not currently being "presented" directly. These appresentations are "co-present," meaning that they are *part of* my experience of the presentation (in the present). In other words, appresentations are what go beyond the actual presentation at hand, and yet, as possibilities or extensions, they are embedded in the momentary presentation. They are, as it were, the spatial and temporal horizons of the current presentation. It is for this reason that, while attending to a presentation right now (say, the front side of my coffee cup), I notice that part of that presentation goes beyond itself to other possible presentations not currently "present" (the other sides, bottom, and interior of my coffee cup that are not presently in view, but are *implied* by my present view).

These horizons within my presentation of an object rest upon my temporal structure of consciousness; appresentations require protention and retention in order to exist as horizons. Through phenomenology, we have been able to ascertain certain passive aspects of temporality which contribute to the foundation of a temporal consciousness which is usually considered to be purely active. With this, we have indicated the interrelation of temporal consciousness with an intersubjective world. Having established the passive and active aspects of temporal consciousness at this point, we now move on to a discussion of the body and its passive and active natures, eventually attempting to re-integrate a notion of temporal consciousness into an understanding of the body.

The Activity and Passivity of the Body

In order to begin a discussion of the interactions of temporality and corporeality, we must admit that they can only be hypothetically distinguished; in actuality, they are always intertwined. If temporality is based somewhat upon the flow of sensations, either constituted or unconstituted, then the foundation of temporality is not only found partially in the hyletic flow (along with constituting consciousness) but also in the perception of that flow through the *body*. Thus we must address the body as both *perceiving* and *perceived*, and its relation to constituting consciousness. We will work with a specific example, that of the person with an eating disorder, since this situation intensifies the relation between body and consciousness, bringing their active and passive tendencies to the fore.

As we noted in the introduction, active temporality has often been opposed to a passive corporeality; this produces themes like "mind over matter," and the philosophical "mind/body split," The body of the eating disordered person—and for this paper, the emphasis will be on the anorexic person—stands clearly as physical evidence for such themes. The active will, which arises from our constituting temporality (in a couple of senses, to which we will return), has applied itself to the body and has affected it quite extremely. But this picture shows the body to be passive—it does *not* show the struggle the body puts up. It does not show what is actually a battle between time and physical being, a battle that is still continuing (and must continue, because we can never lose a phenomenal amount of weight and then just relax), a battle where the body is not passively submitting but instead is actively fighting—and sometimes is losing. Susan Bordo describes this fight in several ways. Here she cites Barbara, from Dalma Heyn's "Body vision" and then responds: "'. . . my breasts, my stomach—they're just awful lumps, bumps, bulges. My body can turn on me at any moment; it is an out-of-control mass of flesh.' . . . I want to consider [these images] as a metaphor for anxiety about internal processes out of control—uncontained desire, unrestrained hunger, uncontrolled impulse. . . . The ideal here is . . . a body that is protected against eruption from within, whose internal processes are under control."[11] Later Bordo also points out: "In cultural fantasies [such as *Vision Quest* and *Flashdance*], self-mastery is presented as an attainable and stable state; but . . . the reality of the contemporary agonism of the self is another matter entirely."[12] In these descriptions we see both temporality and corporeality as active, but as opposed to one another. This opposition results, however, from a fundamental definition of the body as passive, as a mere receptor for hyletic data; thus, when the body is active (i.e., "bulging"), it cannot be "me"—in fact, it can "turn on me." What "I" am is consciousness, I am pure mental activity and will—which excludes the body. When the body "becomes" active (although it may already have been active, I now suddenly perceive it as such), it must be something "other than me." "I" must fight against the bulges resulting from that "other." The body therefore becomes perceived as an "other" that has a will of its own; in the case of the eating disordered person, the body's will contradicts "my own." Furthermore, the body is opposed even more intensely precisely because it is manifesting itself *as active*.

Women, in many cultures, are associated with their (passive) bodies—are often *only* their bodies—so in a society where women begin to explore their power of mind (perhaps aided by their entering the job market, or having access to contraception), one possible result is that they minimize the body to an extreme. It is because of the body's assumed passivity, and the association of women with their bodies, that women are those most often affected by eating disorders, for when they employ their active consciousness, they often apply it to and against their bodies, fighting off or against what has been the reason for their "necessary" passivity. This effect is propagated by two means: first, the women who take up the freedoms associated with the *masculine* (such as financial independence or no fear of pregnancy) also usually assume the symbolic and cultural split between mind and body; second, women face media images that try to control the *feminine* by suggesting a necessary slenderness for them. As "masculine," women must focus on the intellect and reject the body. As "feminine," they interpret—or have interpreted for them—their femininity as "slenderness." Both of these can result in an extreme denial of, or an attempt to have control over, the body. And although the compulsive need for thinness with relation to femininity has been determined as a form of disease in our society, the masculine tendency to *deny* the body might also be termed a disease—in this case one that affects mostly men. This second "disease," however, *gives* (or continues) a social power, instead of taking it away—perhaps for the very reason that it is considered normal or ideal, not abnormal. Therefore, a woman's denial of her own body could be seen as an (abnormal) attempt to *normalize* herself, according to a masculine paradigm.

The above situation reveals both temporality and corporeality as active. In this case the body is interpreted as passive but, ironically, is discovered as quite active through its strong resistance to dangerous change. A rather subtle effect of this situation, we began to see, is a splitting of the subject. We pointed out that the body, when it resists the will, is interpreted as "other" than me—because its "will" is other than "my own." But this split is not merely a split between mind and body. Instead, the body has its own will and, correlatively, its own temporality. In other words, there is a temporal "sensing" associated with the body which is other than my "own" temporal consciousness which opposes it. This "other" temporality is also active and passive: it takes up the flow of sensations and constitutes objects just as "I" do. The "otherness" arises in the fact that the two temporalities effect different and opposing constitutions of the one body involved. One constitutes the body as "fat," the other as "starving." Each has a different constitution of hunger, of energy reserves, of needs to excrete or purge. The split, then, takes place in temporal constitution, but not in the body itself. I do not separate myself just from my body, but more importantly, from my body's temporal constitution.

Bordo suggests that women find a source of empowerment through "subduing" their own bodies. In some cases, this empowerment results from a rejection of the traditional "maternal" values that accompany the "softness" of breasts and stomach. Importantly, these maternal values are also associated with women's lack of power because women are often defined as potential mothers, and only that. In other cases, this empowerment comes simply through achieving a set goal—succeeding obviously, visually, physically. In a sense, such women have beat societal images at their own game. Bordo cites one woman who describes this dangerous game in exactly such terms: "From what I've seen, more people fail at losing weight than at any other single goal. I found out how to do what everyone else couldn't . . . And that meant I was better than everyone else."[13] Extreme thinness is thus evidence of several types of power: my power over my own body, my power to reach very difficult goals and maintain them, my power to distinguish myself from my own mother and from maternal roles, and finally, my power to enter into the male arena, having attained a masculine distance from the body as well as an almost-male body, and having attained a body suggested to me as the ideal body-type by media images. Unfortunately, while such women may have attained power in these senses, they are far from having the power of a "body-less" man. Instead, they are still women, and in some cases, very ill women. What they have discovered, though—which some men may never discover—is the power of the body's own will, the will of the body that must be subdued by my active temporal consciousness.

Bordo argues that it is during periods of social vulnerability that cultural norms demand that its women be overly thin, primarily due to a fear of female desire and the resulting insecurity or lack of control.[14] In such cases, women are required to overcome the active nature of their bodies because of a fear of that active nature's "uncontrollable" desire.[15] Here it is a different external force that turns a woman's mind against her body, and in this case, importantly, her body is *recognized as active*. The battle does *not* begin through a woman's recognition of her temporal consciousness, and her fight against her supposedly passive corporeality. Instead, the battle begins through an external, i.e., social, recognition of active female desire, which results in an attempt to subdue it (using the women themselves to execute the subduing). In this case, then, women's bodies are seen as active forces, not passive, but they are still opposed to the activity of the individual's constituting and temporal consciousness. Perhaps female desire is considered to be so dangerous because it becomes apparent during periods when gender roles are already being challenged, perhaps also because it challenges a very fundamental assumption that the female body is passive.

One could argue, looking at the above, that we are hardly talking about temporal consciousness, but instead are talking more about "the will." Admittedly, the link between temporal consciousness and the will has merely been intimated so far. Now, however, we are much better able to flesh out this relationship. Husserl claims that the act of objective constitution is a "pure" function of consciousness. Discussions of language and its influence (clearly intersubjective) are rejected, because the constitution of objects supposedly happens at a prelinguistic (and pre-egoic) level for Husserl. I have been arguing that there *is* a mutual influence of subjectivity and intersubjectivity at the level of objective constitution. In the case of one's own body[16] (here the woman's body), the interpretive aspect of objective constitution is evident. The anorexic person *sees* and *feels* her body as fat. It is *constituted as fat*—she does not see her body and then decide she would like to *interpret* it as or *call* it fat. It just *is* fat. The judgment comes alongside, that fat is bad. Through a mutual dynamic of her own power of constitution and the intersubjective, constitutive powers around her, the anorexic woman *perceives* herself in this way. The temporal, constitutive function, then, involves both my own activity and the power relations around me. It is an agreement, of sorts, between the individual and certain intersubjective relations.[17] Furthermore, this temporal level of constitution is what underlies all judgments made, i.e., temporal consciousness underlies the will.

Societal images of femininity (and masculinity) are therefore *appresented* along with the presentation of one's own body. In other words, certain intersubjective interpretations of women's bodies are part of the horizons of an individual's constitution of her own body. In the case of the anorexic, though, these appresentations are more than mere horizons. Instead, they become the ideal for the presentation of her body, and they become a permanent judgment on her body as needing to fit a certain role and image. The anorexic subject's temporal consciousness, then, makes possible the infiltration of societal decisions about femininity and women's bodies into her constitution of her own body, because these expectations are appresented *along with* the presentation of her own body. In this way, her body is constituted as fat or as needing some sort of control. By integrating certain intersubjective beliefs about the female body, an individual's temporal consciousness can thus oppose the "consciousness" of her own body that insists it is *not* fat.

Let us focus on the split temporalities that occur in these situations. When the subject turns against her body in the case of the eating disorder, her temporality splits upon her recognition that her body is not passive, but instead is quite active (actively resistant). The temporality splits into two different ways of constituting the subject's body: one, as "fat" or "uncontrollable," the other, as "surviving" or "desiring." The first becomes "my" constitution of my body, the second, in some sense, is my own body's constitution of itself. So far, in the sense of the function of constitution, we have interpreted both split temporalities as active and relating to an active body. Earlier, though, we introduced the notion of passive temporality, which reveals itself both at the unconstituted and at the constituting level. At the unconstituted level, we pointed out, temporality is understood as a pure "flow of sensation," one which can never be directly experienced, only theorized. At the level of constitution, though, we noted the passivity of temporal consciousness through the influence that objects bring to their constitution as well as the influence of intersubjective meanings. But then we might say that the temporality that split off as "my own" is actually much more a passive temporality than my body's constitution of itself. "My" temporality constitutes my body very much in accordance with media images, following others' attitudes about femininity and women, and not in accordance with my own body or myself as a whole entity. The appresentation of societal images of the feminine, in other words, become even more powerful than the actual presentation of my own body. Clearly, in constituting objects, the subject is always somewhat influenced by intersubjective interpretation (and necessarily so), but in the case of this split in the eating disordered subject, the constituting temporality appropriated as "my own" is actually an intensification of certain public images. The eating disordered subject takes up society's mode of constitution of female bodies and, rather than interpreting it in conjunction with her self and her body, she makes those societal appresentations into her own presentations—ironically, as a form of self-empowerment.

Through this analysis, we can see that constituting temporality is hardly "purely" individual (much less solipsistic), but rather is always already intersubjectively involved. Further, intersubjective interpretations of the body can sometimes be so influential that they cause a splitting of an individual temporal consciousness. This splitting occurs when an intersubjective constitution is antagonistic to the subject in some way and yet is appropriated, and intensified, by the subject. In an effort at survival, the two modes of constitution, temporal consciousness and body-consciousness, split from one another and oppose one another. Neither temporal constitution is the "true" subject in the sense of "pure" subject, as all constitution involves intersubjectivity to some extent. But we can say that one form of constitution is more dangerous to the subject than the other, because it leads to the subject's turning against her own body, and in some sense, her self.

While I would like to argue that there are many ways of constituting the "self" that flows through the intersubjective world, I would like to avoid, with Bordo, any assertion that these different interpretations are all equal, that they are all harmless, or that they are all "playful."[18] Indeed, the interpretation of the feminine "self" that we have been addressing can lead to severe illness or even death. The next question, then, would be how to filter those appresentations of societal demands to control femininity without destroying my own temporal consciousness or my body-consciousness. Perhaps the analysis carried out in this paper, of the effects of some interpretations of the self (or of the feminine self) on my temporal constitution, can aid in the creation or constitution of more holistic images of body and self. We cannot reject intersubjective influences, as they are part of the foundation of our temporal constitution, but we can examine those influences that are dangerous, as Bordo and other feminist philosophers have done, and search for influences that are helpful rather than harmful. Then we need to seek interpretations that include the active bodys constituting temporality as well as its interface with individual and intersubjective constitution, revealing harmonious interaction, rather than antagonistic.

It is not the goal of this paper to create new images of the feminine and masculine, however; instead, this analysis of the interrelation of temporality and corporeality is meant to re-introduce the notion of temporal consciousness into feminist dialogues in philosophy of the body. Temporal consciousness is essential not only as the form of objective constitution, but also because it can reveal the interrelation of the subject with intersubjectivity, and the notion of the body as itself actively temporal. An understanding of phenomenological temporality, then, precisely because it discloses so many new interrelations, could be a valuable tool to feminist philosophers, as it was here.

Notes

1. Aristotle, *Physics* Book IV, 223a, 22—29.

2. Luce Irigaray, "Sexual Difference," in *The Irigaray Reader*, ed. Margaret Whitford (Oxford: Blackwell Publishers, 1991), 167.

3. I have in mind here such early Continental feminist philosophers as Edith Stein, Simone de Beauvoir, and Luce Irigaray. These names, of course, barely touch the surface of the contributions made to feminist philosophy that challenge traditional philosophical divisions between masculinity and femininity as well as time and space.

4. The majority of my argument is based on Husserl's published work on temporality: Edmund Husserl, *Zur Phänomenologie des inneren Zeitbewusstseins (1873–1917), Husserliana X*, ed. Rudolf Boehm (The Hague: Martinus Nijhoff, 1966); *On the Phenomenology of the Consciousness of Internal Time (1873–1917)*, trans. John Barnett Brough, (The Netherlands: Kluwer Academic Publishers, 1991). The notion of "intersubjective temporality" comes from my own work, *Intersubjective Temporality: (It's About Time)*, forthcoming.

5. Susan Bordo, "Reading the Slender Body," in *Body and Flesh· A Philosophical Reader*, ed. Donn Welton (Malden, Mass.: Blackwell Publishers, 1998), 291–304.

6. Note the paradox here: Husserl makes an explicit move to separate his analysis of temporality from anything spatial, and at the same time his dependence on sensual experience for any notion of temporality at all requires the involvement of my body.

7. We will set aside Husserl's discussion of recollection and anticipation for this discussion.

8. Klaus Held, *Lebendige Gegenwart· die Frage nach der Seinsweise des transzendentalen Ich bei Edmund Husserl, entwickelt am Leitfaden der Zeitproblematik* (Den Haag: Martinus Nijhoff, 1966), 17–24 Many forms of this term, "living present," are used throughout Husserl's manuscripts; this term is clarified and formalized by Klaus Held in his *Lebendige Gegenwart*

9. We have concentrated up to this point on temporal objects; we will turn to spatial objects in a moment.

10. Because of the limitations of this project, we are setting aside a discussion of the philosophical difficulties of Husserl's notion of the hyle or hyletic flow. In his later manuscripts, Husserl considered whether the hyletic flow might be of already constituted objects, and tried to correct this through the introduction of an "Urhyle," a notion which merely continues the problem rather than taking care of it.

11. Susan Bordo, "Reading the Slender Body," in *Body and Flesh A Philosophical Reader*, ed Donn Welton (Malden, Mass.: Blackwell Publishers, 1998), 293—294, modified.

12. "Reading the Slender Body," 296, modified.

13. "Reading the Slender Body," 298–299

14. This is taken from Mary Douglas' two works, *Natural Symbols* (New York: Pantheon, 1982) and *Purity and Danger* (London: Routledge and Kegan Paul, 1966).

15. It is interesting to note that in societies where men's desire is considered uncontrollable it is often still the women who are covered by clothing or are controlled by other means.

16. For the moment, we are assuming the body can be constituted as any other object (a modern assumption). Clearly, the fact that the body is its own constituting temporality will complicate our analysis, but we cannot take up such complications in detail here.

17. Some other examples that support this argument: 1) upper body strength, i.e., well-developed arms and shoulders, is considered "strong" in our society, whereas lower body strength, in the legs and abdomen, usually goes unnoticed. This, again, falls along gendered lines, as men are often stronger in the upper body but can be weak in the legs, while women usually have strong legs and abdomens. The constitution of something as supposedly neutral as "strength" is simultaneous with intersubjective interpretation. 2) Constitution of the enemy in wartime as "beasts" or "evil" is often brought about through lengthy training or propaganda. Once the war is over, however, this constitution of members of a certain race or country often remains intertwined with wartime images.

18. Susan Bordo, "'Material Girl,'" in *Body and Flesh: A Philosophical Reader*, ed. Donn Welton (Malden, Mass.: Blackwell Publishers, 1998), 45–59.

Bibliography

Aristotle, *Physics,* Book IV.

Bordo, Susan. "'Material Girl:'" The Effacements of Postmodern Culture." Pp. 45–59 in *Body and Flesh: A Philosophical Reader*, edited by Donn Welton. Malden, Mass.: Blackwell Publishers, 1998.

———. "Reading the Slender Body." Pp. 291—304 in *Body and Flesh: A Philosophical Reader*, edited by Donn Welton. Malden, Ma.: Blackwell Publishers, 1998.

Douglas, Mary. *Natural Symbols* New York: Pantheon, 1982.

———. *Purity and Danger* London: Routledge and Kegan Paul, 1966.

Held, Klaus. *Lebendige Gegenwart die Frage nach der Seinsweise des transzendentalen Ich bei Edmund Husserl, entwickelt am Leitfaden der Zeitproblematik.* Den Haag: Martinus Nijhoff, 1966.

Husserl, Edmund. *Zur Phänomenologie des inneren Zeitbewusstseins (1873—1917), Husserliana X.* Edited by Rudolf Boehm. The Hague: Martinus Nijhoff, 1966.

———. *On the Phenomenology of the Consciousness of Internal Time (1873—1917).* Translated by John Barnett Brough. The Netherlands: Kluwer Academic Publishers, 1991

Irigaray, Luce. *"Sexual Difference."* Pp. 165–177 in *The Irigaray Reader,* edited by Margaret Whitford. Oxford: Blackwell Publishers, 1991.

Contributors

Karen Barad is Professor of Women's Studies and Philosophy at Mount Holyoke College. She also teaches in the Critical Social Thought Program. Her Ph.D. is in theoretical particle physics. Her research in physics and philosophy has been supported by the National Science Foundation, the Ford Foundation, the Hughes Foundation, the Irvine Foundation, the Mellon Foundation, and the National Endowment for the Humanities. She is the author of numerous articles on physics, philosophy of science, cultural studies of science, and feminist theory. Her forthcoming book is entitled *Meeting the Universe Halfway*.

Jana Evans Braziel is Assistant Professor of English at the University of Cincinnati where she teaches Caribbean, diasporic, and hemispheric American literatures. Her published and forthcoming articles appear in *Small Axe*; *Callaloo*; *Comparative American Studies*; *Women & Performance*; *Meridians: feminism, race, transnationalism*; *Journal of Haitian Studies*; *Popular Music and Society*; *A/B: Auto/Biography Studies*; *Tessera*; *Journal x*; *Studies in the Literary Imagination*; and *The Journal of North African Studies*. She has also coedited three collections: *Race and the Foundations of Knowledges: Cultural Amnesia in the Academy* (University of Illinois Press, forthcoming 2005); *Theorizing Diaspora: A Reader* (Blackwell, 2003); and *Bodies Out of Bounds: Fatness and Transgression* (University of California Press, 2001). Most recently, Braziel has completed two book manuscripts: *Rethinking the Black Atlantic: Race, Diaspora, and Cultural Production in Haiti and Haiti's 10th Département*, which forms a critical rejoinder to Gilroy's theorizations of the black Atlantic by focusing on Haiti and Haiti's diasporic extra-territorial "tenth department;" and *Haiti's Gwo Nègs ("Big Men"): Haïtiannité and the Trans-American Politics of Black Masculinities in Diaspora* which explores cultural constructions and performative instantiations of black masculinity in diaspora through the Haitian Kreyòl concept of gwo nègs—or "big men"—, the literary texts of Dany Laferrière, the musical remix of Wyclef Jean, the artistic deformations of Jean-Michel Basquiat (as well as post-mortem revenants of Basquiat in literature), the drag queen performances and poetry of Assotto Saint, and the queer drag king performances of Dréd.

Louise Burchill currently teaches at the *Université d'Evry*, France. She has published several essays on contemporary French philosophy, of which the most recent are "In-between 'Spacing' and the '*Chôra*' in Derrida: A Pre-originary Medium?", *Intermediality as Inter-esse: Philosophy, Arts, Politics*, ed. Henk Oosterling, Hugh Silverman and Ewa Plonowska-Ziarek (forthcoming Continuum Press), and "*Le deuxième sexe et le personage conceptual du feminine: l'autrui sexué selon Beauvoir, Deleuze et au-delà*" in *Cinquartenaire du deuxième sexe*, ed. Christine Delphy and Sylvie Chaperon (Syllepse, 2002). She has worked as a research assistant and translator for Julia Kristeva. She has translated and prefaced Alain Badiou's *Deleuize: The Clamor of Being* (University of Minnesota Press, 2000) and is currently translating a series of books by Isabelle Stengers, to be published under the title *Cosmopolitics* by Continuum Press.

Annemie Halsema teaches philosophical anthropology and women's studies at the department of philosophy, University of Tilburg (The Netherlands). She is the author of *Dialectics of Sexual Difference. The Philosophy of Luce Irigaray* (Boom, 1998), and several publications in the field of feminist theory.

Deborah Orr wrote her doctoral thesis on concepts of understanding in the mature philosophy of Wittgenstein. Professor Orr teaches in the areas of gender, ethics, and embodiment in the Division of Humanities at York University in Toronto, Canada. She has published in various journals in the areas of Wittgenstein, pedagogy, moral logic, and moral development. Recent work includes "The Crone as Lover and Teacher: A Philosophical Reading of Zora Neale Hurston's *Their Eyes Were Watching God*," *Journal of Feminist Studies in Religion* (18/1: 25–50); Developing Wittgenstein's Picture of the Soul: Toward a Feminist Spiritual Erotics, in *Feminist Interpretations of Wittgenstein,* ed. Naomi Scheman and Peg O'Connor (The Pennsylvania State Press, 2002); *Holistic Learning and Spirituality in Education: Breaking New Ground,* coedited with Jack Miller, Diana Denton, Salia Karsten, and Isabella Kates (SUNY, 2005) which includes her "Minding the Soul in Education: Conceptualizing and Teaching to the Whole Person"; and "The Uses of Mindfulness in Feminist Anti-Oppressive Pedagogies: Philosophy and Praxis," *Canadian Journal of Education* 27(2). She is working with Dianna Taylor on a second volume, *Identities and Differences* (Forthcoming, 2006, Rowman & Littlefield), from the IAPh Conference in Boston. She is also working on a book about embodied spirituality with the working title *The Art of Love: The Logic of a Feminist Spiritual Erotics* and a book about the use of yoga and meditation in anti-oppressive pedagogy with the working title *Mindful Pedagogy*. She also teaches yoga and meditation in Toronto.

Lanei Rodemeyer received her Ph.D. in Philosophy from the State University of New York at Stony Brook, having written her dissertation on

Edmund Husserl's phenomenology of inner time-consciousness and intersubjectivity. She is currently Assistant Professor at Duquesne University, in Pittsburgh, and is completing revisions of her book on Husserl for publication. Her future work will continue in phenomenology, applying it to philosophy of the body as well as to critical theories of race and sexuality.

Bettina Schmitz is teaching philosophy at the University of Würzbur. Her main areas of research and teaching are contemporary French philosophy, poststructuralism, especially Julia Kristeva, feminist philosophy, practical philosophy, and philosophy and psychoanalysis (psychic bisexuality). She has former research projects on Hannah Arend's narrative notion of the political, and another one on philosophy and literature and on philosophical and poetic language. She is the founder of the Chrysothemis Circle for feminist theory in Würzburg; Member of the board of International Association of Women Philosophers. Selected Publications include *Psychische Bisexualität und Geschlechterdifferenz. Weiblichkeit in der Psychoanalyse*, 1996; *Arbeit an den Grenzen der Sprache Julia Kristeva*, 1998; *Die Unterwelt bewegen Politik, Psychoanalyse und Kunst in der Philosophie Julia Kristevas,* 2000; "Nehmen Sie's wie ein Mann, Madame..." Geschlechterdifferenz—Geschlechtsidenität—eschlechtergleichheit Einige dissidente Anmerkungen", *Streit—Feministische Rechtszeitschrift,* Heft 3 / 2002; "Die Philosophinnengemeinschaft Diotima aus Verona," *Information Philosophie*, Heft 1, 2003, S. 20–26; Das Ich als Schnittstelle. Schmerz und Erfahrung im Bedeutungsprozess, *Journal Phänomenologie*, Heft 17/2003.

Margrit Shildrick teaches and researches in the interdisciplinary fields of recent continental philosophy, feminist theory, and cultural studies. Her publications include *Leaky Bodies and Boundaries: Feminism, Postmodernism and (Bio)ethics* (Routledge, 1997), *Embodying the Monster: Encounters with the Vulnerable Self* (Sage, 2002), as well as two edited collections (with Janet Price) on the body and another due (with Roxanne Mykitiuk) on postmodern bioethics. Her current research project centres on the disabled body.

Käthe Trettin teaches philosophy at the University of Frankfurt am Main, Germany. Her main interests are ontology, philosophy of mind, epistemology, and feminist philosophy. She has published several articles in all these fields— in the last years, first and foremost, on ontology.

Tonja van den End defended her philosophical dissertation on Luce Irigaray in 1999 at the Dutch University for Humanist Studies. Since then she has been working at that university as a philosophy lecturer, as researcher, and as editor of the *Journal for Humanistics*. Since October 2003 she has held a research position financed by the Netherlands Organisation for Scientific Research, to investigate diversity and normative professionality at Dutch humanist organisations.

Veronica Vesterling is associate professor in the Department of Philosophy and the Center for Women's Studies at the University of Nijmegen, the Netherlands. She is director of the research project "Feminist Hermeneutics and Phenomenology." Her publications are in the field of contemporary philosophy and gender theory (Butler, Arendt, Heidegger, Lyotard).

Saskia Wendel, Dr. of philosophy, Dr. of theology. habil.; since 2003 professor for systematic philosophy, metaphysics, and philosophy of religion at the faculty of theology of the university of Tilburg, Netherlands. Recent Publications *include Affektiv und inkarniert. Ansätze Deutscher Mystik als subjekttheoretische Herausforderung,* Regensburg, 2002; *Feministische Ethik zur Einführung,* Hamburg, 2003; *Inkarniertes Subjekt,* in: DZPh 4/2003, 559– 569; *Hat das moralische Subjekt ein Geschlecht?* in: *Theologische Quartalsschrift* 1/2004, 3–17.

Index

abject, 41, 177, 178; abjected
    bodies, 158, 171. *See also*
    Kristeva
abstraction theory, 187
agency, 5, 8, 31n7, 181n13,
    183n19; and discursive
    conditions, 164; and
    intentionality, 181n12; and
    language, 172-76; of language
    and culture, 12, 22, 27;
    material-discursive forms of,
    28; materiality as effect, 29; as
    resignification, 34n31, 35n34
agential realism, 5, 17-21, 23-24,
    26, 29-30, 35n37
agential separability, 21, 28, 30,
    35n37
Alcoff, Linda, 109
the anarchic, 104, 113, 116, 117
Anzaldua, Gloria, 5, 42, 118n28
appearance, 2, 15, 166, 167
appresentation, 201-2, 205, 206
the archic, 104, 113, 116, 117
Arendt, Hannah, 138, 179, 181n13,
    182n19
Aristotle, 32n14, 40, 46n4, 65,
    99n42, 99n43; and time, 117n2,
    198
atomism, 15, 19, 33n16
Augustine, 3, 46n4, 117n2

Austin, J. L., 32n8
Bacon, Francis, 42
Baudrillard, Jean, 39
Beauvoir, Simone de, 4, 51, 160n4,
    185; *The Second Sex*, 8, 152;
    Temps et l'Autre, 2
becoming, 117, 117n2, 133
becoming one's gender, 153-55,
    158, 159
becoming woman, 82, 86, 88, 95n2
Being and Time. See Heidegger
Bell, Shannon, 75n2
Benhabib, Seyla, 6, 163-64
Bergson, Henri, 104, 117n2
Berkeley, George, 8-9, 187, 189-90
Bernal, Martin: *Black Athena*, 114
Best, Sue, 109
Bigwood, Carol, 113
binaristic logic, 1, 2, 4, 5, 60, 64.
    See also linguistic binarism
bodily ego, 169
Bodies That Matter (Butler), 32n8,
    46n3, 99n42, 110-11, 114-15,
    142, 167; agency, 172, 173;
    givenness, 169; law of sex, 177-
    8; materialization, 163, 188;
    prediscursive body, 156, 165;
    radical constructivism, 163;
    symbolic order, 181n10;
    unintelligible body, 170-1;